4/25/2009

IN

SATAN'S

FOOTSTEPS

**What every Christian needs to know
to filter truth from deception**

**by
THEODORE SHOEBAT**

*"...Secrecy is the keystone of all tyranny. Not force, but
secrecy...censorship. When any government, or any church for
that matter, undertakes to say to its subjects, 'This you may
not read, this you must not see, this you are forbidden to
know,' the end result is tyranny and oppression, no matter
how holy the motives."* – Robert A. Heinlein

Cover design: Graphics by Sher

Book design and layout: Cheryl Taylor

For more information, please e-mail the author at ted@insatansfootsteps.com

ISBN: 978-0-9771021-5-0

1st Edition

Printed in the United States

Acknowledgements

I want to thank God, my father, and the Christian side of my family. I would also like to thank all my school teachers and fellow students who have upset my inner soul and provoked me to search for the truth in order to refute and expose their error. To them I say "Your hatred towards God has motivated me."

As the Good News in God's Word the Bible states:

> "And we know that God causes all things to work together for good to those who love God, to those who are called according to His purpose." (Romans 8:28, NAS)

Theodore Shoebat

Introduction

Indiana Jones and the Last Crusade is one of my favorite movies, and a favorite scene is when the S.S Officer questions Indiana's father Henry (played by Sean Connery), and he responds:

S.S. Officer: You have the diary in your pocket.

Henry laughs genuinely, believing himself to be laughing at the expense of the S.S. Officer.

Henry: You dolt! You think my son would be that stupid that he would bring my diary all the way back here?

At which point an awful thought strikes Henry.

Henry: You didn't, did you? (a beat) You didn't bring it, did you?

Indy: Well, uh...

Henry: You did!!

Indy: Look, can we discuss this later?

Henry: I should have mailed it to the Marx Brothers.

Indy: Will you take it easy...?

Henry: Take it easy?! Why do you think I sent it home in the first place? So it wouldn't fall into their hands!!

Indy: I came here to save you.

Henry: Oh, yeah? And who's gonna come to save you, Junior?

Indy: I told you...

Indy's eyes blaze with anger, he rips a machine gun from the hands of one of the startled soldiers. Indy turns and sprays the room with machine gun fire, killing all three Nazis.

Indy: ...don't call me Junior.

Indy: She ransacked her own room, and I fell for it.

Indy: How did you know she was a Nazi?

Henry: She talks in her sleep.

Indy nods, and then the statement catches up with him. He looks at Henry with surprise.

Henry: (to Indy) I didn't trust her. Why did you?

Man in Chair: Because he didn't take my advice.

Indy: Donovan!

Donovan: Didn't I tell you not to trust anybody, Doctor Jones?

Henry: I misjudged you Walter. I knew you would sell your mother for an Etruscan vase. But I didn't know you would sell out your country and your soul to the slime of humanity.

THE SLIME OF HUMANITY

The question I always ask myself is, who are the slime of humanity? And why is it that it takes so long for so many to realize who they are? Why is it that at times these "slime" are disguised as geniuses, leaders, prophets, and even gods? How can we recognize the slime from the good fruit?

Well, I believe the answer is simple. Perhaps I could jump in and provide a simple way as to how to recognize good fruit from slime mixed with honey. It's called the fruit of the Spirit which are love, joy, peace, patience, kindness, goodness, gentleness, faithfulness, and self-control. Anything offered in the swap-meet of religions and man-made systems that is void of these, must be considered nothing more then pure slime mixed with a little dose of cyanide, and that makes a deadly cocktail of poison. It doesn't take a rocket scientist to figure that out. In fact a simple child like myself can figure that out by instinct.

I am a firm believer that human origin and destiny are not an accident. If we believe we came from slime, unfortunately we will also act like slime. I also believe that evil does exist. How else can we explain monsters like Hitler or Stalin. I also believe that scientific knowledge is not enough to know good from evil. Human minds cannot fully grasp or even interpret what is wholly good, or what is wholly evil. How else can we explain the fact that people have lived in turmoil throughout history? Why does life from the beginning always seem to zigzag from century to century, with so many wars and holocausts? How is it that humanity, which claims itself to be good, succeeds in committing the same evils, again, and again, and again?

Even within the last century we can find numerous cults that have ended in self-destruction – mass suicides in Jonestown, Waco, suicide bombings by Muslim fanatics, suicides by the German Nazi elite including Hitler, the founder of the Nazi-cult. And, why is it that evil is always clocked in a "great ideology?" or even in "important scientific research?"

Even great civilizations such as the Mayans with pyramid structures which were considered by many archaeologists to be observatories, are now thought to have been used for Human sacrifice with rituals of plucking out hearts and chopping off heads. I will never forget my first trip to the Pyramids in Chichenitza Mexico, seeing the ritual alters and the gigantic water-hole where they would throw the bodies. Sure, the Mayans had acquired great scientific knowledge, yet their science was intertwined in evil that was so deep it's shocking.

Yes, it's true, nothing is new. Germany, which was hailed as a beacon of knowledge and science, allowed itself to be caught up in the spell of one of the worst slimes in history – Adolf Hitler. In this book I thought it necessary to expose many systems that are still thought to be beacons of wisdom.

What force really inspired such cults? The quest leads us to ask – is there a devil? Can we trace his footsteps? What are the common denominators between these cults?

While we cannot capture any devils, perhaps we can trace their footsteps, and through all the research that I've done, I've come to conclusion that "monsters" are real – the link between evil people who are thought to be great by many and evil itself is mind-blowing.

Within this research you will find a quagmire of evil so intertwined that it will make even a hardened skeptic acknowledge that a devil does exist. Evil so intricate, that it has entangled itself and cloaked its image in science. The evidence even points to religions – that which on the surface is seen as peace-loving and spiritually longing to attain a higher-power, yet leads to a single source of evil. The facts, and history, will show how these "man-inspired" religions are paralleled in so many ways – the same old smelly stuff, simply repackaged with pretty cellophane wrapping, and followers simply look at the glittery cover without digging deeper into the stuffing.

Only a few who seriously seek to search further will find that what is inside the package is simply the old rehashed and regurgitated evil. Once you examine our findings you will conclude that the same signature was chiseled on all these cults long ago. They are simply copies of something very old.

Take the 'New Age Movement' as an example, it's the same as the 'Old Age Movement' we know as Hinduism. The New Age Movement with it's astrology and channeling has simply been re-packaged. Mediocre minds would think that Hinduism is nothing more than a peace-loving aspiration to reach out to a higher source. Yet, mediocre minds are no match for professional deception. Similarly, Islamic Tasawwuf or Sufiism, an established mystical movement within ancient Islam, has re-surfaced in the New Age Movement, with meditation, yoga, Zen, hypnosis, transpersonal psychology, and positive thinking. What is astonishing is that these exercises, no matter how innocent one thinks they are, do connect to a higher-power. As you will see, what seems to the follower as tapping into positive thinking, can thrust them unaware into a controlling force which can take over one's existence, with repercussions so great that could destroy life itself.

Table of Contents

Chapter One – My Struggle

I became tired of dealing with the hypocrisy of my school teachers. One teacher ripped a page out of my brother's daily journal for writing the words "Father God" in it. The teacher objected on the grounds we have "separation of church and state." If separation of religion from school is a mandate, then why is it that we can have a "mother earth" and earth worship? If religion is to be removed from schools, shouldn't it be all religious ideas? Is it possible they are promoting an agenda of atheism?

The lies don't end there. Fellow students and some teachers stated this country deserved 9/11. They said there was a government conspiracy, that the Twin Towers contained missiles. These lies were spewed without a single objection from my teachers. Yet they seemed to conspire to eradicate God out of our minds. Why? One school I attended took us to a local daycare center and assigned us a child with whom we spent time. While I was talking with the younger child, I told him that one day teachers will try to tell him that he came from a monkey. He was quite surprised. I told him not to believe it, explaining to him that once they told me this, but I didn't believe it. The concept of rejecting the idea that we came from monkeys or slimy algae was unthinkable to him. Most students in my school had become so brainwashed with political correctness, and blindly accepted what the teachers said, that when another student heard me say this, she reminded me that we were here to help them, and not to spread negative things about evolution. I ignored her of course. Before I left the classroom, this child told me that one of his favorite holidays was Easter, because of all the candy eggs. I responded by asking him what was the reason we celebrate Easter. He gave a simple answer about the Easter bunny, then I was able to tell him it wasn't about Easter eggs and bunnies, but about the death and resurrection of Jesus Christ as an atonement for our sins. The same politically-correct girl then responded to this by telling me that we were not there to talk about religion. "I am free to help him out as I see fit!" I responded.

There was another situation I remember, when I entered a science classroom for a test. At that time the classroom was empty, so I decided to take a look around. Looking at the posters I saw one labeled, "The History of Life." The poster contained a tube scrolling to the bottom connecting to a little shiny star that resembled the earth. In the tube there were all different kinds of animals. As I looked at the bottom of the tube, it was filled with a green algae primal soup. The algae was entering into the earth as the first organism in history. The poster was practically telling us that the algae formed into greater organisms until it eventually formed into everything we see now. Another poster glued to the wall contained words of wisdom about "mother" earth: "Give unto the earth and the earth will give unto you." No one complained about posters of "earth-worship." When the teacher walked in I asked her, "so we came from algae?" Her response was affirmative. I countered with another question, "where did the algae come from?" She responded that it came from bundles of energy. "Where did these come from?" I responded. Then before she could answer, I asked her if the poster was based on a theory or fact. She responded that it was based on truth!

Truth? It seems that truth is in the eye of the beholder. I tried explaining to her that Somebody had to create all these things – and that was God! I told her that everybody should have a choice – either you want to learn evolution as truth if indeed it is, or you want to learn Creationism. She responded back, "You can learn that in church." (There goes that separation of church and state again!) Was she saying, my truth was not allowed to be substantiated but hers was? Then why was our classroom participating in a "church worship" of Mother Earth? Before I left the classroom I asked her why we couldn't have God in school but she has an earth-worship poster in the classroom. "It's like worshipping the earth," I stated. She quickly responded, "well... I don't see it that way!" So the question is, is it simply the way she sees things which constitutes truth?

This confrontation with my teacher reminds me of a joke. One day a group of scientists representing the global seven got together for their annual convention. They decided that they did not need God anymore and voted on the measure with a resolution that read: "We have found the cure for, and eradicated, all diseases and disorders. We are able to feed every human. We have repaired the ozone layer. We have corrected the problems which made mother earth mad at us, and global warming is history. Having agreed to these accomplishments and are satisfied with the results, we hereby declare that we no longer need God."

The scientist passed this resolution and set a date to meet with God to tell him of their decision. On the day they were scheduled to meet with God, the lead scientist stepped forward with the resolution in hand, ready to read it, when God showed up. When He got their attention he asked: "I see that you are prepared to tell me that you do not need me anymore, is that correct?" The lead scientist said yes, and commenced reading the whereas' of the resolution. At the end of the reading, the lead scientist told God, "we hereby declare we do not need you any more."

To that God said, I'll tell you what!!! I will go away and never ask you to worship and praise me for all of the grace and mercy I have bestowed upon you as you performed these wonders, but only if you can create a man. The scientist responded, "but God, we just told you that we found and eradicated diseases, we did that by designing our own male/female."

To that God said, "Yes, but can you really create a man?" The scientists huddled, then responded in agreement – "yes, we can." God said, "Okay let me see you make a man just like I did when I created Adam." The scientists huddled again. This time two scientists teamed up together and scooped up some dirt – to which God said, "Hold on, make you own dirt!"

How can evolution, which contends we all came here by chance from an ancient explosion, explain things like love, imagination, or thoughts and dreams? How can evolution explain that both sperm and egg contain twenty-three chromosomes? And when they are put together they become one whole cell? Why do we have just algae and not organisms which are half human and half algae? If the world was just one big green, slimy orgy, then I could consider the thought of evolution as being true – but that's not the case! If scientists have found fossils which are "forty-billion" years old, then why aren't they presenting any fossils which are half-human and half-primate? Because there is no such thing. The Bible actually tells us about the formation of the human body: Job 10:11 reads: "You clothed me with skin and flesh, and you knit my bones and sinews together." This verse is quite amazing, because Job – the oldest book in the Bible – is talking about sinews, which actually are (according to a medical dictionary) a band of tough, inelastic fibrous tissue that connects a muscle with its bony attachment and consists of rows of elongated cells, minimal ground substance, and densely arranged, almost parallel, bundles of collagenous fibers.[1] This proves that the Bible contains scientific information; therefore, why not teach creationism in schools? Unlike Darwin's first book *The Origin of Species* which was published in 1859, the Bible was written thousands of years ago, the book of Job's origin ranges from 1500 B.C. to 600 B.C.[2] I often wonder about what impassions evolutionists to protect their theory so much. Why is there such an eagerness to remove creationism and God from our educational systems. If God does not exist, why would they fear that students would think about faith in Him? To evolutionists, degrading people by telling them they evolved from apes, also furthers the assumption that there is no afterlife. As Christians, however, we believe that salvation is far more than just the knowledge we were created in the likeness of God. If evolutionists are really as tolerant as they claim, then why not allow the teaching of creationism? Why is there such an effort to blot out only the Biblical God? How is it that currently the study of Allah and Islam is required in the history curriculum in California schools? This is the gap I'm trying to expose: there is some dark power pulling the majority of people to protect every belief system known to man, except for Christianity. There is an attempt to blot out only one system – the Biblical account of life and destiny.

Destiny is such an important part of this struggle, yet little is said about it. It was the very reason why my father left Islam and embraced his life in the Biblical faith. The Jewish people have returned to their homeland and have made it a state, just as the Bible foretold. Psalm 22 was written about Christ's crucifixion, long before He ever came to earth; saying (in Christ's words): "They part my garments among them, and cast lots upon my vesture." This is just as it happened when Christ was crucified. That cannot be a coincidence. I don't believe in chance or coincidence. I believe in purpose. To look at people all around you and believe in a doctrine called evolution is difficult to fathom. To believe that there is no divine purpose, no point to living in this world, is most demeaning. The same people who criticize the Bible for God choosing Israel as a "racist" state also believe in Darwinism, which has much racism in it. To say that the first evolved humans were African is surly bigoted and racist to say the least. Has anyone ever noticed that the very accusations they use against us are their own folly? Where are the voices to speak out against this? Where is Jesse Jackson? Al Sharpton? Where are the Blacks that you see on T.V. complaining of how Christmas is a racist holiday because of its white snow and white Santa? Is it possible evolutionists forget that it was the Bible that eradicated racism? "...neither Jew nor Greek, there is neither slave nor free, there is neither male nor female; for you are all one in Christ Jesus." (Galatians 3:28) Did they forget that this was the basis of Abraham Lincoln's belief system to eradicate slavery?

I have put up with this type of bigotry in two schools. In one of the schools, the teacher was discussing the case about Terry Schiavo. She stated concerning that situation, she agreed letting Terry Schiavo die would be justifiable. When asked why, she responded that if she was in Terry Schiavo's shoes she would want to die. "But you're not" I responded. Who would give you the right to decide someone else's life? In another class with the same teacher, she was discussing her support for homosexuality, that "it was all right for us to experiment with our sexuality." Of course, with books like *The Joy of Gay Sex* in the children's school library, it was the politically correct thing to say.

There was a literary teacher who skipped the Biblical poems in the text-book since they were from the Psalms. It's hard to believe the writings of king David and Solomon, his son, were rejected in my class. Yet, Middle Eastern myths, Italian and Shakespearian sonnets, were included. Only Biblical poetry was skipped, and that was "to dig deeply into Japanese and Chinese poetry." I had to put up with her views on South Dakota banning abortion; she spoke about how there were some "Christian" fundamentalists who were against abortion, and how Christian conservatives must have control of the government there, and so on, and so forth. Yet, we were supposed to have her liberal views control our thinking and our mind. Do we, even as children, have no rights to express our views and feelings?

I believe that some of the most wicked among us are the evolution-supporting authors who write how evolution is the supreme theory and they portray it as fact. I was at the Barnes & Noble one night and I spotted a book called *Finding Darwin's God* by Kenneth R. Miller. As I was reading the first page I realized that Miller went so far as to jeopardize the very thing the human soul seeks: spiritual fulfillment. He went on to talk about his childhood, where he would ask questions like: "Who made us?" then receiving the answer of, "God made us" (page 1). Miller explains that there is more than just "God made us." But, how is that possible when the book of Genesis never says anything about Adam and Eve coming from Primates.

In the documentary *The Root of All Evil?*, Richard Dawkins inconclusively makes Christian and Jewish children look like victims who are being indoctrinated with myths. He tries to depict them as being segregated from the teaching of evolution, which Dawkins views as truth, rather than what it really is: a mere theory. How could anybody accept that assumption as truth? Scientists erect statues and hang paintings of what we supposedly looked like before we evolved fully into humans. But how could they know what we looked like? Darwin himself said that we could, only to a degree "recall in imagination the former condition of our early progenitors."[3] It's interesting that in the documentary, most of the time Dawkins interviews Christians and Jews, apparently in an attempt to make them look foolish or evil, but he only interviews one Muslim, and only slightly talks about the dangers of fundamentalist Islam within his own nation of England; this he portrays as being too religious, trying to focus more on Christianity while giving little attention to the real problem – Muslim terrorism. Then he portrays the Jewish and Christian religions as being sexist; but he doesn't even mention Islam's horrible treatment of women. Dawkins is a hypocrite to say that he is concerned about Christian and Jewish children, who he claims are being indoctrinated. When I'm at the zoo looking at the monkeys, there's a large poster with pictures showing an array of faces evolving from the monkey to a full human face. And what do children think when they see an ape standing in a pit of dirt, surrounded by old trees with piles of ape feces? Is it any wonder there is so much violence in school? If you teach kids they come from monkeys, it's pretty certain they'll act like it. If we're not going to teach creationism *and* evolution in class and present them both throughout society, then we shouldn't teach any part of the "where we came from" lesson at all. It would be better to let people decide on their own. We must never forget the Columbine massacre, and one of the killers (Harris) who wrote in his journal that "Sometime in April [of 1999] me and V will get revenge and will kick natural selection up a few notches."[4]

School was not about fact but liberal indoctrination. One day I had a discussion with my homeless-appearing art teacher Mr. Gross. I explained to him that I did not agree with abortion but did agree with the death penalty. He said my viewpoint was conservative garbage – that conservatives think they should choose who lives and who dies. I guess he thinks it's all right to kill little babies, but hardened criminals deserve to live. Another teacher agreed with Mr. Gross, saying, "Ted, you've obviously never been pregnant." I said, "you're still killing a baby," it was like pouring holy water during an exorcism, she instantly snapped with a screech and screamed from the top of her lungs "a fetus is not human." It was as if the devil had jumped right out of her, and I was the exorcist.

According to my teacher Mr. Gross, there was no justification for the Israelis to assassinate the wheel-chaired Ahmad Yassin – he deserved a fair trial, no matter how many innocent lives Yassin snuffed out by his suicide bombers. If I disagree with his opinion about killing innocent babies, I'm scorned, and if I object to terrorists being released even though they are responsible for killing civilians, I am also scorned.

My speech therapist, who always accused me of being obsessed with violence for discussing the evils of terrorism or asking her if she watched the movie *The Pianist,* had no problem discussing her agreement with supporting assisted suicides. Yet, as she was harassing me, there were other students hooked on, and selling drugs. One troubled student stabbed another with a pencil in my math class. There were three suicides in one year during my ninth grade. My school was ranked as having the highest number of suicides in the district, yet it was rated as the second best school in our city. But even with the large diversity of students in my school, just bringing in my Bible one day to read it on my break seemed to get me into trouble. One student saw me reading and said "I'm going to get my Muslim friends on you."

I was referred by my teacher to the school psychologist who diagnosed me with a learning disability called *Asperger's Syndrome* and I was sent to special ed. In a meeting my parents had with the school board to "discuss my problem," my teacher Ms. Bruno was rushing over to turn on the heat as she began to complain to my father about my problem – that I was always going against the tide. She gave the example that I was always arguing against global warming. My father jokingly responded "If we have global warming, then how come you were in such a rush to turn on the heat?"

In my special ed. class there was a self-hating Jew named Andrew who had such a deep hatred of himself that he could not wait for the Jewish race to be annihilated. He once went so far as to try to strangle himself in the classroom. With his asphyxiated-looking face, and his hands around his neck as he was turning blue, teachers were trying to pry his hands off his neck. All along he was screaming, "I want to kill myself!!" He once talked about how he wanted to kill his Jewish mother, and said he couldn't wait for another Holocaust.

I was accused of being a sexist by a teacher because I said "women in America shouldn't complain about their rights, since they already have them." But at the same time they teach Darwinism, dismissing that in Darwin's *The Descent of Man,* he states "man might have become as much superior to woman in mind, as the peacock surpasses the peahen in plumage."[5]

Just recently, I asked two fellow students, one of them a radical atheist, if they believed in evolution. They both said yes. When I told them that I believed natural selection was brutal, one of the two asked why. I replied that it was "the superior over the inferior." He said, "if you're retarded you're going to die, and that's the way it is." I also stated that evolution was racially prejudiced, because it promulgates the idea that Africans were the first evolved from the primate. He said "how is that racist?" I replied, "its saying that the Blacks are the closest to the primate, but that Whites are supposedly fully evolved." We then debated the fact that Darwin in *The Descent of Man* referred to Blacks as "anthropomorphous apes." He replied by saying, Darwin the founder of evolution was a racist, but evolution is not!

Evolutionists would argue that "most evolutionists aren't violent," but that does not mean that evolution itself is void of what causes violent behavior. This is especially true if one accepts that we come from slime and will end up as dirt in the ground. Evolution has brought nothing but a cluster of assumptions and a quagmire of meaningless life where the brain only thinks of its own survival and selfish desires. It has also brought a justification for taking life: the darwinian struggle is defined as the struggle for existence between the superior over the inferior. Almost indistinguishable to the ideas in Hitler's *Mein Kampf* – which claims the Asyans are the superior race, and the *Jihad Struggle* – in which Muslims claim their superiority.

We should stop thinking that fascist ideologies are only in the world of the Muslim extremist or fanatical North Korea. In our own nation, fascist ideologies are being taught in our school systems under the guise of evolution. In *Mein Kampf* (My Struggle), Hitler used the German word for evolution, entwicklung, many times, citing "lower human types." He criticized the Jews for bringing "Negroes into the Rhineland" with the aim of "ruining the white race by the necessarily resulting bastardization." He spoke of "Monstrosities, halfway between man and ape." He lamented the fact of Christians going to "Central Africa" to set up "Negro missions," resulting in the turning of "healthy...human beings into a rotten brood of bastards." In the chapter entitled "Nation and Race" he states, "The stronger must dominate and not blend with the weaker, thus sacrificing his own greatness. Only the born weakling can view this as cruel, but he, after all, is only a weak and limited man; for if this law did not prevail, any conceivable higher development (hoherentwicklung) of organic living beings would be unthinkable." Not many pages afterward, he stated, "Those who want to live, let them fight, and those who do not want to fight in this world of eternal struggle do not deserve to live."[6]

Yet I ask why am I having such a struggle? Why do I meet with so much hostility for believing in the Bible and creation? But I know I'd rather believe in the Messiah and His second coming which will liberate the true believers from this self-inflicted decaying world. A world which contains the gap of darkness that I am so futilely trying to fill.

Resources

1. The Free Dictionary, By Farlex, Medical Dictionary, Sinews, Tendon.

2. Who2, Job, Biblical Figure.

3. The Descent of Man, by Charles Darwin, 2nd ed. [1874], at sacred-texts.com, Chapter XXI, General Summary and Conclusion.

4. CNN.com/U.S., Columbine killer envisioned crashing plane in NYC, December 6, 2001 Posted: 12:54 AM EST (0554 GMT).

5. Darwin's "The Descent of Man and Selection in Relation to Sex" (S186: 1871).

6. Evolution or Creationism?, Hitler, Darwinism and The Holocaust, "Ascent of Racism," Paul G. Humber.

Chapter Two – Mormonism is Islam, Re-Packaged

MUHAMMAD – JOSEPH SMITH'S ROLE MODEL

What's interesting is that many cultists are inspired by other cults. Take Islam, for example: hardly anyone knows that Joseph Smith, the founder of Mormonism, was highly inspired by the Islamic prophet Muhammad with all the jihad and utopian attempt to establish a global Mormon hegemony.

A famous speech by Joseph Smith entitled "Alcoran [the Quran] or The Sword," boosted the morale for the Danites who packed a punch in the battlefield on account of this morale-boosting, holy jihad-like event. Initially, the Mormons attempted to establish a government for themselves:

> "We are an injured people, from county to county we have been driven by unscrupulous mobs eager to seize the land we have cleared and improved with such love and toil. We have appealed to magistrates, judges, the Governor, and even to the President of the United States, but there has been no redress for us."

As you see from above, this is similar to Muhammad's plight from Mecca to Medina. Joseph Smith wanted a new identity with a new homeland and a base to begin his wars. As seen in this statement, he eloquently explains himself, drawing a connection to Muhammad and Islam:

> "As Joseph neared the end of his speech, all of his anger erupted from his mouth. 'If the people will let us alone, we will preach the [Mormon] gospel in peace. But if they come on us to molest us, we will establish our religion by the sword. We will trample down our enemies and make it one gore of blood from the Rocky Mountains to the Atlantic Ocean. I will be to this generation a

second Muhammad, whose motto in treating for peace was the Alcoran [The Quran] or the sword. So shall it eventually be with us – Joseph Smith or the Sword!'"[1]

ISLAM'S AMAZING SIMILARITIES WITH MORMONISM

Not only did Mormonism adopt the sword, but also the holy jihad wars. It is interesting to find so many striking similarities between the two:

Islam's founder: Muhammad dissatisfied with the world of different beliefs and supposed evil, he regularly attended and meditated at a secluded place called "Ghar-Hira" – a cave near Mecca, in an attempt to seek God's will. He saw a magnificent bright angel of light, "Gabriel." The Islamic traditions record that his excitement took the shape of a trance or vision. The "Wahi" or angel overtook him and instructed him to "arise and preach." He was taught by the angel that all Christians and Jews in his time were wrong, thus Islam was established.

Mormonism's founder: Joseph Smith, as recorded in his testimony, was dissatisfied with the world of different beliefs, he regularly attended the same secluded place alone, and began to offer up his desires to God. He immediately seized upon some power which put him into a trance-like experience in which he saw a bright Angel of Light "Moroni." He was taught that all the current Christian beliefs were wrong, thus Mormonism was established.

Islam's holy book: Muhammad received revelations which were given from original engraved stone tablets in heaven called *Al-Lawh Al-Mahvouth* (The Sacred Tablet). A new replica was established on earth called the Quran, which was a replica of the original. This supersedes all previous God-inspired books.

Mormonism's holy book: Joseph Smith received his revelation from the original engravings on tablets of various metals, delivered by the "Angel of Light." A replica was established on earth called The Book of Mormon. It supersedes all the previous God-inspired books.

Islam's re-direction of holy places: The Islamic religion which Muhammad promoted changed the "holy city" from Jerusalem to Mecca, with Kaaba as the holiest place.

Mormonism's re-direction of holy places: Joseph Smith changed the coming of Christ from Jerusalem to Independence, Missouri, and promoted "Salt Lake City" as the central headquarters for Mormons.

Islam's re-direction of Biblical stories: In the Quran, main Biblical stories were changed to present their prophets and country as being God's choice for His message. According to the Quran, Abraham built the Kaaba with his son "Ishmael" as the first place of worship. The Arabs who are descendents of Ishmael then suddenly became the chosen people, alongside converts who established the Islamic *Umma* (Muslim Nation). Israel, who is of the lineage of Jacob (Ishmael's younger brother) became replaced by Muslims as being the chosen people of God. Consequently, Israel no longer has any significance. Muslims now are God's instrument to deliver truth to the world by invitation to Islam first, then jihad. The prophet and his language have become significant and no one can worship without praying in Arabic. The world was to be unified under a one government system with one language. Arabic is now God's chosen heavenly language with the Quran superseding the Bible.

Mormonism's re-direction of Biblical stories: Joseph Smith's Book of Mormon has the tribes of Israel living in America as the American Indians. Biblical characters like Jesus supposedly visited America in the past and are depicted by the Mayan god Quetzalcoatl, and will come back to Independence, Missouri. The Book of Mormon is an additional testament to be added to the Bible and supersedes it. Mormons are now the chosen people of God, Nephites and Lamanites (American Indians) are the real Israelites and Mormons are the chosen vessel in charge of the holy message that must be delivered as truth to the world.

Islam's main arguments were with the Judeo-Christian faith: The main arguments the Quran has are with the Judeo-Christian faith. Most of the arguments revolve around Muhammad's prophethood, and his new revelations which supersedes the Bible. True Christianity was lost, and all of today's Christians are "Mushrik" (associate more than one god in the godhead). Interestingly, the Quran never condemned the Bible as a source, yet the majority of Muslims believe that the Bible, as we know it, was corrupted by Jews and Christians, wth the original text lost. Muhammad accused the Judeo-Christian believers with twisting God's word which led the Christians and Jews astray.

Mormonism's arguments were mainly with the Judeo-Christian faith: The main arguments of Joseph Smith were with the Judeo-Christian faith. Most of the arguments revolve around Joseph Smith's prophethood, and his new revelations (the Book of Mormon) which supersedes the Bible and is a later testament of Jesus Christ. True Christianity was lost, and all churches were corrupt. It is interesting that the Book of Mormon never condemns the Bible as a source. However, the key elements in the Bible were altered dramatically. Jesus became a brother of Lucifer, the Lamanites and Nephites (Indians) were Israelites who immigrated to America. Joseph Smith's diatribes were mostly regarding his claim to prophethood, and the corrupt Christian churches.

Islam and women: Women became unimportant. Muhammad received revelations from the Angel of Light "Gabriel" to take the wife of his adopted son "Zayed." He promoted polygamy, and married several women: Khadija, Sawda, Aesha, Omm Salma, Hafsa, Zaynab of Jahsh, Howarya, Omm Habiba, Safia, Maymuna of Hareth, Fatema, Hind, Asma of Saba, Zaynab of Khozaymia, Habla, Asma of Muman, Maria Al-Kibtia, Rayhana, Omm Sharik, Maymuna, Zaynab (The 3rd one), and Khawla. Polygamy was promoted in Islam for the believers (4 wives for each man). Only the prophet had the privilege of marrying so many. (As a side-note: Muhammad took Aesha as his wife when she was only 6 to 7 years old.[2]

Mormonism and women: Women became unimportant. Joseph Smith received revelations from the Angel of Light "Moroni" when he desired to take a woman from someone else. He also practiced polygamy and married several women; Louisa Beman, Fanny Alger, Lucinda Harris, Zina D. Huntington, Prescindia L. Huntington, Eliza Roxey Snow, Sarah Ann

Whitney, Desdemona Fullmer, Helen Mar Kimball, Eliza M. Partridge, Emily D. Partridge, and many others. Polygamy was promoted in Mormonism, and a Mormon can marry several wives.

Fortunately, Mormonism never took a foothold in America. Today, Mormonism is attempting to legitimize itself as another "Christian" faith, and most Mormons simply do not adhere to the old model and seem to have omitted many of the old practices. Most Mormons today would view Warren Jeff, a Mormon fundamentalist, as a heretic.

Although one could point to differences between Islam and Mormonism, nevertheless, the main tenets of each faith are very similar. Could the reason be the inspiration has come from the same source? Both Books, The Quran and The Book of Mormon, claim to believe in the Bible, yet a close study reveals that both books reject the most essential teachings of the Bible, as you will further discover.

Resources

1. No Man Knows My History, The Life of Joseph Smith, By Fawn M. Brodie, First published in 1945 – revised in 1970, Chapter XVI, The Alcoran or the Sword, Pages 229 230 and 231, As related to George Hinkle and James B. Turner, in Correspondence and Orders, etc., pp. 125-129, 139-140, and by John D. Lee: Mormonism Unveiled, pp. 73-74.

2. Nessa Allnabi, Chapter 2, book by Dr. Aisha Abdulrahman (3): Aissa Bent Abu Bakr.

Chapter Three – Encountering Fallen Angels

COULD MUHAMMAD HAVE ENCOUNTERED AN ANGEL FROM GOD?

The striking similarities between Joseph's encounters with an Angel of Light to Muhammad's is quite amazing. In Islam, after Muhammad "saw" the angel Gabriel in the cave of Hira, he told his wife: "I do not know what has happened to me. I fear for myself." He poured out his mental confusion, as reported by Ibn Ishaq, the best collector of Muhammad's deeds, "I'm afraid I'm going out of my mind and being possessed by an evil spirit."

WHO DID MUHAMMAD ENCOUNTER?

This is a depiction of the supposed Angel Gabriel as understood within Islam. He is identified as "Ameer Al-Wahi" (The princely spirit), "Khazen Al-Quds" (The keeper of holiness), "Al-Ruh Al-Ameen" (The trusted spirit) "Al-Ruh Al-Qodos" (The holy spirit), "Tawoos Al-Malaeka" (The peacock of all angels), "The Highest of all Angels," *Most Beautiful of all Angels.* The peacock may also be the symbol of pride. In the account, it also states that when this angel came it instilled terror in their hearts.

IT WAS NONE OTHER THAN BAD, OLD LUCIFER

The one we know to be Lucifer (Satan) in the Bible, is depicted in Islam as the good angel, Gabriel. Just as the Bible describes Lucifer as the most beautiful of all angels, so Islam describes the angel Muhammad encountered. Of Lucifer, God said:

> "You had the seal of perfection, full of wisdom and perfect in beauty. You were in Eden, the garden of God; every precious stone was your covering: the ruby, the topaz, and the diamond; the beryl, the onyx, and the jasper; the lapis lazuli, the turquoise, and the emerald; and the gold, the workmanship of your setting and sockets was in you. On the day you were created they were prepared. You were the anointed cherub who covers, and I placed you there. You were on the holy mountain of God; you walked in the midst of the stones of fire. You were blameless in your ways from the day you were created, until unrighteousness was found in you." (Ezekiel 28:12-15, NAS)

How could Islam identify an angel as The Holy Spirit, which is a title that belongs to God? How could any angel (and especially Satan) be identified as *Khazen Al-Quds,* the keeper of all holiness? These are titles that belong to God alone. Notice in the passage below, the Bible depicts Satan's forces as birds:

> "And he cried mightily with a strong voice, saying, Babylon the great is fallen, is fallen, and is become the habitation of devils, and the hold of every foul spirit, and a cage of every unclean and hateful bird." (Revelation 18:2)

THE SOURCE OF ALL EVIL – AN ANGEL OF LIGHT

When it comes to Mormonism, fourteen-year-old Joseph was "chosen" to receive certain secrets from an "angel of light." But before this episode took place, he was determined to know which of the many religions he should join. He questioned himself "If any one of them be right which is it? And how shall I know it?"[1] Then he encountered a passage in the Bible from the book of James chapter 1 verse 5: "If any of you lack wisdom, let him ask of God, that giveth to all [men] liberally, and upbraideth not; and it shall be given him."

Like Muhammad who secluded himself in Ghar Hira, early one morning in the spring of 1820, Joseph went to a secluded woods (which is now labeled as "The Sacred Grove") to ask God which church he should join.

A darkness gathered around him, and Smith believed that he would soon be totally destroyed. He continued his prayer non-verbally, asking for God's aid, feeling hopeless and resigned to destruction. At this moment, he reported that a light brighter than the sun descended towards him. With the arrival of the light, Smith reported he was delivered from the evil power:

> "Immediately I was seized upon by some power which entirely overcame me, and had such an astonishing influence over me as to bind my tongue so that I could not speak. Thick darkness gathered around me, and it seemed to me for a time, as if I were doomed to sudden destruction."[2]

ONLY CHRISTIANITY IS CORRUPT AND ONLY THEIR RELIGION IS TRUE

The main theme shared by all cults is that Christianity has been corrupted. Islam is famous for such accusations, as well as Mormonism. Only Christianity seems to stand alone against them all, yet they all seem to be unwilling to expose each other. If they are all truly inspired from God, how come they don't agree on the basic essentials with each other? My guess is demons won't busy themselves fighting other demons.

JOSEPH SMITH'S ENCOUNTER WITH THE ANGEL OF LIGHT

In the light, Smith "saw two personages standing in the air" in front of him. One pointed to the other and stated that this was his "Beloved Son." (Smith reported that the two beings were God the Father, and Jesus.) As Smith could now speak, he asked to know which religious sect he should join. Smith claimed he was told that all existing religions had been corrupted from Jesus Christ's teachings.[3]

"I was answered that I must join none of them, for they were all wrong; and the Personage who addressed me said that all their creeds were an abomination in his sight; that those professors were all corrupt; that: 'they draw near to me with their lips, but their hearts are far from me; they teach for doctrines the commandments of men, having a form of godliness, but they deny the power thereof.'[4]

"He again forbade me to join with any of them: and many other things did he say unto me which I cannot write at this time. When I came to myself again, I found myself lying on my back looking up into heaven."[5]

ALEISTER CROWLEY'S ENCOUNTER WITH THE ANGEL

In 1904, a man by the name of Aleister Crowley, claimed to have a mystical experience. This led to his establishing a new religion, Thelema. Shortly thereafter, he had voices reciting to him, which he wrote down. Just as Joseph Smith had secrets "which I cannot write at this time," so too, Aleister Crowley can be linked to Smith, as he was given the instruction not to decode the ciphers. His rules in conversation of having a "holy guardian angel" in which "it is impossible to lay down precise rules by which a man may attain to the knowledge and conversation of His Holy Guardian Angel; for that is the particular secret of each one of us; as secret not to be told or even divined by any other, whatever his grade. It is the Holy of Holies, whereof each man is his own High Priest, and none knoweth the Name of his brother's God, or the rite that invokes Him."[6] This Satanic secret rule of demon conversation, as you can see, wasn't originally written by Aleister Crowley, but a decree of the demon world as you've read from Joseph Smith.

ASA WILD'S ENCOUNTER WITH THE ANGEL

This decree can also be read from Asa Wild, who, similarly to Joseph Smith spoke with "the awful and glorious majesty of the Great Jehovah," he was influenced by this vision "and learned that every denomination of professing Christians had become extremely corrupt. That two-thirds of the world's inhabitants were about to be destroyed and the remainder ushered into the millennium." Wild said that "much more the Lord revealed, but forbids my relating it in this way. I shall soon publish a cheap pamphlet, my religious experience and travel in the divine life."[7]

MY OWN FAMILY'S ENCOUNTER WITH THE ANGEL

My grandfather, a devout Muslim, once told me that his angel comes to him and talks with him. This angel had a "secret name" which he could not reveal. This angel also interpreted the Quran to him.

My father, Walid Shoebat, in the days prior to his conversion to Christianity in Bethlehem, was with his friend Ramzi Hilal. Both were pinned to the ground as they were invoking the spirits. My father asked his friend "what do you see?" His friend answered, "the light," confirming the same thing my father saw. It was such a bright light they couldn't look at it. They were frozen there, unable to move for hours – both of their bodies went into convulsions with tears running uncontrollably like water. Continual connection to abusive and controlling angels is always a sign of meddling with the demonic world.

MUHAMMAD'S ENCOUNTER WITH THE ANGEL

The prophet Muhammad allegedly had a connection with the Angel Gabriel. Muhammad often visited the cave of Hira in the mountain of Jabal Nur (Mountain of Light), within the Hejaz region outside of Mecca, in what was called *tahannuth* (devotion). He would stay in the cave for several days, to pray and meditate, often to struggle with doubts about his self-confidence, and the temptation to commit suicide, then return home. In the year 610 A.D. when Muhammad was about forty, he was suffering one of these psychological and mental traumas.[8] While Muhammad was in the cave, he received a visit from Taus Al-Malaeka (Peacock angel).

"The angel came to Muhammad and asked him to read. The Prophet replied, *ma ana bi-qari* 'I do not know how to read.'" (The Prophet added), "The angel caught me (forcefully) and pressed me so hard that I could not bear it anymore. Then he released me and again asked me to read. I replied, 'I do not know how to read,' whereupon the angel caught me again and pressed me a second time till I could not bear it anymore. He then released me and asked me again to read, but again I replied, 'I do not know how to read.' Thereupon he caught me for the third time and pressed me and then released me and said, 'Read: In the Name of your Lord, who has created (all that exists). Has created man from a [blood] clot. Read and your Lord is most generous, who taught man by the pen which man knew not.' Then Allah's Apostle returned with the Inspiration, his neck muscles

twitching with terror till he entered upon Khadija (his wife) and said *dathireene* 'Cover me.' They covered him till his fear was over and then he said, 'O Khadija, what is wrong with me?' Then he told her everything that had happened and said, 'I fear that something may happen to me.' Khadija said, 'Never! But have the glad tidings, for you are by Allah, Allah will never disgrace you as you keep good relations with your kith and kin, speak the truth, help the poor and the destitute, serve your guest generously and assist the deserving, calamity-afflicted ones.'"9

The Cave of Hira

Khadija then accompanied him to her cousin Waraqa bin Naufal bin Asad bin 'Abdul 'Uzza, who, during the Pre-Islamic period became a Christian and used to write the writing with Hebrew letters. He would write from the Gospel in Hebrew as much as Allah wished him to write. He was an old man and had lost his eye sight. Khadija said to Waraqa, "Listen to the story of your nephew, O my cousin!" Waraqa asked, "O my nephew! What have you seen?" Allah's Apostle described whatever he had seen. Waraqa said, "This is the same one who keeps the secrets (angel Gabriel) whom Allah had sent to Moses."10

Again, this angel was the keeper of secrets. Mormons were required to recite an oath of secrecy for their endowment rituals: "We and each of us, covenant and promise that we will not reveal any secrets of this...should we do so, we agree that our throats be cut from ear to ear and our tongues torn out by their roots."11

SH-H-H! IT'S A SECRET!

Why does Islam have so much in common with Mormonism? What were the reasons that Joseph Smith and Muhammad became curious about this angel of light that visited them? Why are so many religions riddled with secrets? Enticing elements mixed with secrecy is what attracts people to a deadly concoction. The Masonic lodge, Mormonism, and the Quran, all have supposed secrets. Unlike these religions, in the Bible, God does not reveal His secrets to man, but freely gives to man some of His knowledge, and declares they are not secret:

> "The secret things belong unto the LORD our God: but those[things which are revealed belong unto us and to our children for ever, that we may do all the words of this law." (Duet 29:29)

God also clearly stated that he is not into doing the "secret" things:

> "I haven't spoken privately or in some dark corner of the world. I didn't say to Jacob's descendants, 'Search for me in vain!' I, the LORD, speak what is fair and say what is right." (Isaiah 45:19)

And in the Old Testament, when God spoke concerning His nature, being a Triune God, He clearly stated it wasn't in secret: "Come ye near unto me, hear ye this; I have not spoken in secret from the beginning; from the time that it was, there am I [The Son]: and now the Lord GOD [The Father], and His Spirit [The Holy Spirit], hath sent Me [The Son]." (Isaiah 48:16)

The God of the Bible wanted to share with us that which we can fathom, and things that we will fathom – later.

SECRETS IN THE NAZI CULT

Even Hitler expressed he had his own secrets, saying that, "There will be a class of overlords, after them the rank and file of the party members in hierarchical order, and then the great mass of anonymous followers, servants and workers in perpetuity, and beneath them again all the conquered foreign races, the modern slaves. And over and above all these will reign a new and exalted nobility of whom I cannot speak."[12]

COULD JOSEPH SMITH HAVE ENCOUNTERED AN ANGEL FROM GOD?

Similar to Muhammad, the prophet of Islam, in the first part of Joseph Smith's revelation, Smith speaks of the dark power, and of non-verbally asking God for aid:

> "Immediately I was seized upon by some power which entirely overcame me, and had such an astonishing influence over me as to bind my tongue so that I could not speak. Thick darkness gathered around me, and it seemed to me for a time as if I were doomed to sudden destruction."

If Joseph Smith really asked God, why then did a demonic force suddenly appear to him? How could these angels of light be God the Father and Jesus when the Bible tells us there will be no more revelations to people who seek signs and wonders and create separate sects from Christianity after Jesus's resurrection? When these angels said that the Christian faith was corrupted, did that mean God forgot to, or failed to, protect His original Messianic message?

As Jesus clarifies to his disciples in Mathew 16:4:

> "A wicked and adulterous generation seeketh after a sign; and there shall no sign be given unto it, but the sign of the prophet Jonas. And he left them, and departed."

Jesus then says in Mathew 12:40:

> "For as Jonas was three days and three nights in the whale's belly; so shall the Son of man be three days and three nights in the heart of the earth."

Why would Joseph Smith claim to be a follower of Christ, then ask God which religion should he join? What was he prior to his prayer request? If he believed in the true God, then why not just believe in His Holy Bible instead of manufacturing another?

If a Muslim asks Allah who cannot be the Biblical god: which religion should I join? Allah would obviously lead him to Islam. Why would the true God guide you to a religion that goes against His scriptures? Why should we pray to God, and ask Him about the things that are obvious? Jesus said in Mathew 16:18:

> "And I say also unto thee, That thou art Peter, and upon this rock I will build my church; and the gates of hell shall not prevail against it.

No other religion can claim to be a second part of Christianity. How could Jesus promise to build his body of believers (The Church), then renege on His promise to protect His message?

BACK TO THE FRUIT OF THE SPIRIT

In Mathew 7:17 and 18 Jesus clearly proves that Smith's prayer simply could not have been a prayer to God:

> "Even so every good tree bringeth forth good fruit; but a corrupt tree bringeth forth evil fruit. A good tree cannot bring forth evil fruit, neither [can] a corrupt tree bring forth good fruit."

If Joseph Smith was really a "good tree" which brought forth "good fruit" why would he call on a holy war, divide women as property, and be seized by a dark force? Instead of righteous wisdom he received a darkness that seized his body, terrifying him and making him feel as if his life was close to destruction. Why would God want to put fear into someone who is asking for wisdom – and then turn into an angel of light?

In second Corinthians 11:13 and 14 it reads:

> "For such [are] false apostles, deceitful workers, transforming themselves into the apostles of Christ. And no marvel; for Satan himself is transformed into an angel of light."

How can this vision of angelic light be of Jesus? Christianity was the first to worship Jesus Christ. How can Mormonism suddenly create their own doctrine about Jesus? Here's a quote from Brigham Young:

"Some of our old traditions teach us that a man guilty of atrocious and murderous acts may savingly repent when on the scaffold; and upon his execution will hear the expression – "Bless God! he has gone to heaven, to be crowned in glory, through the all-redeeming merits of Christ the Lord." This is all nonsense. Such a character never will see heaven. Some will pray, "O that I had passed through the vail on the night of my conversion!" This proves the false ideas and vain notions entertained by the Christian world. They have no good sense pertaining to God and godliness."[13]

John Taylor, a Mormon leader stated "What! are Christians ignorant? Yes, as ignorant of the things of God as the brute beast.[14] That with all the mockery of Jesus Christ Himself who was portrayed as a polygamist, this is an argument I present to every Mormon who believes in Mormonism which teaches that Jesus was married to Mary, Martha, and Mary Magdalene.[15]

Since many Mormons consider themselves Christians, and accept that Joseph Smith really did see Jesus Christ and God The Father, I would like to share how his vision had absolutely no Biblical connection whatsoever.

Even though Joseph Smith claims that he connected with God during that vision and that he was encouraged to pray after reading James 1:5; it is impossible that he was praying to the Biblical God, the God of Abraham, Isaac, and Jacob. Rather, he had to be connecting with the dark spiritual forces. Jesus explains to his disciples what they should watch out for before his second coming:

"For there shall arise false Christs, and false prophets, and shall shew great signs and wonders; insomuch that, if it were possible, they shall deceive the very elect." Mathew 24:24.

Joseph Smith came after Jesus; therefore there cannot be any more prophets or visions.

In Mark 13:21 through 23, Jesus explains this again but in more detail:

"And then if any man shall say to you, lo, here is Christ; or, lo, he is there; believe him not: For false Christs and false prophets shall rise, and shall shew signs and wonders, to seduce, if it were possible, even the elect. But take ye heed: behold, I have foretold you all things."

--------- **Resources** ---------

1. Wikipedia, Joseph Smith.

2. Encyclopedia of Mormonism, Vol. 1, First Vision, Backman, Milton V., Jr. Joseph Smith's First Vision. Salt Lake City, 1980. Smith, Joseph. The Personal Writings of Joseph Smith, comp. and ed. Dean C. Jessee. Salt Lake City, 1984.

3. All Experts: Encyclopedia, BETA, Summary of Joseph Smith Jr.'s official account of the First Vision.

4. The Church of Jesus Christ of Latter-day Saints, Joseph Smith's testimony, Joseph Smith's first account.

5. The Mormon Doctrine of God, This article originally appeared in The Salt Lake City Messenger, Issue No. 87, December 1994, Joseph Smith's Vision, The Pear of Great Price, Joseph Smith-History 1:14, 16-20.

6. Wikipedia, Holy Guardian Angel, Methods of achieving knowledge and conversation, Book 4, "One Star in Sight."

7. Man Knows My History, The Life of Joseph Smith, By Fawn M. Brodie, First published in 1945 – revised in 1970, chapter II: Treasures in The Earth, page 22-23, See the Wayne Sentinel, October 22, 1823, for Wild's account.

8. The Great Divide, By Alvin J. Schmidt, Chapter 1, Jesus and Muhammad: Polar Opposites, Religious Callings, Page 11.

9. A Mountain Out of a Molehill, Muslims protest cartoons, ignore Guantanamo, By Mona Eltahawy.

10. Muhammad And The Demons, By Silas, Quoting from the Hadith of Bukhari, 9.111: Narrated 'Aisha, Guillaume's "The Life of Muhammad," page 106.

11. University of Southern California, USC-MSA Compendium of Muslim Text, Translation Sahih Bukhari, Volume 1, Book 1: Revelation, Book 1, Number 3: Narrated 'Aisha.

12. A livingstonemusic.net article, Hitler and the Nazis, The 'Supermen.'

13. Remarks by President Brigham Young, made in the Tabernacle, Great Salt Lake City, May 20, 1860, as reported by G. D. Watt.

14. A Sermon by Elder John Taylor, delivered in the Tabernacle, Great Salt Lake City, November 1, 1857, as reported by G. D. Watt

15. The role of women in Mormonism, By Jessica Longaker, Religious Studies 263 march 27 1995, Women and Mormonism, Snowden 141.

Chapter Four – Who Is This Allah?

ALLAH IS THE BIBLICAL SATAN

"I saw another beast coming up out of the earth. He had two horns like a lamb, and he spoke like a dragon." (Revelation 13:11)

In other words, at the ends of days, there will be a demonic cult which seems like a lamb possessing the appearance of a seemingly true faith, yet what proceeds from it is demonic.

Yet, we almost always hear this phrase during religious discussions: "We all worship the same God," or "Muslims believe in Abraham too," or "Muslims also believe in Jesus." How is it they believe in Abraham, who they claim lived in Mecca, when the Biblical truth is Abraham lived in Israel? And, exactly what is it they believe about Jesus?

This is a most interesting story. According to Muslim writers, whose stories differ drastically from the truths in the Bible, the Kaaba was first built in heaven (where a model of it still remains), two thousand years before the creation of the world. Adam then erected the Kaaba on earth, but it was destroyed during the flood. According to Islam, Abraham (who the Bible tells us lived in Israel) was instructed to rebuild it in Mecca and he was assisted by his son Ishmael. Later, Abraham was buried there with his entire family. While looking for a stone to mark the corner of the building, Ishmael met the angel Gabriel, who gave him the "Black Stone" which was at the beginning "whiter than milk. It was only later that it became black from the sins of those who touched it." (*Why I Am Not A Muslim,* by Ibn Warraq, *The Origins of Islam, The Problem With Sources, Muhammad and His Message The Koran.*)

NAMES OF ALLAH

In today's world there are so many different views of God. But the Bible gives us a clear understanding of who God is. Here are just a few names of God which tell us of His character: Alpha and Omega (the beginning and the end), Creator, Healer, Comforter, Protector, Almighty, Everlasting Father, Truthful, Just, Righteous, Immutable, and the list could go on, forever. Here's a list of some of the names and descriptions of Allah. They "pack a punch" giving us insights into the true character of Islam, and Westerners need to understand this. Here are a few:

KHAYRUL MAKIREEN
(Arabic)
THE GREATEST DECEIVER
SCHEMER
CONNIVER

The first verse above from the Quran describes Allah as *khayru al-makireen*. Translation: Allah is "the best deceiver/schemer/conniver." (cf. S. 3:54; 8:30)

All four main interpreters of the Quran, Ibn Katheer, Al-Tabari, Al-Jalalyn, Al-Qurtubi, interpret this as "Allah, the great deceiver, deceived everyone by making observers believe that he was crucified, yet a likeness of Christ was crucified, and not Christ himself." From a Christian perspective, Allah removes the path of salvation since Christ, according to Muslims, never died for the sins of mankind.

AL-MUMEET

THE CREATOR OF DEATH
THE SLAYER
THE LIFE-TAKER

AL-DHARR

THE DISTRESSER
THE AFFLICTER
THE PUNISHER

AL-MUTAKABBIR

PRIDE FILLED
THE MOST PROUD

Muslim apologists claim: "This proves that Allah is the truth, while any idol they set up beside Him is falsehood, and that Allah is the Most High, Most Great (Al-Kabeer)." Quran 31:30 Yet *Al-Kabeer* and *Al-Mutakabbir* are different as some Muslim scholars will declare, and even quote the prophet Muhammad himself:

"Allah's Prayers and Peace be upon him, Allah says: 'Pride is My Wear, Supremacy is My Dress, I will break anyone who vies with Me for them and I do not care.'"[4]

"Glory be to the One who rightfully deserves to be called the Most PROUD, He is Allah." (Islam basics Library)

The very statement yelled by jihadists in every operation, Allahu Akbar (Allah is greater) and has been described by Muslim scholars:

"Majesty and glory belong to Allah alone. From this quality comes the command to magnify Allah by saying the takbor, Allahu Akbar, Allah is Greater. This is pride in the purest sense of the word. It is inconceivable of anyone except Allah in an absolute sense."[2]

AL-MALEK

THE KING

The title of king also includes information regarding his kingdom, which includes both humans and demons, a concept rejected by a Judeo-Christian perspective.

MUSLIMS SEEK PROTECTION FROM ALLAH'S EVIL POWERS

Allah creates evil? Muslims even seek refuge from Allah's evil, to protect them from it:

> "Say: I seek refuge with [Allah] the Lord of the Dawn from the mischief of the evil he created...the mischievous evil of Darkness, as it becomes intensely dark." (Quran 113:1-3)

The "evil he created" refers to the Muslim god, Allah. Seeking refuge in the lord of the dawn (morning star) who created evil and mischief is contrary to Judeo-Christian theology, which considers such descriptions better suited to Satan than to God.

ALLAH IS THE LORD OF THE DEVILS

> "Say: I seek refuge with the lord of the multitudes, the king of multitudes, the god of multitudes, from the mischief of the whisperer (of evil), who whispers into the hearts of the multitude, the multitude of demons and people." (Quran 114:1)

The Quran further defines this king and lord:

> "This is a message sent down from the lord of men and jinn [demons]." (Quran 69:43)

> "I only created jinn [demons] and man to worship me." (Quran, Adh-Dhariyat, 56)

> "Say: It has been revealed to me that a band of the jinn [demons] listened and said, 'We have heard a most amazing recitation. It leads to right guidance so we believe in it and will not associate anyone with our lord.'" (Quran, chapter of the Jinn)

Here demons heard the Quran recited and followed Allah their lord:

"An imp of the jinn said, 'I will bring it to you before you get up from your seat. I am strong and trustworthy enough to do it.'" (Quran, The Ant)

ALLAH IS SATAN IN DISGUISE

There is a marked difference in the Judeo-Christian concept of God and Satan. How could God, as understood in the Bible, bring evil, affliction, destruction and death to the very souls He sent His Son to the cross to die for? It is the Islamic pride-filled god, the causer of death and affliction, who is none other than Satan – who hailed himself as the "most proud," caused the death of mankind in the garden of Eden, and afflicted Job. In Isaiah, Satan is described as "the son of the dawn who brings all evil and destruction." Yet in the Quran it is the Muslim god, Allah, who is described as the "bringer of evil."

There are other passages from the Quran which depict Allah as Satanic.

"Say: I seek refuge with (Allah) the lord of the dawn, from the mischief of the evil he created... the mischievous evil of darkness as it becomes intensely dark, and from the mischief of those who practice the evil of malignant witch-craft and blowing on knots, and from the mischievous evil of the envier when he covets." (Quran 113:1-3)

"So, since we (jinn/demons) have listened to the guidance (of the Quran), we have accepted (Islam): and any who believes in its lord (Allah) has no fear of loss, force, or oppression." (Quran 72:13)

"I swear by those (demons) who violently tear out (the souls), and drag them to destruction." Quran 79:1

"I swear by the dawn, and the ten nights, and the even and the odd, and the night when it departs." Quran 89:1

Seeking refuge in the "lord of the dawn" (morning star) who created evil and mischief is in complete opposition to Christian theology, which sees such descriptions as given to Satan.

"Say: I seek refuge in the lord of men and jinn [demons], the king of men and jinn, the ilah (God) of men and jinn." Quran 114:1

"This is a message sent down from the lord of men and jinn [demons]. Quran 69:43

The Biblical Lord God Almighty is not the lord of demons!

ALLAH IS A WAR GOD

The concept of God in the West has developed from the Judeo-Christian heritage. One cannot deny the influence of Christian thinking in the West. The attributes of God from the Western tradition have come as a result of a rich background in both Jewish and Christian concepts. In the Bible we do not have among the attributes of God, "great deceiver," or "the Lord of demons."

However, god (Allah) as defined in the Quran is quite different. The concept of god which arises from Islamic traditions is multi-conflicting with the true Biblical God. This lord in the Quran possesses diverse characteristics, many of which require bloodshed and war; and this war is also against the people of the Bible:

"Believers! Wage war against such infidels (unbelievers) as are your neighbors, and let them find you rigorous." (Sura 9:124)

"You shall fight back against those – who do not believe in god (Allah), nor in the last day, nor do they prohibit what god and his messenger have prohibited, nor do they abide by the religion of (Islamic) truth, among those who received the scripture – until they pay the due tax (Jizia), willingly or unwillingly." (Sura 9:29)

And instead of reaching out to unbelievers as prescribed in the New Testament, the Quran calls for fighting them in jihad wars:

"Fight against them until idolatry is no more and Allah's religion reigns supreme. But if they desist, fight none except the evil-doers." (2:193)

"Say to those Arabs of the desert, who took not the field, ye shall be called forth against a people of mighty valour. Ye shall do battle with them, or [other translations have "until"] they shall profess Islam." (Sura 48:16)

"O Prophet! Strive hard against the disbelieves and the hypocrites, and be harsh against them." (9:73)

"O you who believe! Fight those of the disbelievers who are close to you, and let them find harshness in you, and know that Allah is with those who are the pious." (9:123)

"Kill the disbelievers wherever we find them." (2:191)

"Fight and slay the pagans (unbelievers), seize them, beleaguer them, and lie in wait for them in every stratagem." (9:5)

"Slay or crucify or cut the hands and feet of the unbelievers, that they be expelled from the land with disgrace and that they shall have a great punishment in world hereafter." (5:34)

"Be harsh with unbelievers." (48:29)

The Quran also instructs them to be "disobedient towards the unbelievers and their governments and strive against the unbelievers with great endeavor." (25:52)

Muhammad prescribes Muslims to fighting and tells them that:

"It is good for us, even if we dislike it." (2:216)

Then he advises Muslims to "strike off the heads of the disbelievers;" and after making a "wide slaughter among them, carefully tie up the remaining captives." (47:4)

Jihad is mandatory and Muslims are warned that "Unless we go forth, (for jihad) he (Allah) will punish us with a grievous penalty, and put others in our place." (9:39)

"And He orders us to fight them [on] until there is no more tumult and faith in Allah is practiced everywhere." (8:39)

"God has bought from the faithful their selves and their belongings against the gift of paradise; they fight in the way of Allah; they kill and get killed; that is a promise binding on Allah." (Repentance 9:110)

"And that god (Allah) may test those who believe, and destroy the infidels." (3:141)

"Relent not in pursuit of the enemy." (4:104)

"O Prophet! MAKE WAR on the infidels (unbelievers) and hypocrites, and deal rigorously with them." (Sura 66:9)

The concept of jihad is foreign to the Judeo-Christian viewpoint. With Islam, we are not dealing with a personal religion, but one that has within its tenets a war system. Some argue that these verses were given for a specific time in Muslim history. The problem is, this is not how it is being taught in the mosques or religious academies in the Middle East now, nor from the beginning of Islam. The verse is taught very clearly:

"O you who believe! Fight those of the disbelievers who are close to you."

Ibn Kateer, interprets this verse in Sura 9 as:

The order for jihad against the disbelievers, the closest, then the farthest areas. Allah commands the believers to fight the disbelievers, the closest in area to the Islamic state, then the farthest. This is why the messenger of Allah started fighting the idolaters in the Arabian Peninsula. When he finished with them and Allah gave him control over Makkah, Al-Madinah, At-Ta'if, Yemen, Yamamah, Hajr, Khaybar, Hadramawt and other Arab provinces, and the various Arab tribes entered Islam in large crowds, he then started fighting the people of the (Biblical) scriptures. He began preparations to fight the Romans who were the closest in area to the Arabian Peninsula, and as such, had the most right to be called to Islam, especially since they were from the people of the scriptures. After his death, his executor friend, and Khalifah, Abu Bakr...started preparing the Islamic armies to fight the Roman cross worshippers, and the Persian fire worshippers. By the blessing of his mission, Allah opened the lands for him and brought down Caesar and Kisra and those who obeyed them among the servants. Abu Bakr spent their treasures in the cause of Allah, just as the messenger of Allah had foretold would happen. This mission continued after Abu Bakr at the hands of he whom Abu Bakr chose to be his successor...With 'Umar, Allah humiliated the disbelievers, suppressed the tyrants and hypocrites, and opened the eastern and western parts of the world. The treasures of various countries were brought to 'Umar from near and far provinces, and he divided them according to the legitimate and accepted method. 'Umar then died as a martyr after he lived a praise-worthy life. Then, the companions among the muhajirin (immigrants) and ansar (helpers) agreed to choose after 'Umar, 'Uthman bin 'Affan, leader of the faithful and martyr of the house – may Allah be pleased with him. During 'Uthman's reign, Islam wore its widest garment and Allah's unequivocal proof was established in various parts of the world over the necks of the servants. Islam appeared in the eastern and western parts of the world and Allah's Word was elevated and His religion apparent. The pure religion reached its deepest aims against Allah's enemies, and whenever Muslims overcame an umma (community), they moved to the next one, and then the next one, crushing the tyrannical evil doers. They did this in reverence to Allah's statement, ("O you who believe! Fight those of the disbelievers who are close to you.")

It is clear from the most notable interpreters of the Quran, how Muslims view the interpretation of these verse.

Resources

1. Narrated by Muslim Abu 2620, Abu Daud 4090, Turmuthy 24,92, Ibn Maja 4174, and Ahamad 8677.

2. Sahih Muslim, Hadith collector, Transliteration, Beautiful names.

Chapter Five – The Crescent Connection and Astral Worship

THE CRESCENT IN ISAIAH

As mentioned earlier, Satan is called an "angel of light." (2 Cor. 11:14) But the prophets gave Satan different names for the time when he will embody the Antichrist: "Gog,"[1] "The Assyrian,"[2] "The Antichrist,"[3] "Son of Perdition,"[4] "Lucifer,"[5] and more. It is also important to point out that in Isaiah 14:12, the word "Lucifer" in Hebrew is *"Hilal ben Sahar."* Hilal also means "the brightness" and in Aramaic/Arabic it means "Crescent Moon." Studying these two words, "Hilal" and "Sahar," we find:

1. Helel, or Heylel (morning star) have possible links with Akkadian elletu (Ishtar) and *Arabic hilal* (new moon). [6] The worship of the moon is also attested to by proper names of people such as *Hilal*, a crescent; *Qamar*, a moon; and so on.[7] "Hilal" means "the shining one" in Hebrew and Arabic, and in Ethiopian it means "Moon crescent." He is a Moon-god."[8]

2. "Sahar" or "Shahar" is Hebrew for dawn or morning star.

It is noteworthy that the meaning of these two words combined, make up the Satanic symbol – crescent moon and star as described in chapter 13. These are also the same symbols which sit over most Islamic mosques and fly on the flags from many Muslim countries.

The Quran mentions the "rising of the dawn" in a night called "the night of vision:"

"We have sent it to thee in the Night of Vision, what do you know of this Night of Vision. The Night of Vision is better then a thousand months. The *angelic hosts descend* [to earth] in it with *the Spirit* by command *of their Lord*. Peace shall it be until *the rising of the Dawn* (Morning star)"[9] The morning dawn (star) and the crescent moon are important symbols to Muslims everywhere. Even when terrorists from over 40 different organizations assembled in Tehran, they gave the name of the summit "Ten Days of Dawn."[10] The italicized words could very well have come out of Scripture regarding Satan and his fallen angels, cast out of heaven (dawn, the spirit, their lord).

HOLY RAMADAN?

The above verses refer to *Ramadan*, a time for Muslims to fast, when the crescent moon appears with Venus (morning star), which is the symbol of Satan as written by Isaiah. Muslims wait until the late hours of the night, gazing at the sky, waiting to see the sky open and the angelic host descend. Prior to my father's conversion, when he was Muslim, he would go up on the roof with his family during the "Night Vision," gaze at the sky and wait for this heavenly sight.

Another reference to the god of Islam as being the "lord of dawn" or "lord of daybreak," the one who brings evil, can be found in Sura 113:

> "Say: 'I seek refuge in the lord of the *Daybreak*, from the *evil of what he has created;* and from the evil of the night when it comes on; and from the evil of the witches who blow upon knots, and from the evil of the envious when he envies.'" Here he is described as the lord of the "daybreak," or of the morning – the son of the morning.

THERE WERE OTHERS WORSHIPPED AS THE LORD OF THE DAWN *MESOAMERICAN GOD QUETZALCOATL IS ALSO LORD OF THE DAWN.* Quetzalcoatl was the "feathered serpent" god of the Aztecs 2000 years ago. Also defined as the morning star, he was known by the title Tlahuizcalpantecuhtli, meaning "lord of the star of the dawn." (Wikipedia, Quetzalcoatl, Attributes)

ALEISTER CROWLEY AND THE LORD OF THE DAWN

In *The Confessions of Aleister Crowley* it reads:

*"O Thou dew-lit nymph of the Dawn, that swoonest in
the satyr arms of the Sun! I adore Thee,
I adore Thee, IAO!"*
(The Confessions of Aleister Crowley, 544)

The most well known Islamic song, which came from Islam's founders, is called "Tala'al-Badru."[11] I have provided the English translation: *O you who were raised amongst us is Muhammad.*

ARABIC	ENGLISH
Tala'al-Badru 'alayna	O the White glowing Moon rose over us
min thaniyyatil-Wada'	From the Valley of Wada'
wajaba al-shukru 'alayna	And we owe it to show gratefulness
ma da'a lillahi da'	Where the call is to Allah
Ayyuha al-mab'uthu fina	O you who were raised amongst us
ji'ta bi-al-amri al-muta	coming with a work to be obeyed
Ji'ta sharrafta al-Madinah	You have brought to this city nobleness
marhaban ya khayra da'	Welcome! Best Call to Allah's Way

In Isaiah 14, the *"king of Babylon"* is identified as Satan:

"O shining star, son of the morning! How you have fallen from heaven," and to him the Bible says, "You shall be cast from your grave" and, "You shall not be united with them (the other kings of the earth) in burial, because you ruined your land and you have slain your people."[12]

This agrees with Revelation 19, where we see the Antichrist thrown alive into the Lake of Fire. It is the embodiment of Satan as the Antichrist, Satan in the flesh deceiving people as the false Messiah.

"I will break the Assyrian in My land, and tread him underfoot."[13]

Here, Satan (Lucifer) is addressed as a man. "They that see thee shall narrowly look upon thee, [and] consider thee, [saying, is] this the *man* that made the earth to tremble, that did shake kingdoms?"[14] The question is, when did this angelic 'Lucifer' become man? Clearly, this is Satan-in-the-flesh.

Thus, the Babylonian king is not Nebuchadnezzar or any other ruler of ancient Babylon. Isaiah 14, verse 14, all the way to verse 23, is about Satan, and then suddenly verses 24 and 25 use end-time terminology:

> "As I have purposed, it shall rise; to break Assyria in My land, and on My mountains I will trample him...this is the purpose that is purposed on all the earth, and this is the hand that is stretched out on all the nations."

The text suddenly goes from describing the Antichrist's destruction to describing the destruction of Assyria without any apparent break. In Isaiah, "the king of Assyria" is very descriptive of the Antichrist.

Isaiah 30:30-31 confirms this:

> "Yahweh (God) will make the majesty of His voice heard; the lowering of His arm He will show, with raging anger, and a consuming flame; cloudburst and storm and hailstones. For by the voice of Yahweh, Assyria is crushed."

It's that unmistakable terminology signifying the Day of the Lord, where "His arm" is referring to Jesus, as is the case throughout Isaiah, including Isaiah 3:1. This is not the Assyria of the moment, but an end-time Assyria which is destroyed at the fiery coming of Jesus on dark and tempestuous clouds, when He destroys Satan by a "breath of His mouth" and "sword out of His mouth."

Isaiah reveals the outcome for the man who would be a modern "Nebuchadnezzar" and threaten all of creation with his terrible weapons: "For I will rise up against them, says the Lord of Hosts, and cut off from Babylon its name and remnant, and offspring and posterity, says the Lord...I will sweep it with the broom of destruction..."[15]

The broom of destruction. Anyone who has seen footage of a nuclear bomb explosion knows how the ominous cloud sweeps up everything in its path.

CRESCENT MOON AND MYSTERY BABYLON

Revelation 17 presents a snapshot of the entire Babylonian influence and of human sin, stretching over time to encompass the empires of Daniel with their false religions. Islam's crescent moon, in reality, stems from Babylonian, modern day Iraq. In 217 AD, Emperor Caracala was killed after he was returning from visiting the temple of the moon god in Haran, Iraq. In 363 AD, Emperor Julian paid his respects to the temple of sin. The moon god, in fact, was the most WORSHIPPED god in Roman times. It is reasonable to connect the Roman Empire's religious worship from Babylon to Islam, which adopted this symbol. The moon god at Haran was described by the Doctrine of Addai, Jacob of Searug, and others.

Islam is simply a revival of a Babylonian religion. The moon god with the crescent moon and star symbol originated in Babylon (Iraq) and was one of the 360 idols in the Kaaba (Mecca) before Muhammad destroyed them. In Babylon, the moon god was called "Sin."

G. Caton Thompson's book, *The Tombs and Moon Temple of Hureidha*, discusses the uncovering of a temple of the moon god in southern Arabia. The symbols of the crescent moon and no less than twenty-one inscriptions with the name "Sin" were found in this temple.

An idol, which may be the moon god himself, was also discovered. The Arabic word for 'god' is 'Ilah' and the moon god became synonymous with "al-Ilah," meaning "the god;" pagan Arabia believed that the moon god was the greatest of all the gods, hence the phrase "Allahu Akbar," meaning "Allah is greater."

This is what led Muhammad to go one step further and proclaim in the Quran that "la ilaha ila Allah" – there is no god but Allah.

Inscriptions of "al-Ilah" have been found on an idol with the crescent moon and star symbols. The pagan Arabs used "Allah" in naming their children. For example, Muhammad's father was called Abdullah, meaning "servant of Allah."

Even the killing of converts was not unusual in pre-Islamic practice in Arabia, just as it is not unusual today. There is the story of Sylleus the Arab, who fell in love with Salome in Herod's kingdom, but he would not convert at her request for fear of being stoned by his people, the Arabs.[16]

Sir Leonard Woolley excavated a temple of the moon god in Ur (Babylon). His findings are displayed in the British Museum. In the 1950s, a major temple of the moon god was excavated at Hazer in "Palestine." Two idols of the moon god were found. Each was a statue of a man sitting upon a throne with a crescent moon carved on his chest, and the inscriptions confirm the items were idols. They also found several smaller statues bearing inscriptions identifying them as the "daughters" of the moon god.[17]

In Saudi Arabia before Muhammad was born, there were three sisters, al-Lat, al-Uzza and Manat, who many speculated were the daughters of Allah. They are depicted together with Allah, the moon god, represented by a crescent moon above them. The daughters themselves have the symbol of a star. Even the Quran, in Sura 53:19-20, mentions them by name, not to mention the abrogated "Satanic verses" which give additional weight to the fact that Allah was the moon god. Idols of al-Lat, al-Uzza and Manat were also WORSHIPPED in the Kaaba and, lo and behold, Sura 53 is titled "An-najm," meaning "the star."

This "Mystery Babylon" stemmed from Babylon and lived throughout history in every empire in the east. The fall of "Mystery Babylon" as prophesied could likely mean "the fall of Islam."

Dr. Arthur Jeffrey, professor of Islamic and Middle East Studies, one of the world's foremost scholars on Islam, said that the name "Allah," and its feminine form, "Allat," were well known in pre-Islamic Arabia and were found in inscriptions uncovered in North Africa: it "is a proper name applicable only to their peculiar god." He adds, "Allah is a pre-Islamic name...corresponding to the Babylonian god known as Bel."[18] "Bel" simply means "lord" and this is a title of reverence to the moon-god "Sin."

And the name *Sanballat the Arab* mentioned in the Bible harassing Israel while rebuilding the Temple is a derivative of two words, the Sin (moon god), and Allat, the feminine of Allah, one of his three daughters. This shows that such names existed way before Muhammad, just as his father's name, Abd-*Allah*, meant "slave of Allah," the moon god.

The worship of the moon god came from Ur of the Chaldees in Babylon. Abraham is the first to mention it in his account of his journey in Genesis 12:1.

Nabodnidus elevated the moon god, Sin, to the top of the Babylonian pantheon in an effort to make the Babylonian religion more acceptable to the Arabs and Armadas. The emblem for the god Sin, the *Controller of the Night*, was the crescent moon, which became the primary religious symbol of Islam. The Islamic calendar is based on the lunar cycle, and may have relevance to moon god worship. In Arabia, he was known as "Hubbell," al-Allah, "the god."

In Sura 106, the Quran commanded Quays, Muhammad's clan, to *"worship the lord of this shrine"* (i.e., the Kabana) which can mean only the moon god. It is only after this Sura was revealed that Muhammad came back to destroy the idols in the Kabana and fight the people that refused to accept his status as prophet. There is no mention in the Bible of God ordering anyone to erect a shrine in Arabia, so who really is *"the lord of this shrine?"*

ISLAM CONSTITUTES BLASPHEMY

The Bible clearly states: "Who is a liar but he that denieth that Jesus is the Christ? He is Antichrist that denieth the Father and the Son." (1 John 2:22)

To blaspheme God is to deny His attributes – to deny that He is the Father, that He has a Son, and that Christ, the Word of God, took on human flesh. Islam is actually a polemic against Christianity. It is the only religion with the central purpose of denying that God is our Father and that He has a Son who came in the flesh.

THE HEAVENLY BADGE AND THE MARK OF THE BEAST

"And he causeth all, both small and great, rich and poor, free and bond, to receive a mark in their right hand, or on their foreheads:

And that no man might buy or sell, save he that had the mark, or the name of the beast, or the number of his name." (Revelation 13:16)

There are three choices which the dammed would wear on their foreheads or hands indicating allegiance to the beast, the mark, the name, or the number.

The Greek word *charagma* used for "mark" is actually a "badge of servitude" or of allegiance and servanthood. *Strong's Hebrew Lexicon* defines *charagma* as "the mark stamped on the forehead or the right hand as the badge of the followers of the Antichrist." Note that the phrase "right arm" is from the Greek *dexios*, which could also be translated "right side."[19] The Islamic Shahadatan (I declare no god but Allah and Muhammad is his messenger) is actually a declaration of allegiance and servitude (Submission/Islam) to Allah and Muhammad; the inscription of this declaration is worn by millions on the forehead or right arm. It can be seen on Muslim demonstrators and jihadists who wear badges and banners on their foreheads today. Contrary to many speculations today, there is absolutely nothing in the text of Revelation 13 to suggest that followers of the Antichrist will be required to have a chip implanted in their foreheads or their hands (arms).

Islam and Mormonism share a further similarity with "certificates" or "badges" to heaven. Muhammad stated:

"Allah will save a man from my nation above all creation on Judgment Day. In front of him will be laid 99 registers for his sins. Every register is as long as the eye can see. Then he is asked "do you deny any of these?" then he says "no O lord," then he is asked "do you have any excuse?" in which he responds "no lord," then he is told "you have but one good deed and there will be no condemnation for you today." A badge is brought forth on it "No god but Allah, and Muhammad is His messenger." Then he is asked to bring forth his deeds, then he asks "O lord, what is this badge that is with these registers?" then he is told "you will receive no condemnation," then the deeds are put on one hand,

and the badge in the other, then the registers will float and the badge will outweigh the registers.[20]

Brigham Young stated "No man or woman in this dispensation will ever enter into the celestial kingdom of god without the consent of Joseph Smith...Every man and woman must have the certificate of Joseph Smith, junior, as a passport to their entrance...I cannot go there without his consent...He reigns there as a supreme being in his sphere, capacity, and calling, as God does in heaven.[21]

ISLAM DENIES RIGHTS TO WOMEN

The Antichrist will have no regard for women's rights. Women will have no voice in his empire, just as it is in Islam.

"Neither shall he regard the gods of his fathers nor the desire of women." (Daniel 11:37)

ISLAM HONORS A GOD OF WAR

"...nor [shall he] regard any god; for he shall magnify himself above all. He will exalt himself above all gods." (Daniel 11:37)

The Antichrist is Satan personified and he is the god of war – jihad.

"But in his estate shall he honor the god of forces: and a god whom his fathers knew not shall he honor with gold, and silver, and with precious stones, and pleasant things." (Daniel 11:38)

Interestingly, all Muslims are required to honor Allah once a year by fulfilling one of the five pillars of Islam called *Zakat*, the requirement that each Muslim give a percentage of his wealth from money, gold, silver, or any other resources.

THE NAZIS AND ASTRAL WORSHIP

The party elite in the Nazi SS were taught knowledge of the psychic, tapping into the "Vril Force," self-denial, brotherhood mission, medieval lore, fearlessness of death. The innermost circle was privy to the hard-core gnostic teaching on the grail, immortality and godhood. Many neo-Nazi groups continue to pursue these topics with devotion. But under it all was the invisible presence of "Unknown Superiors" who taught Hitler himself and who were assumed by his associates to endow him with his uncanny hypnotic power.[22]

The vril force or vril energy was said to be derived from the Black Sun, a big ball of "Prima Materia" which supposedly exists in the center of the Earth, giving light to the vril-ya and putting out radiation in the form of vril. The Vril Society believed that Aryans were the actual biological ancestors of the Black Sun.[23]

With the origin of Nazi doctrine came of a mix of ideologies – the Vril Society and the Freemasons. These teachings are not recent, they were known to the ancients under many names. They have been called Chi, Ojas, Vril, Astral Light, Odic Forces and Orgone. In a discussion of the 28th degree of the Ancient and Accepted Scottish Rite of Freemasonry – called "Knight of the Sun" or "Prince Adept" – Albert Pike said, "There is in nature one most potent force, by means whereof a single man, who could possess himself of it, and should know how to direct it, could revolutionize and change the face of the world."[24]

Astral light? That should sound familiar – the sun is a star, and in these societies they WORSHIPPED the Black Sun. Just as the Nazis believed the power of the Black Sun formed the Aryan race that lived on earth, the Muslims believed in the power of the Black Stone – an asteroid piece of star (sun) which fell from heaven and crashed on earth.

BAPHOMET VS. ISLAM'S GABRIEL

Even Baphomet (meaning Satan or demon, a member of the hierarchy of Hell) (A) which is used by Satanists would have much in common with the angel whom both Muhammad (B) and Joseph Smith encountered. Note in the second illustration of Baphomet (C) there are two crescent moons around it, and the star on its forehead represents blasphemy. The two horns are symbolic representing an attack on Heaven. The chain which Muhammad described – what seems like two intertwined snakes – is seen on both the Muslim angel and Baphomet, as coming out of the chest area.

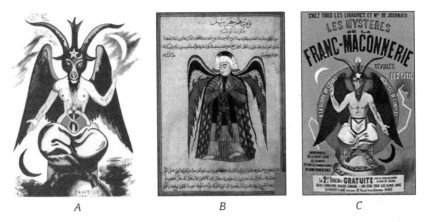

A   B   C

The crescents have played an intricate roll in all cults from ancient Egypt, Babylonian, Assyrian, Grecian, Roman, Islamic, Mormon, and Satanist.

Roman Coin. Hadrian, AD 117 – 138

Typical of many LDS churches, there are numerous stars around the church building, representing the starry heavens above.

In this picture of a Mormon church, one can see the pentagram stars on top and crescent on the bottom; the same pentagram is on the forehead of Baphomet. Within Mormonism there are three levels to which some people will be assigned after Judgement Day. The celestial kingdom is the highest level, for the sun (thought to be the highest because it's nearest God); the terrestrial kingdom is the second, or intermediate level, for the moon; and the telestial kingdom is the third, or lowest level, for the stars. On the Mormon Church in Nauvoo, Illinois, Joseph Smith arranged these symbols in different order – from the ground level up: the moon in the base; sun in the capital, and the stars in the frieze.[25]

Mormonism's Doctrine and Covenant 88: 7, 8 and 9 reads:

> "Which truth shineth. This is the light of Christ. As also He is in the sun, and the light of the sun, and the power thereof by which it was made. Also He is in the moon, and is the light of the moon, and the power thereof by which it was made; As also the light of the stars, and the power thereof by which they were made."[26]

The Christ and Abraham of Islam and Mormonism are not to be confused with the same people as in Bible. Cults always use the Biblical names of real people in the Bible. However, they possess totally different attributes and history. In fact, the Christ and Abraham of Islam and Mormon are depicted as being opposite the Biblical characters. These cults even go so far as to take what is described as most evil in the Bible, and try to make them appear most holy. Often, the antithesis of Christ (The Antichrist) is described as the holy one within these cults. Here is but one example. In the Book of The Law it reads:

> "Now ye shall know that the chosen priest and apostle of infinite space is the prince-priest the beast; and in his woman called the scarlet woman is all power given. They shall gather my children into their fold: they shall bring the glory of the stars into the hearts of men. For he is ever a sun, and she a moon. But to him is the winged secret flame, And to her the stooping starlight."[27]

Yet, in the Bible this is the ultimate evil:

> "So he carried me away in the Spirit into the wilderness. And I saw a woman sitting on a scarlet beast *which was* full of names of blasphemy. And the woman was arrayed in purple and scarlet color, and decked with gold and precious stones and pearls, having a golden cup in her hand full of abominations and filthiness of her fornication." (Revelation 17:3-4)

The Book of The Law also states:

> "For perfume mix meal and honey and thick leavings of red wine: then oil of Abramelin and olive oil, and afterward soften and smooth down with rich fresh blood." (Chapter 2, #23)

While the Bible states:

> "And I saw the woman drunken with the blood of the saints, and with the blood of the martyrs of Jesus: and when I saw her, I wondered with great admiration." (Revelation 17:6)

Why would The Book of The Law used by witches, Mormonism, and Islam choose what is evil in the Bible and announce it as godly?

ISLAM'S MESSIAH IS ANTICHRIST

Most Christians know that the Antichrist, or the incarnation of Satan, will appear on the earth to establish a seven year reign in which after 3½ years of false peace there will be tyranny and destruction. (Daniel 9:27) After that, the Antichrist will be removed by Christ who will finally establish true peace. When Ahmadinejad addressed the United Nations General Assembly in October of 2005, he ended his speech with a prayer imploring god to hasten the return of the 12th Imam. Ahmadinejad refers to the return of the 12th Imam, also known as the Mahdi, in almost all his major speeches. In the Islamic faith, the Mahdi is the ultimate savior of mankind. His appearance will usher in an era of Islamic justice and bring about the conversion of the heathen amidst flame and fire. The Mahdi will establish Islam as the global religion and will reign for seven years before bringing about the end of the world. Muhammad, the prophet of Islam states: "He will fill the earth will equity and justice as it was filled with oppression and tyranny, and he will rule for seven years." (Narrated by Abu-Daud)

Muhammad the prophet of Islam also stated:

> "Allah will expand that day to such a length of time, as to accommodate the kingdom of a person from my Ahlul-Bayt (household of Muhammad) who will be called by my name. He will fill out the earth with peace and justice as it will have been full of injustice and tyranny (by then)." (Sahih al-Tirmidhi, v. 2, p. 86, v. 9, pp. 74-75)

THE BLACK STONE, AND SATAN (THE STAR) THAT FELL FROM HEAVEN

This very Mahdi, could be Satan who is depicted in the Bible as the "great star that fell from heaven:"

In Revelation 8:10, "And the third angel sounded, and there fell a great star from heaven, burning as it were a lamp and it fell upon the third part of the rivers and upon the fountains of waters." Besides a literal star (asteroid), the fallen star is synonymous with Satan and his fallen angels. A metaphorical interpretation would be that Satan (morning star, angel in heaven) appears as a lamp (angel of light) and is cast down to deceive the world. (Isaiah 14)

Since the death of one-third of the population will occur by rise of the eighth empire (see Revelation 17, which is one of the seven heads [mountains] the woman rides), which will be Islamic, we must correlate these verses with this Scripture. The fallen star, the destroyer who is unleashed, must lead the "mountain" (empire), causing one-third of mankind to die. This is the same force that lead all past empires and will all come up in the end. For a more detailed study on this please refer to *Why I Left Jihad* (W. Shoebat, 2005). Revelation 17:9 is not speaking of literal mountains. "Here is the mind which has wisdom: The seven heads are seven mountains on which the woman sits. They are also seven kings." A "Mountain" is a kingdom ruled by kings. This would resemble all seven empires which ruled the ancient world – Egyptian, Babylonian, Assyrian, Medo-Persian, Grecian, Roman, and Muslim which will arise again as the eighth:

> "And the beast that was, and is not, even he is the eighth, and is of the seven, and goeth into perdition." (Revelation 17:11)

This last empire will be ruled by the most ruthless man who will be possessed by the "star" (Satan) who will want his image to be WORSHIPPED. An asteroid is a logical assumption as this symbolic star, since the Black Stone itself is evidently a meteorite and undoubtedly owes its reputation to the tradition that it fell from the "heavens." (see Acts 19:35)

It is doubly ironic that Muslims venerate this piece of rock as that given to Ishmael by the angel Gabriel to build the kaaba, since, to quote Margoliouth (a professor of Arabic, Oxford University, 1889-1937), "...it is of doubtful genuineness, since the Black Stone was removed by the...Qarmatians in the fourth (Muslim) century, and restored by them after many years: it may be doubted whether the stone which they returned was the same as the stone which they removed."

This asteroid stone caused a great portion of mankind to be spiritually poisoned. When Muslims pray, they bow towards this Black Stone to worship Allah five times a day. Yet the Bible offers a similar symbol for Satan (the star) being cast out to dwell on earth where he demands worship. This is a most interesting story. According to Muslim writers, the kaaba was first built in heaven, (where a model of it remains), two thousand years before the creation of the world. Adam allegedly erected the kaaba on earth but it was destroyed during the flood. After that, Abraham was instructed to rebuild it where he was assisted by Ishmael. While looking for a stone to mark the corner of the building, Ishmael met the angel Gabriel (Lucifer in disguise), who gave him the *Black Stone, which was then whiter than milk; it was only later that it became black from the sins of those who touched it.*

In other words the pilgrims who venerate the Black Stone have emptied their sins into it. This is why in Islam, it's crucial for Muslims to go to Mecca at least once in their lifetime, usually when they are older, so as to ensure a sinless life before they die. This cleansing ritual offers a new life for the Muslim. This veneration of an asteroid would be blasphemous in Christian theology, especially since Jesus was the only one who took upon Himself the sins of the world, and not Satan. In other words, the Black Stone is believed by Muslims to have come down from heaven, and takes upon itself the sins of mankind.

THE IMAGE OF THE BEAST

This story is nothing new. The Book of Acts spoke of this very issue:

"At last the mayor was able to quiet them down enough to speak. 'Citizens of Ephesus' he said. "Everyone knows that Ephesus is the official guardian of the temple of the great *Artemis, whose image fell down to us from heaven*." (Acts 19:35)

Artemis, in Ephesus (modern day Turkey), was often depicted with the crescent moon on her forehead and was sometimes identified with Selene (goddess of the moon) who the people in Ephesus WORSHIPPED. It is likely that Turkey's crescent symbol is a throwback to those ancient times. Could this image *"the image of the beast"* be a crescent moon? Only time will tell.

CYBELE

Also known as Kybele, is interestingly the same word Muslims use for the direction of prayer towards the Black Stone (Al-Qibla). Likewise, ancient worship of Cybele was also associated with a Black Stone or meteorite that had fallen from the sky:

"Varro states that the goddess was brought from a shrine called the Megalesion in the city of Pergamon while Ovid located the Mother's home on Mount Ida near the ancient city of Troy, which was under Pergamene control at that time. Livy seems to combine the two traditions in reporting that the Romans sought the help of the Pergamene King Attalos I in obtaining the goddess from Pessinous. Precisely what the Romans obtained is described in several sources: it was a small dark sacred stone not formed into any iconographic image, that had fallen to the shrine of Pessinous from the sky." (*In Search of God the Mother*, Roller, p. 265.)

The stone associated with Cybele's worship was, originally, probably at Pessinus but perhaps at Pergamum or on Mount Ida. What is certain is that in 204 B.C. it was taken to Rome, where Cybele became 'Mother' to the Romans. The ecstatic rites of her worship were alien to the Roman temperament, but nevertheless animated the streets of their city during the annual procession of the goddess's statue. Alongside Isis, Cybele

The crescent moons (Hilal) are easily viewed at the top of each dome. The stars are seen on the exterior walls.

Up-close photo of a star on a mosque wall.

A photo of a crescent moon taken in Nauvoo, IL. The symbol of the crescent can be linked to the Muslim Hilal.

Muslim minaret with crescent moon and star on top.

retained prominence in the heart of the Empire until the fifth century B.C. – when the stone was lost. Her cult prospered throughout the Empire and it is said that every town or village remained true to the worship of Cybele.[28]

The area of Masjid al-Harem, or the Sacred Mosque, surrounds the Kaaba. According to Islamic theology, the mosque was first built by the angels before the creation of mankind when God ordained a place of worship on

Earth. This place of worship was to reflect the house in heaven called al-Bayt-al-Mamur, which translates to 'The Worship Place of Angels' and is directly above the Kaaba in heaven.[29]

The Quran:

> "I swear by the heaven and the comer by night; and what will make you know what the comer by night is? the star of piercing brightness; there is not a soul but over it is a keeper."[30]

HITLER AND THE MOON

Hitler himself wrote of a certain mystical power of the moon. Here is a poem he wrote after over five years of study in Vienna where St. Germain and Kaballists reigned supreme:

> "I often go on bitter nights To Wotan's oak in the quiet glade. With dark powers to weave a union – The runic letter the moon makes with its magic spell and all who are full of impudence during the day are made small by the magic formula."[31]

ANCIENT EGYPT AND THE MOON

Thoth is an Egyptian moon god. Over time, he developed as a god of wisdom, and came to be associated with magic, music, medicine, astronomy, geometry, surveying, drawing and writing. Thoth was also a god of the underworld, where he served as a clerk who recorded the judgments on the souls of the dead.[32]

THE STAR OF SIRIUS

In Friedrich Nietzsche's book, *Thus Spoke Zarathustra,* Nietzsche writes:

From Crystallinks.com, Thoth depicting the crescent moon on his head.

> "When Zarathustra was thirty years old he left his home and the lake of his home and went into the mountains. Here he enjoyed his spirit and his solitude and for ten years he did not

tire of it. But at last his heart transformed. One morning he arose with the dawn, stepped before the sun and spoke thus to it: 'You great star! What would your happiness be if you had not those for whom you shine? For ten years you have come up here to my cave: you would have tired of your light and of this route without me, my eagle and my snake. But we awaited you every morning, took your overflow from you and blessed you for it. Behold! I am weary of my wisdom, like a bee that has gathered too much honey. I need hands that reach out. I want to bestow and distribute until the wise among human beings have once again enjoyed their folly, and the poor once again their wealth. For this I must descend into the depths, as you do evenings when you go behind the sea and bring light even to the underworld, you super-rich star! Like you, I must *go down* as the human beings say, to whom I want to descend.'"[33]

Quran 91:1-2 reads: "I swear by the sun and its brilliance, And the moon when it follows the sun,"

It's interesting what the members of the Order of The Solar Temple believed in – they looked up on the star of Sirius which is the brightest star of the night-time sky.

From 1994 to 1997, the Order of the Solar Temple's members became so paranoid they began a series of mass suicides, which led to roughly 74 deaths. Farewell letters were left by members, stating that they believed their deaths would be an escape from the "hypocrisies and oppression of this world." Adding that they felt they were "moving on to Sirius."[34]

THE STAR OF SIRIUS IN ISLAM

It's interesting that the Quran also mentioned Sirius, saying: "And that he [Allah] is the lord of Sirius" وَأَنَّهُۥ هُوَ رَبُّ ٱلشِّعْرَىٰ [35] The same god of Sirius (Satan) was the god of many other cults and Satan worshippers. The Hindu god's name is Shiva and is also called *Chandrashekhara* which literally means "one whose crest is the moon" because the crescent moon of the fifth day (panchami) sits in his hair.

HADIT, NUIT AND THE KAABA

Aleister Crowley's *The Law is for All* describes Hadit and Nuit. Nuit, the feminine side of the great astuteness known as creation, asserts in verse 21: "I am nothing: they do not see me. They are as upon the earth; I am Heaven and there is no other god than me, and my lord Hadit." She goes on in verse 22 to say: "I am infinite space, and the infinite stars thereof..."[36]

He [Hadit] identifies himself as the point in the center of the circle, the axle of the wheel, the cube in the circle, "the flame that burns in every heart of man, and in the core of every star," and the worshipper's own inner self. Thelema connects the sun-god Hadit with every individual star. Furthermore, *The Book of the Law* says, "Every man and every woman is a star."[37]

An aerial view of the Kaaba shows the millions of worshippers that go in a circle around the cube (Kaaba).

The Pilgrimage to Makkah

The Kaaba could possibly represent the cube in the circle of people (stars) which Hadit (the spirit) is in every man who is possessed with the spirit of Hadit.

The Book of The Law states: "I, Hadit, am the complement of Nu, my bride. I am not extended, and Khabs is the name of my House. In the sphere I am everywhere the center, as she, the circumference, is nowhere found. Yet she shall be known and I never."[38] Hadit does not represent the sphere itself – but the spirit within the sphere. Also, the words Khabs and Kaaba sound almost alike. Khabs is the house of Hadit, while the Kaaba carries the nick name *Baytullah*, which means House of Allah.

Nu, representing Satan's bride, is the circle of people who either worship towards it, or circulate seven times around it, during the *Hajj*. This bride of Satan is the circumference surrounding his house (the Kaaba) and within it is the Black Stone, which is his representation on earth. This attempt to be parallel to the bride of Christ (Believers in Christ) is quite interesting to say the least. As Christ through the Holy Spirit dwells in believers, so does Satan attempt to have a demon (star) dwell in every man and woman "Every man and woman is a star."

The description of the *Hilal* where it reads the "new moon" (Arabic hilal – new moon) has a possible connection with a text written by Aleister Crowley:

> "In the Daylight I see not Thy Body of Stars, O Beloved. The little light of the Sun veils the Great Light of the Stars, for today Thou seemest distant. The Sun burns like a great Torch, and Earth seems as one of His little Spheres, filled with life. I am but a tiny spermatozoon, but within me is the fiery and concentrated essence of Life. Draw me up into Thyself, O Sun! Project me into the Body of Our Lady Nuit! Thus shall a new Star be born, and I shall see Thee even in the Daylight, O Beloved." And to this one as well: "Thus shall a new Star be born, and I shall see Thee even in the Daylight, O Beloved."

In Islam, the name for demon is 'jinn.' The word 'jinn' literally means anything which has the connotation of concealment, invisibility, seclusion and remoteness.[39] The Quran explains the way the jinn describe heaven: "We jinn pried into the secrets of heaven; but we found it filled with fierce guards, stern wardens and flaming fires. We used to sit there in, hidden in observatories, trying to steal a hearing; but any who listen now will find a shooting star and a flaming fire watching him, lying in wait as an ambush for him." (Quran 72.8)

Then in Quran 72:1-8, the jinn begin to describe their view of the Quran: (I will also put it in Arabic for accuracy).

"Say (O Muhammad): It is revealed unto me that a company of the jinn gave ear, and they said: Lo! it is a marvelous Quran, Which guideth unto righteousness, so we believe in it and we ascribe unto our Lord no partner. And (we believe) that he, exalted be the glory of our lord! hath taken neither wife nor son. And that the foolish one among us used to speak concerning Allah an atrocious lie. And lo! we had supposed that humankind and jinn would not speak a lie concerning Allah. And indeed (O Muhammad), individuals of humankind used to invoke the protection of individuals of the jinn so that they increased them in revolt (against Allah); And indeed they supposed, even as ye suppose, that Allah would not raise anyone (from the dead). And (the Jinn who had listened to the Quran said): We had sought the heaven but had found it filled with strong warders and meteors."[40]

The Quran speaks of the dawn, when the angelic host came down from heaven. (Quran, Surat Al-Qadr) Here is the portion about the Night of Vision:

"We have sent it to thee in the Night of Vision, what do you know of this Night of Vision. The Night of Vision is better than a thousand months. The angelic hosts descend [to earth] in it with the spirit by command of the their Lord. Peace shall it be until the rising of the Dawn (Morning star)."[41] So according to this verse, the angelic host will come down to earth at night. In Islam – so do devils: Allah's Apostle said, "When night falls (or when it is evening), stop your children from going out, for the devils spread out at that time. But when an hour of the night has passed, release them and close the doors and mention Allah's Name, for Satan does not open a closed door. Tie the mouth of your waterskin and mention Allah's Name; cover your containers and utensils and mention Allah's Name. Cover them even by placing something across it, and extinguish your lamps."[42]

In the dawn, the angelic hosts may possibly represent the jinn. According to the ancient Semites, jinn were spirits of vanished ancient peoples who acted during the night and disappeared with the first light of dawn.[43]

The cult Heaven's Gate (started by Marshall Applewhite and Bonnie Nettles) has also stated something which resembles this. Heaven's Gate had their own web page in order to promote their religion. On the Web page, Applewhite posted six key points, paraphrased as: I and my partner are from the Evolutionary Level Above Human and we took over two human bodies in their forties, which had been tagged at birth as vehicles for our use. We brought a crew of students to Earth with us from the Kingdom of Heaven. Many of us arrived in staged crashes of spaceships and authorities confiscated some of our bodies. Others came before us to tag our bodies with special chips. Before our human incarnation, we were briefed by older beings with details about how to take over the human vehicle. The Kingdom of God is genderless, multiplying through metamorphosis, and its inhabitants have free will.[44]

And this can lead back to the thetans: a body thetan is a thetan who is 'stuck' in, on, or near a body because they have lost their free will as a result of an event in their past. This is an interesting statement because this means that the thetans originally had free will. The jinn are said to be creatures with free will.[45]

Crowley had once said concerning his connection with Nuit: "I am uplifted in thine heart; and the kisses of the stars rain hard upon thy body."[46] In the Bible, stars are usually considered demons and it is a fact that Aleister Crowley was a demon worshipper. Revelation 12:3, 4, talks about stars being demons: "Then another sign appeared in heaven: an enormous red dragon with seven heads and ten horns and seven crowns on his heads. His tail drew a third of the stars of heaven and threw them to the earth. And the dragon stood before the woman who was ready to give birth, to devour her Child as soon as it was born." This is saying that a third of the angels were fallen angles, or demons, and they were cast to the earth. This confirms that the angels of the Night Vision in the Muslim Quran are the fallen angels. "The angelic hosts descend [to earth] in it with the spirit by command of their Lord. Peace shall it be until the rising of the Dawn (Morning star)." When you look at Islam and the Muslim Messiah (Mahdi) through the prophecy spoken by Daniel regarding the Antichrist, one can see that the Muslim Messiah is the Antichrist.

Now to the Thetans. In this story Xenu is considered to be the 'president' of space:

"Xenu was about to be deposed from power, so he devised a plot to eliminate the excess population from his dominions. With the assistance of 'renegades,' he defeated the populace and the 'Loyal Officers,' a force for good that was opposed to Xenu. Then, with the assistance of psychiatrists, he summoned billions of people to paralyze them with injections of alcohol and glycol under the pretense they were being called for 'income tax inspections.' The kidnapped populace was loaded into space planes for transport to the site of extermination, the planet of Teegeeack (Earth)."[47]

The hundreds of billions of captured thetans were taken to a type of cinema, where they were forced to watch a "3-D, super colossal motion picture" for 36 days. This implanted what Hubbard termed "various misleading data" (collectively termed the R6 implant) into the memories of the hapless thetans, "which has to do with God, the devil, space opera, et cetera."[48] There they were, being shown movies of what life on Earth should be like, and they were also shown false pictures of God and Christ to instill a religious fervor in them that would make them less effective and so easier to control.[49] When the space planes had reached Teegeeack/Earth, the paralyzed people were unloaded and stacked around the bases of volcanoes across the planet. Hydrogen bombs were lowered into the volcanoes, and all were detonated simultaneously. Only a few people's physical bodies survived. Hubbard described the scene in his abortive film script, Revolt in the Stars:

"Simultaneously, the planted charges erupted. Atomic blasts ballooned from the craters of Loa, Vesuvius, Shasta, Washington, Fujiyama, Etna, and many, many others. Arching higher and higher, up and outwards, towering clouds mushroomed, shot through with flashes of flame, waste and fission. Great winds raced tumultuously across the face of Earth, spreading tales of destruction. Debris-studded and sickly yellow, the atomic clouds followed close on the heels of the winds. Their bow-shaped fronts encroached inexorably upon forest, city and mankind, they delivered their gifts of death and radiation. A skyscraper, tall and arrow-straight, bent over to form a question mark to the very idea of humanity before crumbling into the screaming city below..." – L. Ron Hubbard, *Revolt in the Stars Treatment*.[50]

This may lead to several things: Xenu represents God giving the account that reads: "pictures of God and Christ to instill a religious fervor in them that would make them less effective and so easier to control."

Satan has a large tendency to switch Biblical terms and apply them to himself, as one can see from Ezekiel 28:4: "Son of man, say unto the prince of Tyrus, Thus saith the Lord GOD; Because thine heart is lifted up, and thou hast said, 'I am a God, I sit in the seat of God, in the midst of the seas;' yet thou art a man, and not God, though thou set thine heart as the heart of God."

As it says in the story: "With the assistance of 'renegades' he defeated the populace and the 'Loyal Officers.' Satan is trying to portray himself as the 'loyal officers.'

"Yes, I've been to Heaven. And so have you. And you have the pattern of its implants in the HCO Bulletin Line Plots. It was complete with gates, angels and plaster saints – and electronic implantation equipment. So there was a Heaven after all – which is why you are on this planet and were condemned never to be free again – until Scientology." – L. Ron Hubbard[51]

The same happened to the Islamic jinns (demons): Here's a piece from Maududi's Quran commentary: "The jinn used to be able to eavesdrop on heaven but suddenly they found that angels had been set as guards and meteorites were being shot on every side so that they could find no place of safety to hear the secret news. They had set about searching for the unusual thing that had occurred on the earth to explain why the security measures had been tightened up. Many companies of jinn were moving about in search when one of them, after having heard the Quran from the Prophet, formed the opinion that it was the very thing which had caused all the gates of the heavens to be shut against them."[52] According to Islam, the "Night of Vision" is when the angelic beings (which are 'good spirits') descend to earth.

As the thetans questioned earth "A skyscraper, tall and arrow-straight, bent over to form a question mark to the very idea of humanity before crumbling into the screaming city below…" so did the jinn question: "They had set about searching for the unusual thing that had occurred on the earth to explain why the security measures had been tightened up."[53]

And how can Muslims refer to the jinn as evil spirits when they themselves (the jinn) are Muslims: "So, since we [Jinn] have listened to the guidance (of this Quran), we have accepted (Islam): and any who believes in his Lord has no fear of loss, force, or oppression." – Quran 72:13[54]

Satan [in Islam] is also a jinn and not an angel as believed in Christianity and Judaism.[55]

In the Islamic story of the Isra and Miraj while he was riding the "al-buraq," a so-called "devil" from the jinn came to him holding a firebrand, every time Muhammad turned, there was the "devil." Gabriel asked him: "Shall I teach you words which, if you say them, his firebrand will go out and he will fall dead?"[56]

Muhammad agreed and Gabriel told him to say this:

> "I seek refuge in the Face of Allah the Munificent (the 'generous') and in Allah's perfect words which neither the righteous nor the disobedient overstep from the evil of what descends from the heaven and the evil of what ascends to it and the evil of what is created in the earth and the trials of the night and the day and the visitors of the night and the day except the visitor that comes with goodness, O Beneficent One!"[57]

Why would evil ascend to heaven? In Islamic terms this may possibly signify the angelic beings from the "Night of Vision." But as we all should know, Satan always tends to grab Biblical terms and apply them to himself. According to Islam, the jinn were shot down to earth from heaven, so this means that Muhammad was asking for protection from the jinn – but why would he want protection from demons who were Muslims? "So, since we (Jinn) have listened to the guidance (of this Quran), we have accepted (Islam): and any who believes in his Lord has no fear of loss, force, or oppression."

In Sura al-Falaq 113:1-5, we read,

> "I seek refuge with The Lord of the dawn, From the mischief of things he created, From the mischief of those who practice magic (blow on knots) and from the mischief of the envious one as he practices envy."[58]

The Bible was written centuries before either the Quran or the Book of Scientology. How could it be a coincidence that what happened in their book is true? In their books, it is said that the beings cast out of the sky are the beings that are the good spirits, the spirits they are instructed to worship. But remember, the Quran is the <u>antithesis</u> of the Bible:

> "And there was war in heaven. Michael and his angels fought against the dragon, and the dragon and his angels fought back. But he was not strong enough, and they lost their place in heaven. The great dragon was hurled down – that ancient serpent called the devil, or Satan, who leads the whole world astray. He was hurled to the earth, and his angels with him. Then I heard a loud voice in heaven say: "Now have come the salvation and the power and the kingdom of our God, and the authority of his Christ. For the accuser of our brothers, who accuses them before our God day and night, has been hurled down." (Revelation 12:17)

Again, in the "Night of Vision" it reads: "The angelic hosts descend (to earth) in it with the spirit by command of the their lord."

The angelic hosts have the same lord, Muhammad said:

"When night falls (or when it is evening), stop your children from going out, for the devils spread out at that time."[59]

TECCIZTECATL

Tecciztecatl, or 'Old moon god.' An Aztec moon god who represents the male form on the planet, even its rising from the ocean. He is called "he who comes from the land of the sea-slug shell" because of the similarity between the moon and

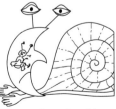

Aztec gods and goddesses 2, Tecciztecatl

the slug. Tecciztecatl portrayed as an old man who carries a large white seashell on his back.[60]

TONATIUH

In Aztec mythology, Tonatiuh was the sun god. The Aztec people considered him the leader of Tollan, their heaven. He was also known as the fifth sun, because the Aztecs believed that he was the sun that took over when the fourth sun was expelled from the sky. According to their cosmology, each sun was a god with its own cosmic era.[61]

Vanderbilt University, Center for Latin American and Iberian Studies, General Information

Nauvoo – Mormon Utopia On The Mississippi, sun gleaming off temple sunstone pilaster. By mtncorg

A close-up photo of the sun limestone in the Mormon town of Nauvoo highlights a parallel to the Aztec's beliefs.

In addition to the Masonic symbols previously discussed, the "all seeing eye" is also a Masonic symbol. Many of these symbols – the sun, moon, stars, all-seeing eye, beehive, and the hand grip – were also placed on the Mormon Temple in Salt Lake City.[62]

Masonic Symbols and the Latter Day Saints Temple, by Sandra Tanner and Morals and Dogma of the Ancient and Accepted Scottish Rite of Freemasonry, by Albert Pike discusses the various Masonic symbols and their meaning.

THE BOOK OF LIES

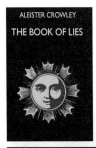

"The Book of Lies," a book written by Aleister Crowley, consists of 93 chapters, each consisting of one page of text of various kinds, including poems, rituals, and obscure allusions and cryptograms.[63]

Vox, My Life in the Sunshine, Book of Lies, Aleister Crowley

This is an artifact from the Cybele cult, their god was "earth mother." You can see on the artifact there is a crescent moon with a star and next to it is a sun.

From Wikipedia, the cult of Anatolian Cybele

CONCLUSION

How can all these religions, Islam, Heaven's Gate, and Scientology explain the 'good guys' as being those that were cast out of, or descended from, Heaven? How is it Christianity, which was established centuries before Mormonism and other cults, declares that demons, or fallen angels, fell from heaven and onto earth?

The Bible talks about false prophets "coming from the desert," Matthew 24:24-26:

"For there shall arise false Christs, and false prophets, and shall show great signs and wonders; insomuch that, if [it were] possible, they shall deceive the very elect. Behold, I have told you before. Wherefore if they shall say unto you, Behold, he is in the desert; go not forth: behold, [he is] in the secret chambers; believe [it] not."

Muhammad was not the only false prophet that has come from the desert. Aleister Crowley performed magical acts and would also recite the Quran while crossing the Sahara Desert. Charles Manson and his cult group, "the family," resided in the Spahn Ranch, (a mountain area in California) and later lived in California's Death Valley desert. Charles Manson told his followers that there was an underground world connected by a hole underneath the desert.

I imagine the question one might be asking is, "Wasn't Joseph Smith in a secluded woods, not a desert?"

In order to answer that question, one can't take the word desert as just a place with sand – we must look at the word through the Greek text. Eremos (er-ay-mos) is the Greek word for desert, which means an area which is solitary, wilderness, desolate or desert; it is a fact that the "Sacred Grove" is defined as a secluded place. Joseph Smith states in the Book of Mormon that he "retired to the woods." "Woods" is just another word for "forest." According to Dictionary.com, the word "wilderness" means, "a wild and uncultivated region, as of forest or desert, uninhabited or inhabited only by wild animals; a tract of wasteland." Also on Dictionary.com the word "woods" means: "large and thick collection of growing trees; a grove or forest" – the secluded woods that Joseph Smith went to is now called the "Sacred Grove!"

It was said by Joseph Smith: "The Lord heard my cry in the wilderness."[64]

When Jesus was in the desert, Satan appeared to him – but unlike any of the others – Jesus did not give in to the temptations.

> "Then was Jesus led up of the Spirit into the wilderness to be tempted of the devil. And when he had fasted forty days and forty nights, he was afterward hungered. And when the tempter came to him, he said, 'If thou be the Son of God, command that these stones be made bread.' But He answered and said, 'It is written, Man shall not live by bread alone, but by every word that proceedeth out of the mouth of God.'" – Matthew 4:1-4

In Matthew 4:8-10 it states:

> "Again, the devil taketh him up into an exceeding high mountain, and showeth him all the kingdoms of the world, and the glory of them; And saith unto him, 'All these things will I give thee, if thou wilt fall down and worship me.' Then saith Jesus unto him, 'Get thee hence, Satan: for it is written, Thou shalt worship the Lord thy God, and him only shalt thou serve.'"

Jesus set the example for us. The example for us is that Satan will come to tempt us – but it is *up to each person to choose if we will yield to Satan's temptation.* If you yield to Satan, that is the area in *your* life he will bombard you, just as Muhammad and Joseph Smith were visited by "angles of light" who were truly Satanic figures.

Muhammad saw Gabriel and then married his adopted son Zayed's wife, then carried out his Jihad expeditions. Joseph Smith Jr. saw two angles of light and thanks to his beliefs, he sparked a Mormon holy war which caused numerous guerrilla battles. Mahmoud Ahmadinejad saw an angel of light and now he wants to wipe Israel off the face of the earth. According to Matthew 7:15-16 we are exhorted to:

> "Beware of false prophets, which come to you in sheep's clothing, but inwardly they are ravening wolves. Ye shall know them by their fruits. Do men gather grapes of thorns, or figs of thistles?"

> "And no marvel; for Satan himself is transformed into an angel of light. Therefore (it is) no great thing if his ministers also be transformed as the ministers of righteousness; whose end shall be according to their works." (2 Corinthians 11:14)

Another thing to remember is that Muhammad and Joseph Smith were both *humans*, which makes them both *sinners* – but God came to us as God in the form of a man, Jesus, to die for us and give us salvation from an eternity in hell. God did not choose a man for us to follow, but He sent His own Holy Son Jesus Christ, to earth.

Resources

1. Ezekiel 38:2, 38:3, 38:14, 38:16, 38:18, 39:1, 39:11, Revelation 20:8.

2. Isaiah 10:5, 10:24, 14:25, 19:23, 23:13, 30:31, 31:8, Ezekiel 31:3, Micah 5:5, 6.

3. 1 John 2:22, 2 John 1:17.

4. John 17:12, 2 Thessalonians 2:3.

5. Isaiah 14:12.

6. Expositor's Bible Commentary, Isaiah 14, General Editor Frank Gaebelein, Zondervan.

7. Ibn Warraq. Why I am not a Muslim.

8. Finn Rasmussen, Early Letter Names.

9. Quran, Sura: 97.

10. Ten Days of Dawn, The Terrorism Research Center, February 1, 1979, Khomeini Returns From Exile Called the Beginning of the Ten Days of Dawn, commemorating the ten days of unrest which ended with Khomeini taking power on February 11 (the Day of Victory).

11. Yousuf Islam, Islamiway.Spyw.com, Jihad Songs.

12. Isaiah 14:19-20.

13. Isaiah 14:24-27.

14. Isaiah 14:16.

15. Isaiah 14:22-23.

16. Josephus, 226, 1987 ed., p 440.

17. Yadin Yigal, Hazor, (New York: Random House, 1975), (London: Oxford, 1972), (Jerusalem: Magnes, 1958).

18. The Hastings' Encyclopedia of Religion and Ethics, volume I, p.326.

19. See Strong's Exhaustive Concordance, number #5480, also see Thayer's Greek-English Lexicon of the New Testament

20. Hadith, as narrated by Turmuthi, 2639

21. On Doctrine, Mormon Church (LDS), Joseph Smith was more successful and of a greater and better moral character then Jesus Christ, Jesus Christ and Joseph Smith compared, LDS president and prophet Brigham Young, Journal of Discourses, vol. 7, p. 289.

22. Philologos Religious Online Books, The Rainbow Swastika, A report to the Jewish People about new age anti-Semitism, The Nazi sacred symbols and concepts, Angeberts, page 178, quoting Rudolf Olden, Hitler the Pawn, written 1936. Rauschning used the same term – page 233, by Hannah Newman.

23. Illuminati, conspiracy archive, The Vril Society, the Luminous Lodge and the Realization of the Great Work, The Vril Force and the Black Sun, Terry Melanson.

24. Ibid

25. Nauvoo Temple Symbolism, By Lisle Brown

26. D&C, Section 88: 7,8,9

27. The Book of the Law, Liber AL vel Legis, sub figura CCXX as delivered by XCIII = 418 to DCLXVI, Chapter I, 15,16.

28. Maarten J. Vermaseren, Cybele and Attis, trans. A.M.H. Lemmers, Thames and Hudson, 1977 cited in Baring and Cashford, op. cit.

29. Wikipedia, Masjid al-Haram, Narrative of origin.

30. Chapter 86: Al-Tariq (The Morning tar), (1) (2) (3), Quran, Chapter 86, Verses 1-4.

31. Gotlinks.com, Hitler Was A Catholic?, By: Robert Bruce Baird, Fri Dec 9th, 2005 08:26:38 PM.

32. Thoth, Egyptian Gods index

33. Cambridge University Press 0521841712 – Friedrich Nietzsche – Thus Spoke Zarathustra A Book for All and None – Edited by Adrian Del Caro and Robert B. Pippin Excerpt, First part, Zarathustra's Prologue, 1.

34. Wikipedia, Cult Suicide, Solar Temple

35. Al Islam, The Holy Quran: Chapter 53: Al-Najm, 53:49

36. Nuit and Hadit, The Sexual Duality Of The Universe, The Law is for All, Aleister Crowley, Copyright – James Donahue

37. Wikipedia, Hadit, Descriptions, Book of the Law 1,3, Book of the Law II,23, Book of the Law II,6, the Old Comment to Liber AL II:22 says this explicitly Book of the Law II,26-27, see http://www.philae.nu/akhet/NetjeruH.html# Horus, Free Encyclopedia of Thelema, Hadit, Retrieved Sept. 4, 2005, Crowley, Aleister, The Book of the Law, York Beach, Maine: Samuel Weiser, Grant, Kenneth, Aleister Crowley and the Hidden God, Grant, Kenneth. Cults of the Shadow Grant, Kenneth. Hecate's Fountain, Grant, Kenneth. The Magical Revival, Grant, Kenneth. Outside the Circles of Time, Thelemapedia, Retrieved April 21, 2006, Retrieved from http://en.wikipedia.org/wiki/Hadit.

38. Secret Center, Had; The Energy of The World, James Donahue.

39. The Root of Terrorism and the Return of Radical Islam, Why I Left Jihad, Chapter 10: The Crescent Connection, Page 280, By Ex-Muslim Terrorist Walid Shoebat.

40. Wikipedia, Genie

41. Prophet of Doom, By Craig Winn, 72: The Jinn, Qur'an 72.8.

42. The Meaning of the Glorious Qur'an, By Marmaduke Pickthall,

43. University of Southern California, USC-MSA Compendium of Muslim Text, Translation of Sahih Bukhari, Book 69: Volume 7, Book 69, Number 527: Narrated Jabir bin 'Abdullah.

44. Court TV, Crime Library, Criminal Minds and Methods, The Real End

45. Wikipedia, Genie, Jinn in Islam

46. Rewards for the Scribe, The Rapture of Hadit in Hiding.

47. Wikipedia, Xenu, Summary, Jon Atack, A Piece Of Blue Sky (Kensington Publishing Corporation, New York, 1990; ISBN 0-8184-0499-X)

48. Wikipedia, Xenu, Summary, Jon Atack, A Piece Of Blue Sky (Kensington Publishing Corporation, New York, 1990; ISBN 0-8184-0499-X)

49. Horrible Truths for Scientologists: Body Thetans, By Roland Rashleigh-Berry

50. Wikipedia, Xenu, Summary, Jon Atack, A Piece Of Blue Sky (Kensington Publishing Corporation, New York, 1990; ISBN 0-8184-0499-X)

51. Ron (and indeed everyone) has been to Heaven, Hubbard Communications Office, Saint Hill Manor, East Grinstead, Sussex, HCO Bulletin of May 11, AD13, Central Orgs, Franchise, Routine 3 Heaven.

52. Prophet of Doom, By Craig Winn, 72: The Jinn, Maududi's Qur'an commentary.

53. Ibid

54. Ibid

55. Wikipedia, Genie, Jinn in Islam

56. Commemorating the prophet's rapture and ascension to his lord, III. The Collated Hadith of Isra' and Mi`raj

57. Ibid

58. Muhammadanism, The Occult in the Qur'an, Muhammad's Fear of the Occult, In Sura al-Falaq 113:1-5.

59. Bukhari 7/527 and Abu Daud 3722

60. Wikipedia, Cult Suicide, Solar Temple

61. Encyclopedia Mythica, Tecciztecatl, By Micha F. Lindemans

62. Masonic Symbols and the LDS Temple, By Sandra Tanner, Morals and Dogma of the Ancient and Accepted Scottish Rite of Freemasonry, discusses the various Masonic symbols and their meaning.

63. Wikipedia, The Book of Lies (Crowley), Crowley, Aleister (1979), The Confessions of Aleister Crowley, London; Boston: Routledge & Kegan Paul Crowley, Aleister (1978), The Book of Lies, New York, NY: S. Weiser.

64. Joseph Smith: America's Hermetic Prophet, By Lance S. Owens, Dean C. Jessee, ed., The Papers of Joseph Smith, Vol. 1 (Salt Lake City: Deseret Book Co., 1989), 6. For a detailed examination of Joseph Smith's early years, see Richard L. Bushman, Joseph Smith and the Beginnings of Mormonism (Urbana: University of Illinois Press, 1984). Despite many interpretive limitations, Smith's best overall biography remains Fawn M. Brodie, No Man Knows My History (New York: Alfred A. Knopf, 1945, 2nd ed. 1971).

Chapter Six – Elevating Men to be Gods

Satan always tempts people with worldly goals – kingdoms and sexual desires that some men will kill for – literally. Becoming a god is probably one of the major concepts in cultic heavens or utopias. Evolutionists try to act as God – they try to create life out of nothing, an attempt that has failed every time. In Mormonism, you must be perfect in order to be a god. In Islam, Muhammad (also known as "his apostle") was the exalted one over Jesus Christ, and considered to be the perfect Adam. Muslims claim they don't worship Muhammad, yet in reality he is portrayed closely akin to god, as if he possessed godly attributes. Here's a quote from the Hadith:

> "While we were in the Mosque, the prophet came out and said, 'Let us go to the Jews.' We went out till we reached Bait-ul-Midras. He said to them, 'If you embrace Islam, you will be safe. You should know that the earth belongs to Allah and His Apostle, and I want to expel you from this land. So, if anyone amongst you owns some property, he is permitted to sell it, otherwise you should know that the earth belongs to Allah and His Apostle.'"[1]

In Christianity the earth belongs to God and no other. It would be blasphemy to say the earth belongs to Muhammad, who in this case claims Christ-like attributes in order to establish a false kingdom for Allah. This is especially true since Muhammad isn't even mentioned by name in the Bible.

In the Hadith of Bukhari, V4B55N651-2: "I heard Allah's Apostle saying, 'I am the nearest of all the people to Jesus. There has been no prophet between me and Jesus. All the prophets are paternal brothers; their mothers are different, but their religion is one.'" However, the Bible is clear that only Jesus can intercede for someone:

"For God so loved the world, that He gave His only begotten Son, that whosoever believeth in him should not perish, but have everlasting life." (John 3:16)

ISLAMIC MARTYRS AS CHRIST

Salvation as understood in Christianity is different than what Muslims believe. In Islam, the idea of Christ dying for all humanity is rejected, which is one reason why Islam was created. Yet, it is shocking to find that Islam offers an assurance to salvation similar to Christian dogma, with a basic difference; it's not the death of Christ that sends you to heaven, but your own.

A martyr in Islam becomes a sacrificial lamb (preferably through acts of jihad), a sacrifice to obtain salvation, this is evident from the cultural term given to a terrorist – "Fida'e" which literally means "the sacrifice." The argument against blood atonement by Islam here is somewhat contradictory to the concept of martyrdom in Islam. Blood atonement is hardly absent from Islam, and in fact it calls for the "blood" of the shahid (martyr). Then 70 members of his/her family who would otherwise enter hell, are able to go to the paradise. So, at least one person in a family is encouraged to intercede on behalf of the other 70 to alleviate their future in hell. It is this thinking by Muslims where they believe they possess certain attributes of Jesus, namely, to be an intercessor. In Islam: "The martyr will intercede to forgive all sin on behalf of seventy members of his family."[2]

In Mormonism, the husband will resurrect his wife (if she's faithful). It is believed the Mormon husband has the power to deny his wife (wives) the privilege to ascend to the celestial heaven:

"Do you uphold your husband before God as your lord? 'What! – my husband to be my lord?' I ask, 'Can you get into the celestial kingdom without him? Have any of you been there?' You will remember that you never got into the celestial kingdom without the aid of your husband. If you did, it was because your husband was away, and someone had to act proxy for him. No woman will get into the celestial kingdom, except her husband receives her, if she is worthy to have a husband; and if not, somebody will receive her as a servant." – Erastus Snow [3]

Similarly, Islam forbids a wife entry into paradise if she is found to have been disobedient to her husband.

SAME OLD TEMPTATIONS

Because of their belief that God is only an exalted man, Mormon leaders teach that He had a mother as well as a wife.[4] "The idea that the Lord our God is not a personage of tabernacle is entirely a mistaken notion. He was once a man."[5]

Mormons believe that God populated the earth by having sex with his plural wives in heaven. Further, they believe this will happen to them when they ascend to heaven.

Here's a quote from the Doctrine and Covenants:

"And again, verily I say unto you, if a man marry a wife by my word, which is my law, and by the new and everlasting covenant, and it is sealed unto them by the Holy Spirit of promise, by him who is anointed, unto whom I have appointed this power and the keys of this priesthood; and it shall be said unto them – Ye shall come forth in the first resurrection; and if it be after the first resurrection, in the next resurrection; and shall inherit thrones, kingdoms, principalities, and powers, dominions, all heights and depths – then shall it be written in the Lamb's Book of Life, that he shall commit no murder whereby to shed innocent blood, and if ye abide in my covenant, and commit no murder whereby to shed innocent blood, it shall be done unto them in all things whatsoever my servant hath put upon them, in time, and through all eternity; and shall be of full force when they are out of the world; and they shall pass by the angels, and the gods, which are set there, to their exaltation and glory in all things, as hath been sealed upon their heads, which glory shall be a fullness and a continuation of the seeds forever and ever. Then shall they be gods, because they have no end; therefore shall they be from everlasting to everlasting, because they continue; then shall they be above all, because all things are subject unto them. Then shall they be gods, because they have all power, and the angels are subject unto them."[6]

SAME TEMPTATIONS OFFERED TO JESUS

The declaration "and shall inherit thrones, kingdoms, principalities, and powers, dominions, all heights and depths" reminds us of a passage in the Bible when Jesus was hungry in the desert for forty days and encounters Satan, who tempts Him:

"And the devil, taking him up into an high mountain, showed unto him all the kingdoms of the world in a moment of time. Again, the devil taketh him up into an exceeding high mountain, and showeth him all the kingdoms of the world, and the glory of them; And saith unto him, All these things will I give thee, if thou wilt fall down and worship me." (Matthew 4: 8-9)

Why would the true God present Mormons with the same temptations as Jesus was faced by Satan?

PRINCIPALITIES ARE DEMONIC

Such principalities as Mormonism describes are the demonic forces described in Ephesians 6:12:

"For we do not wrestle against flesh and blood, but against principalities, against powers, against the rulers of the darkness of this age, against spiritual hosts of wickedness in the heavenly places."

This whole basis of man becoming a god has it's roots in Satan's lie when he told Adam and Eve in the Garden:

"And the woman said unto the serpent, We may eat of the fruit of the trees of the garden: But of the fruit of the tree which [is] in the midst of the garden, God hath said, Ye shall not eat of it, neither shall ye touch it, lest ye die. And the serpent said unto the woman, Ye shall not surely die: For God doth know that in the day ye eat thereof, then your eyes shall be opened, and ye shall be as gods, knowing good and evil." (Genesis 3:2-5)

TYRUS

It seems that every time Satan appears to somebody he tempts them, just as he tempted Jesus in the desert. Now we can say that Joseph Smith, and every cultist who claims to have seen an angelic figure, was simply being tempted by Satan. The Bible describes the anti-Christ as a person who wants to be God:

> "Son of man, say unto the prince of Tyrus, Thus saith the Lord GOD; Because thine heart [is] lifted up, and thou hast said, I [am] a God, I sit [in] the seat of God, in the midst of the seas; yet thou [art] a man, and not God, though thou set thine heart as the heart of God."

The enticement to become a god-like character is also seen in Scientology. Through successful auditing with the spirit of Thetan, you too can become an "Operating Thetan" and wear Scientology's bracelet, a sign that you have reached "total spiritual independence and serenity."[7]

ÜBERMENSCH AS GOD

The philosopher Friedrich Nietzsche, whose writings influenced Hitler, wrote that man has the ability of being an Übermensch or super-human. Nietzsche's motivation for the claim 'God is dead' was the destruction of the Christian conscience, a God-centered way of thinking, coupled with his fateful desire to break out. The symbols he chose for his philosophy were flame and thunder. Only by discarding the idealistic norms can one become Übermensch, which literally means "beyond human."[8]

In Nazism, Adolf Hitler was occasionally compared with Jesus, or revered as a savior sent by God. A prayer recited at orphanages goes as follows:

> "Leader, my Leader, given to me by God, protect me and sustain my life. For a long time you have rescued Germany out of deepest misery, to you I owe my daily bread. Leader, my leader, my belief, my light. Leader my Leader, do not abandon me."[9]

In Hitler's Mein Kampf, it reads: "And this action is the only one which, before God and our German posterity, would make any sacrifice of blood seem justified: before God, since we have been put on this earth with the mission of eternal struggle for our daily bread, beings who receive nothing as a gift, and who owe their position as lords of the earth only to the genius and the courage with which they can conquer and defend it; and before our German posterity in so far as we have shed no citizen's blood out of which a thousand others are not bequeathed to posterity."[10]

Brigham Young had once said: "We are not required in our sphere to be as perfect as gods and angels are in their spheres, yet man is the king of kings and lord of lords in embryo."[11]

Hitler firmly believed in the coming of a new race, the 'Supermen.' He expected them to be a literal 'mutation' of homo sapiens, achieved by arriving at "higher levels of consciousness."[12]

Hitler's personal aide, Hermann Rauschning, was an eye witness of the madness of the Third Reich. In 1939 he wrote this account:

> "What will the social order of the future be like? Comrade, I will tell you. There will be a class of overlords, after them the rank and file of the party members in hierarchical order, and then the great mass of anonymous followers, servants and workers in perpetuity, and beneath them again all the conquered foreign races, the modern slaves. And over and above all these will reign a new and exalted nobility of whom I cannot speak. But of all these plans the militant members will know nothing. The new man is living amongst us now! He is here. Isn't that enough for you? I will tell you a secret. I have seen the new man. He is intrepid and cruel. I was afraid of him" – Adolf Hitler quoted from "Hitler Speaks" by Hermann Rauschning.[13]

Both the Nazi Utopia and Islam are worldly, and focused on pride that invests in worldly desires, offering servants, women and power which appeal only to carnal desires.

DAVID KORESH AS GOD

Twentieth century cult leaders such as Jim Jones and David Koresh have falsely claimed to be the promised Messiah.[14] Since David Koresh was able to give an explanation of the seven seals, Branch Davidians claimed he must be the second Messiah.[15] Koresh himself believed he was the reincarnation of both King David and King Cyrus of Persia, and that he had been appointed by God to rebuild the Temple and destroy Babylon.[16] He prophesied that he would move to Israel and be martyred by crucifixion at the hands of the U.S. Army. Former members claimed that one reason for the martyrdom was jealousy over Koresh's wives and concubines.[17] Because of this, they (Branch Davidians) claim the U.S. Government murdered the "Son of God."[18]

JIM JONES AS GOD

Another cult leader, Jim Jones taught that all people had access to the holy spirit within themselves, but that Jones' healing power demonstrated that he was a special manifestation of "Christ the Revolution." "I am the way, the truth, and the light. No one can come to the father but through me." – Jim Jones.[19]

DORE WILLIAMSON AS GOD

Dore Williamson has proclaimed herself to be the fourth part of the Godhead (trinity). Her anti-Freemason views have landed her the title of "internet kOOk." She has made many 'failed' predictions of end-of-the-world events, including that the world would end in 1999 by a biological war unleashed by Bill Clinton. Among her other claims she says she is the incarnation of Christ, and also that Bill Clinton is the Antichrist.[20]

RAJNEESH AS GOD

Rajneesh believed enlightenment is every person's natural state, but because of our emotional ties and activity of thought to society, one can be distracted from attaining it. He recognized Jesus Christ had attained enlightenment, and believed that he survived his crucifixion and moved to

India where he died at the age of 112.[21] Rajneesh once stated that it was possible to push objects around by will-power alone (psychokinesis).[22]

JOSEPH SMITH AS GOD

Joseph Smith wanted to be seen as a god-like figure to those he knew. A prominent Mormon and well-known gunslinger was O. Porter Rockwell. In a biography of the Porter Rockwell, Smith told Rockwell: "Cut not thy hair and no bullet or blade can harm thee!"[23] Joseph was attempting to be like God talking to Samson. Here's a self-explanatory quote from Joseph Smith:

> "God is in the still small voice. In all these affidavits, indictments, it is all of the devil – all corruption. Come on! ye prosecutors! ye false swearers! All hell, boil over! Ye burning mountains, roll down your lava! for I will come out on the top at last. I have more to boast of than ever any man had. I am the only man that has ever been able to keep a whole church together since the days of Adam. A large majority of the whole have stood by me. Neither Paul, John, Peter, nor Jesus ever did it. I boast that no man ever did such a work as I. The followers of Jesus ran away from Him; but the Latter-day Saints never ran away from me yet. You know my daily walk and conversation. I am in the bosom of a virtuous and good people. How I do love to hear the wolves howl! When they can get rid of me, the devil will also go."[24]

SUN MYONG MOON AS GOD

The above quote from Smith has a definite correlation with Sun Myong Moon. Moon believed that he was selected as "the savior, messiah and king of kings of all of humanity" by God.[25] He would call himself the "father." Moon paralleled Joseph Smith: "Jesus never achieved a thousandth of what Father has done. In his two years and eight months of public ministry, [Jesus] didn't even establish the national foundation. Now, Father has established a foundation of worldwide power that is unprecedented in history."[26]

MICHAEL TRAVESSER AS GOD

His real name is Wayne Bent. Bent claims to be "Michael the Archangel," explaining that, in the book of Daniel, Michael is described as a deliverer who will protect his people – something Michael Travesser says he is doing:

"(…) I was asked by News4 if I were Michael the archangel. I answered, Yes, I am. After Father came upon me to expose the destructive power of that 'Wicked one,' who is now ruling the world, and to feed the Woman (church) in the wilderness for 3½ years, he opened up to me the work that he was giving to me for this time, and anointed me with his spirit to carry it out. That 'Wicked one' is the one mentioned in 2 Thess. 2:8. 'And then shall that Wicked be exposed.' I began to see what my work was and it was the work of Michael mentioned in Revelation 12. It is not my body that is Michael, but the spirit that came into me. My spirit is Michael and Michael speaks in me. I only say what I hear Michael say."[27] In addition to claiming to be 'Michael the Archangel,' Michael also suggests that he is Jesus.[28]

MARSHALL APPLEWHITE AS GOD

Applewhite was the founder of the cult Heaven's Gate. Cult members led an ascetic life, in their efforts to achieve "Human Individual Meta-morphosis" – the transformation into an "Evolutionary Level Above Human." In a September 1995 post to Usenet, Applewhite announced his plan to the general public. Introducing himself as "Jesus, Son of God."[29]

SABBATAI ZEVI AS GOD

Zevi revealed himself to a band of followers as the "true messianic redeemer" designated by God to overthrow the governments of the nations and to restore the kingdom of Israel. Yet, Sabbatai's time of glory was brief. He was arrested at sea by Turkish authorities who had heard rumors that he was conspiring to overthrow the sultan. Summoned before the sultan and ordered to choose between death by torture or conversion to Islam. Sabbatai renounced Judaism for the faith of Muhammad and lived well for a time, but his wanton sexual activity and erratic behavior eventually drew fire from Muslim authorities, who exiled him to the remote Albanian seaport of Dulcigno where he died in loneliness and obscurity.[30]

BEING GOD IN EARTH WORSHIP

In earth worship we learn that sex "is a gift of pleasure and creation. It is survival. Witches are thankful and we celebrate sex. Sex is joy and survival, of our own bodies, of our species. Sex is out of this world, cosmic pleasure! And all acts of pleasure are the acts of the goddess, our mother, our selves. These are pleasures the likes of which produce life. A woman, a witch, should not fear sex and our own pleasures. We create life. We are deity. We are the Goddess."[31]

Earth worship also "teaches us to love ourselves for what we are, to celebrate all aspects of our existence, our femininity and what that means." And also women are "goddess, and likewise, men are god. But they are not god in the terms of patriarchal sky father, waving a big phallus and suppressing women and minorities and poor people. God and goddess are equal, are part of life. Together they are a whole, and they create life."[32]

BEING GOD IN SATANISM

In Anton LaVey's "Satanic Bible," there is a section of the "Book of Lucifer" labeled as "The god you save may be yourself," it follows up on the concept of "I am my own god" with a full explanation of the Satanic egocentric view of the world. This short essay states that as all gods are of human creation, worshipping an external god is to worship another human by proxy; therefore, the sensible, Satanic approach is to create your own god, namely yourself, and to "worship" this god. The result, of course, is to view oneself as the most important of all beings, and to adopt an unapologetically self-centered view of the world and course of action.[33]

Resources

1. The Quran and Ahadith on the Concept of Protection and Friendship, By Sam Shamoun, Narrated Abu Huraira, Sahih al-Bukhari, Volume 4, Book 53, Number 392.

2. Muhammad, the prophet of Islam, narrated by Al-Miqdaam Ibn Ma'di Karib, Tirmidhi & Ibn Maajah).

3. How the LDS Husband Hopes to Resurrect His Wife According to the LDS Temple Ceremony, by Sandra Tanner, Journal of Discourses, vol. 5, p. 291.

4. How the LDS Husband Hopes to Resurrect His Wife According to the LDS Temple Ceremony, by Sandra Tanner, Journal of Discourses, vol. 5, p. 286.

5. Jehovah As Father, The Development of the Mormon Jehovah Doctrine," by Boyd Kirkland, *Sunstone 9.2.*

6. Doctrines and Covenants, Section 132, #20, Jult 12, 1843.

7. Probe Ministries, Scientology: Religion of the Stars, The Worldview of Scientology: Human Nature, Ibid., 150. Written by Don Closson.

8. "The will to destruction," This article is from Wikipedia. All text is available under the terms of the GNU Free Documentation License.

9. Wikipedia, Nazi Maystism, Esoteric Hitlerism 1933-1945, Prayer to Hitler.

10. Adolf Hitler, Mein Kampf (1926), Volume Two, Chapter Fourteen: "Eastern Orientation or Eastern Policy."

11. Mormon Quotes, Journal Of Discourses, Volume: 10, Chapter: 43, Page: 223.

12. A livingstonemusic.net article, Hitler and the Nazis, The 'Supermen.'

13. Ibid

14. Jim Jones, Joseph Smith, and David Koresh, By Rit Nosotro, Robinson, B.A. "The People's Temple," 4 Apr. 2004.

15. Outline of Branch Davidian Teachings, The Seven Seals.

16. Rotten, Library, Biographies, Religion, Cult leaders, David Koresh.

17. The Watchman Expositor, Vol. 10, No. 4, 1993 Articles on Cults and New Religions, David Koresh and Joseph Smith: False Prophets, 7. Both Joseph Smith and David Koresh prophesied of their own martyrdom., Fort Worth Star Telegram, 3 March 1993, p. 19A.

18. Outline of Branch Davidian Teachings, The Seven Seals.

19. Jonestown, Who Was Jim Jones?

20. Answers.com, List of people have claimed to be Jesus, Wikipedia, List of people who have claimed to be Jesus, Dore Williamson, A Brief History of the Apocalypse, 1998 – 1999: The End is Nigh.

21. Religious Tolerance, Osho formally known as Bhagwan Shree Rajneesh, Beliefs and Practices.

22. The Ridiculous Teachings of Wrong Way Rajneesh.

23. Orrin Porter Rockwell: Man of God, Son of Thunder (1966; second edition 1983); and Frank Esshom, Pioneers and Prominent Men of Utah (1913).

24. Mormon Quotes, John Taylor, Journal of Discourses, Volume 6, Page 25.

25. Rotten, Library, Biographies, Religion, Cult leaders, Sun Myung Moon.

26. Ibid.

27. Apologetics Index, Strong City, Michael Travesser, Michael the Archangel, Source: Strong City web site, Michael's Diary – Sunday, November 17, 2002.

28. Apologetics Index, Strong City, Michael Travesser, Michael the Messiah.

29. Rotten, Library, Biographies, Religion, Cult leaders, Marshall Applewhite.

30. 2spare.com, 8 Wackiest self-proclaimed Messiahs, Sabbatai Zevi, the Jewish Messiah who Converted to Islam.

31. www.depts.ttu.edu/wstudies/WS43992006/Lauren.htm.

32. Ibid.

33. Wikipedia, The Satanic Bible, The Book of Lucifer, II The God you save may be yourself.

Chapter Seven – Sex, Money, and Power

There is one thing all cults have in common, that is the desire for power over women and earthly things. In both Mormon and Islamic heavens there is the act of sexual reproduction.

While on earth, ambitious Mormon men must beget many children with as many wives as possible, for "their glory (in heaven) is in proportion to the number of their wives and children."[1] If a man went to heaven with ten wives, he would have more than tenfold the blessings of a mere monogamist, for all the children begotten through these wives would enhance his kingdom.[2] After death, husbands are creating and ruling over planets and women have the questionable honor of bearing his "spirit children" for eternity. These spirit children descend to their Father's planet to inhabit bodies as mortals, who are then ruled over by him. Mormon doctrine states that these celestially married men and women "will live eternally in the family unit and have spirit children, thus becoming eternal fathers and eternal mothers." A man who has multiple wives can beget many more spirit children, making him much more powerful.

In the Mormon heaven it reads, "which glory shall be a fullness and a continuation of the seeds forever and ever." This resembles the Islamic heaven. The Quran states: "Your women are your fields, so go into your fields whichever way you like."[3] Here's a segment from the story of the Isra' and Miraj:

> The gate was opened. The prophet saw Ibrahim the Friend sitting at the gate of paradise on a throne of gold, the back of which was leaning against the Inhabited House (al-Bayt al-mamur). With him were a company of his people. The prophet greeted him and he returned his greeting and said: "Welcome to the righteous son

and the righteous prophet!" Then Ibrahim said: "Order your community to increase their seedlings of paradise for its soil is excellent and its land is plentiful."[4]

The Quran does mention servants and sex slaves in Surah 52: 17 through 24:

"As to the Righteous, they will be in gardens, and in happiness, enjoying the (bliss) which their lord hath bestowed on them, and their lord shall deliver them from the penalty of the fire. (To them will be said:) "Eat and drink ye, with profit and health, because of your (good) deeds." They will recline (with ease) on thrones (of dignity) arranged in ranks; and we shall join them to compan-

إِنَّ ٱلْمُتَّقِينَ فِى جَنَّـٰتٍ وَنَعِيمٍ ۝

فَـٰكِهِينَ بِمَآ ءَاتَىٰهُمْ رَبُّهُمْ وَوَقَىٰهُمْ رَبُّهُمْ عَذَابَ ٱلْجَحِيمِ ۝

كُلُوا۟ وَٱشْرَبُوا۟ هَنِيٓـًٔا بِمَا كُنتُمْ تَعْمَلُونَ ۝

مُتَّكِـِٔينَ عَلَىٰ سُرُرٍ مَّصْفُوفَةٍ وَزَوَّجْنَـٰهُم بِحُورٍ عِينٍ ۝

وَٱلَّذِينَ ءَامَنُوا۟ وَٱتَّبَعَتْهُمْ ذُرِّيَّتُهُم بِإِيمَـٰنٍ أَلْحَقْنَا بِهِمْ ذُرِّيَّتَهُمْ وَمَآ أَلَتْنَـٰهُم مِّنْ عَمَلِهِم مِّن شَىْءٍ كُلُّ ٱمْرِئٍ بِمَا كَسَبَ رَهِينٌ ۝

ions, with beautiful big and lustrous eyes. And those who believe and whose families follow them in faith, – to them shall we join their families: nor shall we deprive them (of the fruit) of aught of their works: (yet) is each individual in pledge for his deeds. And we shall bestow on them, of fruit and meat, anything they shall desire. They shall there exchange, one with another, a (loving) cup free of frivolity, free of all taint of ill."[5]

Could this mean sex without any sexual infection? The word "taint" according to Dictionary.com means infection, and this hadith reads "taint of ill."

> "Round about them will serve, (devoted) to them, young boys (handsome), as pearls well-guarded."[6]

Ali, narrated that the apostle of Allah said, "There is in paradise an open market wherein there will be no buying or selling, but will consist of men and women. When a man desires a beauty, at once he will have intercourse with them as desired."[7]

WHAT IS FORBIDDEN ON EARTH IS PERMISSIBLE IN HEAVEN

What the Muslims complain about when accusing the West of being run by international Zionism, with it's Hollywood and sexual licentiousness, all seems to exist in abundance in the Muslim paradise, with angels and young boys (handsome) as pearls well guarded. (Quran 52:24) Perpetual freshness (Quran 56:17) thou seest them, thou wouldst think them scattered pearls (Quran 76:19) rivers of wine (Quran 47:15) served with goblet filled at a gushing fountain, white and delicious to those who drink it. It will neither dull their senses nor befuddle them. (Quran 37:40-48) Rivers of milk of which the taste never changes; a joy to those who drink; And rivers of honey pure and clear. (Quran 47:15) Bosomed virgins for companions: a truly overflowing cup (Quran 78:31), these virgins are bashful, undefiled by man or demon.

Sexual enticements play an integral element in recruiting jihadists. The late author and journalist Muhammad Galal Al-Kushk wrote:

> "The men in paradise have sexual relations not only with the women [who come from this world] and with 'the black-eyed,' but also with the serving boys." According to Kurum, Al-Kushk also stated, "In paradise, a believer's penis is eternally erect."[8]

A Hamas youth leader in a Gaza refugee camp told Jack Kelley of USA Today that "most boys can't stop thinking about the virgins."[9] Sheikh Abd Al Fattah Jam'an speaking to Muslims in Palestine stated:

> "What is waiting for the suicide bomber in paradise is a harem of beautiful virgins who are delicate and pure, esthetic, passive, with no personality or self or ego, whose only role is to sexually satisfy the shahid and be ever ready to fulfill his desires."[10]

Some delights do not have to wait until paradise:

> Ibn Fahd asking Al-Hajjaj "I have some slave girls who are better than my wives, but I do not desire that they should all become pregnant. Shall I do azl (withdrawal) with them?" Al-Hajjaj asked. "They are your fields of cultivation. If you wish to irrigate them do so, if not keep them dry."[11]

There are a lot of references to sex in the Quran with sexual entitlement that only belonged to Muhammad:

> "Forbidden to you also are married women, except those who are in your hand as slaves, this is the law of Allah for you."

> And Sura: Confederates (al-Ahzab verse 50): "O prophet; we allowed thee thy wives to whom thou hast paid their dowries, and the slaves whom thy right hand possesseth out of the booty which Allah hath granted thee, and the daughters of thy uncle, and of thy maternal aunt, who fled with thee to Medina, and any believing woman who hath given herself up to the prophet, if the prophet desired to wed her, a privilege to thee above the rest of the faithful."

Muslims have no problem with Muhammad taking advantage of this privilege. He married many wives and took several slave girls from the booty he collected from his victorious battles. We never knew how many wives he had, and that question was always a debatable issue. One might debate the numbers yet never question the moral justifications. One of his wives was even taken from his own adopted son, Zayed, as "Allah declared that she was given to the prophet." Others were Jewish captives forced into slavery after Muhammad beheaded their husbands and families.

Banu Al-Mustaliq had a similar fate, especially since Muhammad's army lusted after their women and raped them:

> "We were lusting after women and chastity had become too hard for us, but we wanted to get the ransom money for our prisoners. Therefore, we wanted to use the "Azl" (Coitus Interruptus where the man withdraws before ejaculating)...We asked the prophet about it and he said: "You are not under any obligation to stop yourselves from doing it like that..." Later on the women and children were given for ransom to their envoys. They all went away to their country and not one wanted to stay although they had the choice..."[12]

Abu Sa'id al-Khudri said:

> The Apostle of Allah sent a military expedition to Awtas at the battle of Hunain. They met their enemy, fought with them, defeated them, then took them captive. Some of the companions of the apostle of Allah were reluctant to have intercourse with the female captives in the presence of their husbands who were unbelievers.

> Therefore, Allah, the exalted, sent down the Quranic verse: "And all married women (are forbidden) unto you save those (captives) whom your right hand possesses."

The Quran, and Muhammad confirms:

> "Thus (shall it be), and we will wed them with houris, pure, beautiful ones."[13]...They shall recline on couches lined with thick brocade, and within reach will hang the fruits of both gardens...Therein are bashful virgins whom neither man nor jinnee will have touched before...Virgins as fair as corals and rubies..."[14] "In each there shall be virgins chaste and fair...Dark eyed virgins sheltered in their tents whom neither man nor

jinnee would have touched before. They shall recline on green cushions and fine carpets..."[15]

"We created the houris and made them virgins, loving companions for those of the right hand...That which is coming..." (Quran, 56:36) "As for the righteous, they shall surely triumph. Theirs shall be gardens and vineyards, and high-bosomed virgins for companions: a truly overflowing cup."[16]

The very same Quran and Sunna that served as the rules of conduct in the seventh century remain the basis for Islamic law today. Although many Muslim countries have banned such laws as a result of Western inquisitions. Today the cry of the Muslim fundamentalist it to reinstitute them, including slavery:

A slave is the property of his/her master. He/She is subject to the master's power, insomuch that, if a master should kill his slave he is not liable to retaliation. With female slaves a master has the 'mulk-i-moot'at,' or right of enjoyment, and his children by them, when acknowledged, have the same rights and privileges as his children by his wives. A slave is incompetent to exercise authority over others. Therefore a slave cannot be a witness, a judge, or an executor or guardian to any but his/her master and his children. A slave cannot inherit from anyone, and a bequest to him becomes a bequest to his master.[17]

You might ask, how can people believe this? This is a stubborn reality that eludes many in the modern, secular West. These beliefs seem so bizarre.

Terry Mattingly, a syndicated religion columnist and scholar of media and religion at Palm Beach Atlantic College explains, "If your worldview is essentially materialist, then to be 'real,' something has to present itself in a form that makes sense in a laboratory, or on Wall Street, or in the New Hampshire primary, and anything that can't be explained within those templates doesn't count. Thus we can't seem to understand why people behave in ways that don't serve their self-interest."[18]

Boston University's Landes agrees, saying that the American cultural elite tend to disdain religion, when in fact, it is a major factor in modern history. "When 9/11 happened, one of the questions people asked was, 'is it religious, or is it political?' People are more comfortable explaining it as politics. The very fact that people asked that question shows how little they understand," he says.

> "Since September 11, we have all been brought to the point of recognizing the pervasive power of religions to shape all kinds of events." Weber adds. "We are dealing with ancient religious convictions and memories, and they are driving forces in the modern world. The secular press just doesn't get it, but it seems to me there's no other way to understand this."[19]

DAVID KORESH AND WOMEN

If Muhammad was a true prophet, why is it there appears to be no difference between him and David Koresh, who declared he was owed at minimum, 140 wives, and that he was entitled to claim any of the females in the compound as his. Evidently he had fathered at least a dozen babies by the harem. Some were girls as young as 12 or 13 when they were impregnated by the "Messiah."[20]

Former members reported Koresh prophesied for himself 60 wives and 80 concubines and "virgins without number."[21]

SAME AS JOSEPH SMITH

Joseph Smith received a revelation of a "new and everlasting covenant" which his followers must obey or they "shall be damned." The revelation promoted what has been called the "plural wives" or "spiritual wife" doctrine.[22]

MORMONS, MUSLIMS AND BOOTY

In Islam, Muhammad had married a girl at a very young age: "The Prophet married Aesha in Mecca three years before the Hijrah, after the death of Khadija. At the time she was six."[23] It is also justified to marry your adopted son's wife. Sura 33:37 reads: "Behold! Thou didst say to one who had received the grace of Allah and thy favour: 'Retain thou (in wedlock) thy wife, and fear Allah.' But thou didst hide in thy heart that which Allah was about to make manifest: thou didst fear the people, but it is more fitting that thou shouldst fear Allah. Then when Zayed had dissolved (his marriage) with her, with the necessary (formality), we joined her in marriage to thee: in order that (in future) there may be no difficulty to the believers in (the matter of) marriage with the wives of their adopted sons, when the latter have dissolved with the necessary (formality) (their marriage) with them. And Allah's command must be fulfilled."[24]

In Mauritania, Africa, which is largely a Muslim country, it is common to find brides as young as ten or eleven years of age. Iran's Ayatollah Kohmeini at age twenty-eight married a ten-year old girl, who became pregnant at age 11.[25]

Another form of power that the cults use is the control of its members and family.

Joseph Smith's communal experiment was located in Kirtland, Ohio and was established as part of the "law of consecration," also called the "United Order" or "Order of Enoch." According to the revelation, to avoid the risk of being "cut off" followers had to "consecrate" their possessions to the Bishop who redistributed the property according to the needs of the people.[26]

David Koresh began by requiring 10% of his followers' income, then in the late 1980s required 30%. Finally Koresh demanded 100% of his followers' income and possessions. Former member Michelle Tom explained that after giving all, "Vernon would just give them back an allowance." In Tom's case that was between $2 and $5 a week.[27]

In Islam, Muhammad not only collected 20% of the booty, but through the submission of non-Muslims collected a poll tax called Jizia.

"Fight those who do not believe until they all surrender, paying the protective tax in submission."[28] Muhammad led armed expeditions against various tribal groups, amassing considerable wealth, much of it from the booty they acquired, of which he commonly took one-fifth.[29]

Mormons took booty as well. In "Mormonism Unveiled," John D. Lee (writing as an ex-Mormon) describes a conversation he had with a fellow Mormon named Dan Haight. Their conversation is based upon the Mountain Meadow Massacre in which Mormons and Native Americans allied together in the slaughter of innocent travelers:

> "I at once saw that we were in a bad fix, and I asked Haight what was to be done. We talked the matter over again. Haight then told me that it was the orders of the Council that I should go to Salt Lake City and lay the whole matter before Brigham Young. I asked him if he was not going to write a report of it to the Governor, as he was the right man to do it, for he was in command of the militia in that section of the country, and next to Dame in command of the whole district. I told him that it was a matter which really belonged to the military department, and should be so reported."

He refused to write a report, saying: "You can report it better than I could write it. You are like a member of Brigham's family, and can talk to him privately and confidentially. I want you to take all of it on yourself that you can, and not expose any more of the brethren than you find absolutely necessary. Do this, Brother Lee, as I order you to do, and you shall receive a celestial reward for it, and the time will come when all who acted with us will be glad for the part they have taken, for the time is near at hand when the Saints are to enjoy the riches of the earth. And all who deny the faith and doctrines of the Church of Jesus Christ of Latter Day Saints shall be slain – the sword of vengeance shall shed their blood; their wealth shall be given as a spoil to our people."[30]

Resources

1. The role of women in Mormonism, By Jessica Longaker, Religious Studies 263 march 27 1995, Women and Mormonism, Fife 103, 516.

2. No Man Knows My History, The Life of Joseph Smith, First published in 1945 – revised in 1970, chapter XXI: If a Man Entice a Maid, page 300, For documentation on the details of Joseph's plural wives see Appendix C, By Fawn M. Brodie.

3. "Plowing fields" and marrying little girls in the Quran, By James M. Arlandson, Section 1: A husband has sex with his wife, as a plow goes into a field, MAS Abdel Haleem, The Qur'an, Oxford UP, 2004.

4. Commemorating the prophet's rapture and ascension to his lord, III. The Collated Hadith of Isra and Miraj.

5. Muslim access, At Tûr, Surah 52, the mount.

6. Ibid

7. Al-Quds Al-Arabi London, May 11, 2001

8. Muhammad, Terrorist or Prophet?, Jihad (Holy War) & Islamic Martyrs, Hadith: Al hadiths, Vol. 4, Page 172, No.34: Hozrot Ali (r.a) narrated.

9. USA Today, June 26, 2001.

10. The Jerusalem Post Internet Edition, 9,6,2001

11. Malik 362:1221

12. Narrated Abu Burda. Volume 9, Book 84, Number 58

13. Narrated Anas Bin Malik, Hadith Sahih Bukhari Vol. 1 # 387

14. The Evident Smoke, 44:54 Shakir, Shakir, M. H., "The Quran," Tahrike Tarsile Quran, Inc, Elmhurst, NY, 1993

15. The Beneficent, 55:54-58 Dawood, Dawood, N. J., "The Koran," Penguin, London, England, 1995. Also see Quran, The Beneficent 55:70-77

16. The Tidings, 78:31-33 Dawood

17. p. 367_Digest of Islamic Law_ N. Bailli e, Premier Book House, Pakistan

18. National Review Online, April 11, 2002

19. National Review Online April 11, 2002

20. Rotten, Library, Biographies, Religion, Cult leaders, David Koresh

21. The Watchman Expositor, Vol. 10, No. 4, 1993 Articles on Cults and New Religions, David Koresh and Joseph Smith: False Prophets, 5. Both Joseph

Smith and David Koresh were practicing polygamists., Dallas Morning News, 1 March 1993, p. 13-A, Ft. Worth Star Telegram, 3 March 1993 p. A-19.

22. The Watchman Expositor, Vol. 10, No. 4, 1993 Articles on Cults and New Religions, David Koresh and Joseph Smith: False Prophets, 5. Both Joseph Smith and David Koresh were practicing polygamists., Doctrine and Covenants 132:6.

23. Prophet of Doom, By Craig Winn, 13 The Pedophile Pirate, Tabari VII:7.

24. The following verse is about the story of Muhammad marrying Zainab, the wife of Muhammad's adopted son., Sura 33:37, Contradictions in the Qur'an Answering Islam Home Page.

25. The Great Divide, By Alvin J. Schmidt, Chapter 1, Jesus and Muhammad: Polar Opposites, Page 79, Chapter 3, Women: Veiled or Unveiled?, Nicholas Pythiana, "Moslem Mauritania to Stop Child Brides," Reuters (Nouakchott, Mauritania), October 28, 1996, (Obtained from Lexis-Nexis Internet Service)., Amir Taheri, The Spirit of Allah: Khomeini and the Islamic Revolution (New York: Adler and Adler, 1986), 90-91.

26. The Watchman Expositor, Vol. 10, No. 4, 1993 Articles on Cults and New Religions, David Koresh and Joseph Smith: False Prophets, 4. Both Joseph Smith and David Koresh established religious communes in which followers were asked to give all possessions to the church and share all things in common., Doctrine and Covenants, section 51 and History of the Church, Vol. 1, pp. 364-65.

27. The Watchman Expositor, Vol. 10, No. 4, 1993 Articles on Cults and New Religions, David Koresh and Joseph Smith: False Prophets, 4. Both Joseph Smith and David Koresh established religious communes in which followers were asked to give all possessions to the church and share all things in common, Waco Tribune-Herald 6 March 1993, p. 5A.

28. Prophet of Doom, By Craig Winn, Muhammad's Own Words, Fighting, Qur'an:9:29.

29. The Great Divide, By Alvin J. Schmidt, Chapter 1, Jesus and Muhammad: Polar Opposites, Page 15, Sale, "Life of Mohammad," 192.

30. Mormonism Unveiled or The Life and Confessions of the Late Mormon Bishop John D. Lee, Written By Himself, The Mountain Meadows Massacre, Chapter XIX, Page 251.

Chapter Eight – The Connection Between Delusions & Demonism vs. Drugs & Mental Illnesses

Narcotics and mental problems like mania and schizophrenia can be connected to the act of demon worship. I am not attempting to say that just because a person has depression he or she is possessed by a demon(s). But, I am saying that a person who is demon possessed could be misdiagnosed as being bipolar. Depression can be a chemical imbalance, which is the physical component, but if it starts to affect someone by making the person violent, or start to have hallucinations, then that person's mind can be opened to the demonic realm. Hallucinogens, or psychedelics, are drugs that affect a person's perceptions, sensations, thinking, self-awareness, and emotions. Hallucinogens include such drugs as LSD, mescaline, psilocybin, and DMT. PCP is sometimes considered an hallucinogen because it produces some of the same effects. These drugs cause bizarre sensations and behavior to erupt. The user may feel several different emotions at once or swing rapidly from one emotion to another. The person's sense of time and self change. Sensations may seem to "cross over," giving the user the feeling of "hearing" colors and "seeing" sounds. All of these changes can be frightening and can cause the user to panic.[1]

The scary sensations may last a few minutes or several hours and be mildly frightening or terrifying. The user may experience panic, confusion, suspicion, anxiety, feelings of helplessness, and loss of control.[2] This is basically what happened to Joseph Smith in the beginning of his first revelation. "Immediately I was seized upon by some power which entirely overcame me, and had such an astonishing influence over me as to bind my tongue so that I could not speak. Thick darkness gathered around me, and it seemed to me for a time as if I were doomed to sudden destruction." (JS–H 1:15-17)

Demons terrify their subjects on their first visitations. Just look at what Muhammad felt during his first vision: The angel caught me (forcefully) and pressed me so hard that I could not bear it anymore. He then released me and again asked me to read, and I replied, "I do not know how to read," whereupon he caught me again and pressed me a second time till I could not bear it no more.

Allah's Apostle returned with the inspiration, but his neck muscles were twitching with terror till he entered where his wife Khadija was and said, "Cover me! Cover me!" She covered him till his fear was over. Then he said, "O Khadija, what is wrong with me?" (Bukhari, 1,1,3) Then he told her everything that had happened and said, "I fear that something may happen to me."

LUCY MACK SMITH

Lucy Mack Smith, Joseph Smith's Mother, was also spooked by a vision. Lucy did not feel prepared for death and judgement: "I knew not the ways of Christ; besides there appeared to be a dark and lonesome chasm between myself and the Saviour, which I dared not attempt to pass." By making a gigantic effort, she perceived "a faint glimmer of light." She spent the night pleading with the Lord to spare her life so she could bring up her children, Alvin and Hyrum, and "be a comfort" to her husband.[3]

Many users of LSD experience a dissolution between themselves and the "outside world."[4] This sounds similar to what Lucy Smith (Joseph Smith's mother) wrote about her son: "A short time before the house was completed [1825], a man by the name of Josiah Stoal came from Chenango County, New York, with the view of getting Joseph to assist him in digging for a silver mine. He came for Joseph on account of having heard that he posssessed certain means by which he could discern things invisible to the natural eye."[5] It was said by Islam's Isra and Miraj: "The prophet also saw people whose lips and tongues were clipped with scissors made of fire. Jibril told the prophet, these are the speakers of sedition (fitna) who call people to misguidance."[6] This would definitely indicate Muhammad's disconnection from reality. In the Hadith it reads: "Magic was worked on Allah's Apostle and he was bewitched so that he began to imagine doing things which in fact, he had not done." (Bukhari: V7B71N661)

ARTHUR RIMBAUD

Arthur Rimbaud once wrote: "I became adept at simple hallucination: in place of a factory I really saw a mosque, a school of drummers led by angels, carriages on the highways of the sky, a drawing room at the bottom of a lake; monsters, mysteries; the tide of melodrama would raise horrors before me. Then I would explain my magic sophism with the hallucination of words! Finally I came to regard the disorder of my mind as sacred."[7]

LSD is considered an entheogen because it often brings about intense spiritual experiences where users feel they have come into contact with a greater spiritual, mystical or cosmic order. Some users consider LSD a religious sacrament, or a powerful tool for access to the divine. Many books have been written comparing the LSD trip to the state of enlightenment of eastern philosophy. Such experiences under the influence of LSD have been observed and documented by researchers such as Timothy Leary and Stanislav Grof. For example, Walter Pahnke conducted the Good Friday Marsh Chapel Experiment under Leary's supervision, performing a double blind experiment on the administration of psilocybin to volunteers who were students in religious graduate programs, e.g., divinity or theology.[8]

Here's a excerpt from an interview with Reverend Randall Laakko who was one of the volunteers, explaining his LSD trip:

> "I had a real struggle with the chemical and at one point I thought I had died and I was in hell. I began saying the Bible verse 'For God so loved the world that He gave his only begotten Son, that whoever believes in Him shall not perish but have everlasting life,' and I kept repeating that over and over again and then I came to the awareness that this wasn't helping me at all."[9]

Laakko ran out of the chapel – at this moment he was experiencing a vision of a great 'glow' – enticing him: "Everything in the world just seemed to glow inwardly with life."[10] A parallel experience to that of Joseph Smith in his first revelation: at first experiencing utter panic – then concluding with two bright lights.

MAHMOUD AHMADINEJAD

The tyrant of Iran, president Mahmoud Ahmadinejad claims that he saw a "bright light surrounding him" while he was giving a speech at the UN General Assembly in September 14, 2005. According to Ahmadinejad, a U.N. member had told him that he saw a bright light surrounding him. Ahmadinejad stated in a video interview:

> "I felt it myself. I felt that the atmosphere suddenly changed, and for those 27 or 28 minutes, all the leaders of the world did not blink. When I say they didn't move an eyelid, I'm not exaggerating. They were looking as if a hand was holding them there, and had just opened their eyes to the message of the Islamic Republic."[11]

A women who did not mention her name, said: "I have not had the privilege to see him yet, but I've had many dreams about him. In one of my dreams I saw a big bright light in the sky and this figure standing over me."[12]

There's another story which compares with Laakko's experience, when he describes himself in hell: the Islamic story of the Isra and Miraj. As Muhammad was resting in the kaaba, Gabriel came to him, and brought him the winged steed Buraq, who carried him to the "furthest mosque," where he dismounted, tethered the Buraq, and led the other prophets in prayer. He then got back on the Buraq, and was taken to the heavens, where he toured heaven and hell (described in some detail). He then spoke with the earlier prophets, and with Allah. (Wikipedia.org)

The Buraq had the body of a horse but the face of a human being, with big black eyes and soft ears. Whenever he faced a mountain his hind legs would extend, and whenever he went downhill his front legs would extend.

He had two wings on his thighs which lent strength to his legs.[13] His color was that of a peacock whose plumage was set with red rubies and corals, on which sat a white head of musk on a neck of amber. His ears and shoulders were of pure white pearls attached with golden chains, each chain decorated with glittering jewels. His saddle was made of silk lined with silver and gold threads. His back was covered with green emerald and his halter was pure peridot.[14]

There is a section from the Isra and Miraj that explains in detail the gothic style of visions that Muhammad saw while in the hell-fire: "Also, the Prophet saw people who were drinking from the fluid coming from the bodies of the fornicators, (water mixed with blood). Jibril indicated to the Prophet these were the ones who were drinking the alcohol which is prohibited in this world."[15] And to this line as well: "The Prophet saw angels smashing some people's heads with rocks. These heads would return to the shape they had been, and then the angels would smash their heads again – and so on. Jibril told the Prophet, "These are the ones whose heads felt too heavy to perform prayer – the ones who used to sleep without praying."[16]

Even Joseph Smith had frightening visions. In 1828 Joseph Smith told Emma's cousins Hiel and Joseph Lewis that while trying to get the Plates, he was knocked down three times and a man appeared, like a Spaniard, with a long beard and his throat cut from ear to ear with blood flowing down.[17]

Mesoamerican doctors are called "shamans." They would use narcotics to cure their patients. "Shaman" is understood as being a priestly healer who dealt with certain ailments, the most common of which was the loss of the soul. In order to cure his patients, the shaman turned to psychotropic drugs (peyote, tobacco, red beans mixed with mescaline) and magical manipulations (incantations, offerings).[18]

PCP can produce violent or bizarre behavior in people who are not normally given to these episodes. This behavior can lead to death from drownings, burns, falls (sometimes from high places), and automobile accidents.[19] There is a Biblical story where Jesus is confronted with a demon-possessed boy with these kind of demonic characteristics. "And when they were come to the multitude, there came to him a [certain] man, kneeling down to him, and saying, 'Lord, have mercy on my son: for he is a lunatic, and sore vexed: for oft-times he falleth into the fire, and oft into the water. And I brought him to thy disciples, and they could not cure him.' Then Jesus answered and said, 'O faithless and perverse generation, how long shall I be with you? how long shall I suffer you? bring him hither to me.' And Jesus rebuked the devil; and he departed out of him: and the child was cured from that very hour." (Matthew 17:14-18)

Later we will examine how demonic activity can result in self-affliction. But first we must examine some examples in which PCP causes people to afflict others: "Young man shoots and kills own father, mother and grandfather," "Person sits engulfed in flames, unable to perceive danger," "Pulls out own teeth with pliers," "Mother puts baby in cauldron of steaming water."[20] This evil doesn't simply occur by accident, it takes planning and pre-meditation to boil one's own baby, or to shoot loved ones.

PATRICIDE AND ISLAM

Patricide is one killing their own father and Matricide is when one kills their own mother. My father served on the jury of the Kendra Bernard case in California, in which the daughter killed her own mother, and was responsible for her decapitation. Regardless of the fact that Kendra was high on PCP, the jury found her guilty of murder in the first degree, since the crime was done with pre-meditation, aforethought, and malice. How could Kendra who was high on a drug with her boyfriend, commit her crime with such detail by decapitating head, hands, and feet – separating these from the torso, and dumping them separately in two areas far apart? All parts which identify the body such as fingerprints and teeth had to be removed. If drug addicts are not able to decipher right from wrong, then how does someone commit a crime in such detail? Does the drug inhibit us from thinking straight? Or does it simply affect us to become evil? There are many situations in cult-like encounters when people murder their own relatives. Even in Islam, Muhammad the prophet of Islam states:

"Abdullah b. Zubair reported on the Day of the Battle of the Trench: I and Umar b. Abu Salama were with women folk in the fort of Hassan (b. Thabit). He at one time leaned for me and I cast a glance and at another time I leaned for him and he would see and I recognized my father as he rode on his horse with his arms towards the tribe of Quraizah. Abdullah b. 'Urwa reported from Abdullah b. Zubair: I made a mention of that to my father, whereupon he said: My son, did you see me (on that occasion)? He said: Yes. Thereupon he said: By Allah, Allah's Messenger (may peace be upon him) addressed me saying: I would sacrifice for thee my father and my mother."[21]

This cliché "I would sacrifice for thee my father and my mother" is a common statement made by Muhammad's followers. This was taken literally. In the Battle of Badr, many of Muhammad's colleagues fought and killed their own relatives including fathers and children. Abu Ubaida Amer bin Al-Jarrah killed his father. Abu Bakr Siddiq was about to kill his son. Umar ibn Al-Khattab killed his uncle.[22] All this for Muhammad and for the sake of Islam. Abu Ubaida fought and killed his father because he was an obstacle in the face of Islam and tried to stop Islam from dominating the Arabs at that time.[23]

It is not unusual in Islam to kill their own children if they leave the faith. Honor killings within Muslim societies is not confined to moral issues alone. What gross things that occur in small cults in America are sanctioned by entire nations in the Muslim world. There was a splinter cell of the Community of Christ, founded by Jeffrey Lundgren (more on him later), where he had people killed by his cult-members. He once said: "It's not a figment of my imagination that I can in fact talk to God, that I can hear his voice...I am a prophet of God. I am even more than a prophet." Lundgren also stated, "I cannot say that God was wrong. I cannot say that I am sorry I did what God commanded me to do in the physical act."[24]

Regular PCP use affects memory, perception, concentration, and judgment. Users may show signs of paranoia, fearfulness, and anxiety. During these times, some users may become aggressive while others may withdraw and have difficulty communicating. A temporary mental disturbance, or a disturbance of the user's thought processes (a PCP psychosis) may last for days or weeks. Long-term PCP users report memory and speech difficulties, as well as hearing voices or sounds which do not exist.[25]

Muhammad had heard voices and noises. Here are descriptions of this: "The Revelation is always brought to me by an angel: sometimes it is delivered to me as the beating sound of the bell – and this is the hardest experience for me; but sometimes the angel appears to me in the shape of a human and speaks to me."[26]

"He fell to the ground like one intoxicated or overcome by sleep; and in the coldest day, his forehead would be bedewed with large drops of perspiration. Inspiration descended unexpectedly, and without any previous warning."[27]

If Muhammad was alive today he would possibly be diagnosed with temporal lobe epilepsy. Here are some of its symptoms:

- Hallucinations or illusions such as hearing voices when no one has spoken, seeing patterns, lights, beings or objects that aren't there.

- Sudden, intense emotion such as fear.

- Rhythmic muscle contraction, muscle cramps are involuntary and often painful, contractions of the muscles which produce a hard, bulging muscle.

- Muscle twitching (fasciculation) is the result of spontaneous local muscle contractions that are involuntary and typically only affect individual muscle groups. This twitching does not cause pain

- Abnormal mouth behaviors

- Sweating

- Flushed face

- Rapid heart rate/pulse

- Changes in vision, speech, thought, awareness, personality[28]

All the above symptoms were present in Muhammad during the moments that he was allegedly receiving revelations:

- He had visions (hallucinations) of seeing an angel or a light and of hearing voices.

- He experienced bodily spasms and excruciating abdominal pain and discomfort

- He was overwhelmed by sudden emotions of anxiety and fear

- He had twitching in his neck muscles

- He had uncontrollable lip movement

- He sweated even during cold days

- His face flushed. His countenance was troubled

- He had rapid heart palpitation[29]

Users find it difficult to describe and predict the effects of the drug. For some users, PCP in small amounts acts as a stimulant, speeding up bodily functions. For many users, PCP changes how users see their own bodies and things around them.[30] Muhammad saw bizarre delusional things occurring to his body. One night Muhammad had a bizarre experience where Gabriel cleans his insides: the ceiling of the house in which he was staying was opened, and Jibril descended.[31] "I was lying in the hijr (of the Inviolable Mosque of Makka) when someone [the archangel Jibril] came to me and cut open my chest from throat to belly. He removed my heart and cleaned it with the water of the well of Zamzam before putting it back in its place."[32] Then Jibril brought him a golden vessel filled with "wisdom and belief" which he emptied into his chest. He filled his chest with hilm – "intelligence, patience, good character, knowledge, certainty, and submission," then he closed it up.[33]

The same scenario happened to Muhammad as a youth: "...two men in white clothes came to me with a golden basin full of snow. They took me and split open my body, then they took my heart and split it open and took out from it a black clot which they flung away. Then they washed my heart and my body with that snow until they made them pure." "His [Muhammad's friend's] father said to me, "I am afraid that this child has had a stroke, so take him back to his family before the result appears. She [Muhammad's mother] asked me what happened and gave me no peace until I told her. When she asked if I feared a demon had possessed him, I replied that I did."[34]

In the pre-Islamic era it was believed that the demon spirits of the "jinn" were responsible for diseases and for the manias of some lunatics.[35]

NAVEED AFZAL HAQ

Naveed Afzal Haq – a Muslim man who was angry with Israel barged into the offices of the Jewish Federation of Greater Seattle one Friday afternoon, and opened fire with a handgun, killing one woman and wounding five others before surrendering to police.[36] One of Haq's friends told The Seattle Times that the suspect was taking medication for bipolar disorder, and that he was unhappy with his life and sometimes made offhanded anti-Semitic remarks.[37]

A SPIRIT OF DEPRESSION

Signs and symptoms of the depressive phase of bipolar disorder include (but in no way are limited to): persistent feelings of sadness, anxiety, guilt, anger, isolation and/or hopelessness, disturbances in sleep and appetite, fatigue and loss of interest in daily activities, problems concentrating, loneliness, self-loathing, apathy or indifference, depersonalization, loss of interest or a sudden increased interest in sexual activity, shyness or social anxiety, irritability, chronic pain (with or without a known cause), lack of motivation, and morbid/suicidal ideation.[38]

There is a common phrase that we call "withdrawal" which refers to the characteristic signs and symptoms that appear when a drug which causes physical dependence is regularly used for a long time and then suddenly discontinued or decreased in dosage. The term can also, less formally, refer to symptoms that appear after discontinuing a drug or other substance, and while it doesn't cause a true physical dependence, does cause a psychological dependence.[39]

The drug-abuser becomes addicted to hallucinations or physiological stimulations – such as Muhammad in the Isra and Miraj. Addicts constantly need these narcotics in order to receive euphoria which is a emotional stage of intense happiness. Euphoria is charged by a bodily hormone called dopamine.

Withdrawal symptoms can vary significantly among individuals, but there are some commonalities. Subnormal activity in the nucleus accumbens is often characterized by depression, anxiety and craving, and if the symptoms are extreme, can drive the individual back to continue using the drug in spite of significant harm, or even suicide – thus, the definition of addiction.[40]

Muhammad himself went through a "withdrawal" from the angel Gabriel:

"Waraqa said, 'This is the same Namus (i.e., Gabriel, the Angel who keeps the secrets) whom Allah had sent to Moses. I wish I were young and could live up to the time when your people would turn you out.' Allah's Apostle asked, 'Will they turn me out?' Waraqa replied in the affirmative and said: 'Never did a man come with something similar to what you have brought but was treated with hostility. If I should remain alive till the day when you will be turned out then I would support you strongly.' But after a few days Waraqa died and the Divine Inspiration was also paused for a while and the Prophet became so sad as we have heard that he intended several times to throw himself from the tops of high mountains and every time he went up the top of a mountain in order to throw himself down, Gabriel would appear before him and say, 'O Muhammad! You are indeed Allah's Apostle in truth' whereupon his heart would become quiet and he would calm down and would return home. And whenever the period of the coming of the inspiration used to become long, he would do as before, but when he used to reach the top of a mountain, Gabriel would appear before him and say to him what he had said before."[41]

"The inspiration ceased to come to the messenger of God for a while, and he was deeply grieved. He began to go to the tops of mountain crags, in order to fling himself from them; but every time he reached the summit of a mountain, Gabriel appeared to him and said to him, 'You are the Prophet of God.' Thereupon his anxiety would subside and he would come back to himself."[42]

This may compare with Hallucinogen Persisting Perception Disorder (or HPPD). People with this condition experience perceptual (usually visual) distortions even after the "trip" is over and the drug and its metabolites have left the body.[43] The trips may come back sometimes weeks, months, or even years afterward.[44]

The bouts of depression continued over the next several years, the suicide attempts would follow, and the spirit persisted to soothe him. Muhammad began to believe he was a messenger of god. A messenger of a god who's influence caused him to attempt suicide.[45]

Then he came to a plank in the middle of the road, where not even a piece of fabric or less, could cross it but it would be pierced. He asked, "What is this, O Jibril?" He replied: "This is what happens to those of your community who sit in the middle of the road and cut it." He recited, "Lurk not on every road to threaten wayfarers and to turn away from Allah's path him who believes in him, and to seek to make it crooked."(7:86) [46]

Then he saw people who wore loincloths on their fronts and backs. They were roaming the way camels and sheep roam. They were eating thistles and zaqqum – the fruit of a tree that grows in hell and whose fruit resembles the head of devils (37:62-63) – and white-hot coals and stones of Gehenna. He said, "Who are these, O Jibril?" Jibril replied, "These are the ones who did not meet the obligation of paying sadaqa from what they possessed, whereas Allah never kept anything from them."[47]

For those that don't know what Sadaqa is, it is giving things for Allah, so that Allah will give back to you a reward for committing sadaqa. Since when does God need your possessions in order to send you to Heaven?

HELENA PETROVNA BLAVATSKY

Helena Petrovna Blavatsky was a very sensitive child, often walked in her sleep, and suffered from hallucinations. As an adult she saw herself as a telepath and a psychic. She was also the author of the book "Secret Doctrine." In this book she wrote that during her trip to Tibet, she was led into a secret room underneath a Tibetan monastery where she was shown texts of ancient occult and mystical secrets of the universe, which were also said to lay a route to the future course of history. She was then initiated into the practice of magic, using esoteric symbols which foretold how the human race would once again rise into a pure spirit. She claimed she was in current telepathic contact with hidden masters, who taught her the occult history of the human race.[48]

L. Ron Hubbard was a severe drug addict. In a letter to his wife Mary Sue, Hubbard said that, in order to assist his research, he was drinking a great deal of rum and taking stimulants and depressants – saying that "I'm drinking lots of rum and popping pinks and greys." His assistant at the time, Virginia Downsborough said that he "was existing almost totally on a diet of drugs." It is said that one of the origins of his Xenu story (more on that later) was drugs.[49]

Herbert Spencer suffered from chronic insomnia and could only work a few hours a day. He used fairly substantial amounts of opium. He experienced a strange sensation in his head which he called "the mischief," and was known for eccentricities like the wearing of ear-plugs to avoid over-excitement, especially when he could not hold his ground in an argument.[50]

It is said that Joseph Smith drank alcohol while writing the Book of Mormon. In the History of the Church, Vol. 2, p. 26, we find the following: "The council proceeded to investigate certain charges presented by Elder Rigdon against Martin Harris; one was, that he told A.C. Russell, Esq., that

Joseph drank too much liquor when he was translating the Book of Mormon..."Brother Harris did not tell Esq. Russell that Brother Joseph drank too much liquor while translating the Book of Mormon..."[51]

ALAN GINSBERG AND HIS HALLUCINATIONS

Alan Ginsberg is a famous poet, drug addict, and a man who has boasted about his homosexuality and his attraction to young boys. In his most famous poem, "Howl," Ginsburg writes about a chilling visitation from a 'god' who he describes as "Moloch" (possibly better described as "Baal Moloch"). Jeremiah 32:35 speaks of "the high places of the Ba'al, which are in the valley of Ben-hinnom, to cause their sons and their daughters to pass through the fire Mo'lech; which I did not command them, nor did it come into my mind that they should do this abomination, to cause Judah to sin." Ginsberg had this hallucination by taking the drug peyote. This is part of what he wrote in Howl:

"I saw the best minds of my generation destroyed by
madness, starving hysterical naked,
dragging themselves through the negro streets at dawn
looking for an angry fix,
angelheaded hipsters burning for the ancient heavenly
connection to the starry dynamo in the machinery of night,
who poverty and tatters and hollow-eyed and high sat
up smoking in the supernatural darkness of
cold-water flats floating across the tops of cities
contemplating jazz,
who bared their brains to Heaven under the El [marijuana] and
saw Muhammadan angels staggering on tenement
roofs illuminated," – Howl, by Alan Ginsburg

In 1948 in an apartment in Harlem, Ginsberg had an auditory hallucination of William Blake reading his poems "Ah, Sunflower," "The Sick Rose," and "Little Girl Lost" (later referred to as his "Blake vision"). Ginsberg was reading these poems since he was very familiar with them. At one point he said he heard them being read by a voice that sounded like the voice of God, but he interpreted it as the voice of Blake. It was at that moment he had pivotal revelations that defined his understanding of the universe. He believed he had witnessed the interconnectedness of the universe. He saw the lattice work on the fire escape and realized some hand had crafted that. Then he looked at the sky and intuitively knew some hand had crafted that also, or rather, that the sky was the hand that crafted itself. He explained that this hallucination was not a result of drug use, but admitted he sought to recapture that same feeling later with various drugs. It's interesting to note that music and chanting were both important parts of his poetry readings. He often played the harmonium, and was frequently accompanied by a guitarist.[52]

Resources

1. ADA, As a Matter of Fact..., Hallucinogens and PCP.

2. Ibid

3. Signature Books, Excerpt, Lucy's Book A Critical Edition of Lucy Mack Smith's Family Memoir, Contents, Forward Lucy Mack Smith – First Mormon Mother, Irene M. Bates, Bloch 118.

4. Wikipedia, LSD, Psychological, Linton, Harriet B. and Langs, Robert J. "Subjective Reactions to Lysergic Acid Diethylamide (LSD-25)." Arch. Gen. Psychiat. Vol. 6 (1962): 352-68.

5. Salt Lake City Messenger, April 1999, #95, Was Joseph Smith a Magician?, Biographical Sketches, Lucy Smith, pp. 91-92, as quoted in Early Mormon Documents, Vol. 1, p.309.

6. Miracle of Al-Isra and Al-Miraj, Al-Isra, 10.

7. http://www.songsouponsea.com/Promenade/CirkusA.html, – Arthur Rimbaud, A Season in Hell and The Drunken Boat.

8. Wikipedia, LSD, Spiritual.

9. Yoism, The Marsh Chapel Experiment.

10. Ibid

11. Christian World News, Islam, Waiting For Islam's Messiah, By George Thomas, June 16, 2006.

12. Ibid

13. Commemorating the prophet's rapture and ascension to his lord, III. The Collated Hadith of Isra' and Mi`raj.

14. The Prophet's Night Journey and Ascension, The Buraq (Heavenly Beast).

15. Miracle of Al-Isra and Al-Miraj, Al-Isra, 10.

16. Wikipedia, Mesoamerica, Human Sacrifice, Carmack, Robert; et. al. (1996). The legacy of Mesoamerica: history and culture of a Native American civilization. New Jersey: Prentice Hall. ISBN 0-13-337445-9.

17. Mormon History – A Chronology, 1843.

18. Wikipedia, Mesoamerica, Magic and Logic, Medicine, Carmack, Robert; et. al. (1996). The legacy of Mesoamerica: history and culture of a Native American civilization. New Jersey: Prentice Hall. ISBN 0-13-337445-9.

19. Why Is PCP Dangerous, National Institute on Drug Abuse, 1984

20. The Dusting of America, John P. Morgan, M.D. & Doreen Kagan, M.S. From the Journal of Psychedelic Drugs 12(3-4), Jul-Dec 1980, Gay, B. 1978. The evils of angel dust and other " a P P P drugs," Sepia VOL 27: 17-19, Koper, P. 1978. Angel death. New Times March 20., Table III, Popular Horror Tales of PCP Users.

21. USC-MSA Compendium of Muslim Texts, Translation of Sahih Muslim, Book 31:, Book 031, Number 5940.

22. Zawaj.com, Editorials, Brotherhood – The Basis of Islamic Society, By M. Adil Salahy, The Muslim December-January 1975/6.

23. Hazrat Abu Ubaida ibn Al'Jarrah, 3.

24. News 14 Carolina, Charlotte, Top Stories, Thursday January 18 2007, Cult leader headed to execution, By: Thomas J. Sheeran, Associated Press.

25. Why Is PCP Dangerous, National Institute on Drug Abuse, 1984

26. Faithfreedom.org, Muhammad and Temporal Lobe Epilepsy (TLE), By Ali Sina, The Physical Effects of Muhammad's Ecstatic Experiences, An Introduction to Islam, By Dr. Q Shah Balg, The Archangel Gabriel, Al-Bukhari, 1:2.

27. Faithfreedom.org, Muhammad and Temporal Lobe Epilepsy (TLE), By Ali Sina, The Physical Effects of Muhammad's Ecstatic Experiences, Bukhari 7, 71, 660.

28. Faithfreedom.org, Muhammad and Temporal Lobe Epilepsy (TLE), By Ali Sina, The Physical Effects of Muhammad's Ecstatic Experiences, The following is a partial list of the Temporal Lobe Seizure Symptoms & Signs as defined in health.allrefer.com.

29. Ibid

30. Why Is PCP Dangerous, National Institute on Drug Abuse, 1984

31. Miracle of Al-Isra and Al-Miraj, Al-Isra, 10.

32. Deen Islam, Sadaqah Group "In an age of terror, Reviving Lost Spiritual Knowledge," The Night Journey, The Spiritual Significance of Isra and Miraj, By Shaykh Hisham Muhammad Kabbani.

33. Commemorating the prophet's rapture and ascension to his lord, III. The Collated Hadith of Isra' and Mi`raj.

34. Muhammad And The Demons, By Silas, W. M. Watt's translation of Ibn Ishaq's biography of Muhammad, page 36, Guillaume's translation of Ibn Ishaq, page 72, "The Life of Muhammad," by A. Guillaume, Oxford University Press.

35. Wikipedia, Genie, Jinn in Pre-Islamic Era.

36. Jihad Watch, FrontPageMag.com, By Robert Spencer, By Hugh Fitzgerald, Books Dhimmi Watch Robert Spencer, July 29, 2006, Seattle jihad shooter: "Peace be upon you."

37. Wikipedia, Navved Afzal Haq, Minor Brushes the the Law, "Incidents clash with image suspect conveyed in school," Seattle Times, 2006-07-29. Retrieved on 2006-07-29.

38. Wikipedia, Bipolar, The Depressive Pahse, http://www.mayoclinic.com/health/bipolar-disorder/DS00356/DSECTION=2.

39. Wikipedia, Withdrawal.

40. Wikipedia, Withdrawal, Withdrawal from drugs of abuse.

41. Muhammad's Suicide Attempts, By Silas, Ibn 'Abbas said regarding the meaning of: 'He it is that Cleaves the daybreak (from the darkness)' (6.96) that Al-Asbah. means the light of the sun during the day and the light of the moon at night). Quoted from the Sahih (authentic) Hadith (traditions) of Bukhari, "Sahih al-Bukhari," translated by M. Khan, published by Kitab Bhavan, New Delhi. , Volume 9, number 111.

42. Muhammad's Suicide Attempts, By Silas, Tabari, "The History of al-Tabari," translated by W.M. Watt, published by SUNY., volume 6 page 76.

43. Wikipedia, Hallucinogen persisting perception disorder.

44. Wikipedia, LSD, Flashbacks and HPPD.

45. Muhammad's Suicide Attempts, By Silas, Discussion.

46. Commemorating the prophet's rapture and ascension to his lord, III. The Collated Hadith of Isra' and Mi`raj.

47. Ibid

48. Hitler and the secret Societies, By Wes Penre, Illuminati News, Feb 11, 1999, Madame Blavatsky and the Theosophical Society.

49. Wikipedia, Xenu, Origins of the Xenu story, Corydon, pp. 58-59, 332-333; letter filed as evidence in Church of Scientology v. Gerald Armstrong, 1984, Los Angeles Superior Court, Case No. C420153., Attack, part 4, ch. 1, "Scientology at Sea."

50. Herbert Spencer, Alvin Wee, University Scholars Programme, National University of Singapore, Spencer, Herbert. 'Development Hypothesis' Spencer, Herbert. First Principles 1862. Spencer, Herbert. The Man Versus the State 1884. Young, R.M., The development of herbert spencer's concept of evolution Thoemmes Press Online, Psychology Section Herbert Spencer's Social Darwinism Herbert Spencer (Internet Encyclopedia of Philosophy)

Herbert Spencer. Development of Sociological Theory (University of Minnesota Duluth).

51. The Word of Wisdom, From Mormonism – Shadow or Reality, By Jerald and Sandra Tanner, Chapter 26 – pages 405-413, Joseph's Example, In the History of the Church, Vol. 2, p. 26.

52. Widipedia, Allen Ginsburg, Life, Early Buddhism.

Chapter Nine – The Superman and the Nazi Connection

As was stated earlier, Scientologists believe that anyone can attain a god-like existence by thetan(s). Additionally, in Scientology, the "thetan is not a thing. It is the creator of things."[1] According to L. Ron Hubbard, they are three parts of man: the body, the mind, and thetan; Hadit is the principal speaker of the second chapter of the Book of the law, where he identifies himself as the point in the center of the circle, the axle of the wheel, the cube in the circle, "the flame that burns in every heart of man, and in the core of every star," and the worshipper's own self. Hadit has been interpreted as the inner spirit of man, the "holy ghost," the sperm in which the DNA of man is carried. When juxtaposed with Nuit in Liber Legis, Hadit represents each unique point-experience. These point-experiences in combination comprise the sum of all possible experience, Nuit.[2]

Thetans generated "points to view," or "dimension points" which caused space to come into existence. Thetans agreed that other thetans' dimension points existed, and that agreement brought about reality. Reality, indeed the entire universe, is an "agreed upon apparency," and all matter, energy, space and time exists because thetans agree it exists.[4]

The Scientology term "thetan" is what has commonly come to be known as the "spirit" and it is defined in Scientology as the source of life; in the individual, it is recognized as the core of personality or essence of oneself, quite distinct and separate from the physical body or the brain.[5] Here's a quote from Scientologytoday.org: "Unlike religions with Judeo-Christian origins, the Church of Scientology has no set dogma concerning God that it imposes on its members.

As with all its beliefs, Scientology does not ask individuals to believe anything on faith. Rather, as one's level of spiritual awareness increases through participation in auditing and training, he attains his own certainty of every dynamic and, as he moves from the seventh (spiritual) dynamic to the eighth, will come to his own conclusions concerning the nature of God (or the supreme being or infinity) and his relationship to it."[6]

Consequently, there is no point for anyone to seek salvation or God; instead they should allow themselves to go through auditing and training in order to experience the eight dynamics and restore "free will" into their own thetan. Further, each person is to put their life in the hands of thetan and not God – to let thetan guide you to find God and not yourself. But isn't Scientology a religion too? If so, what God are they being guided to? According to Professor Lonnie Kliever, Department Chair of Religious Studies at the SMU:

> The ultimate goal of the religious life in Scientology is survival "through a Supreme Being" or "as Infinity." As we shall see, auditing and training are the primary forms of worship in the church of Scientology. These worship activities equip and assist the Scientologist to survive and thrive across all eight dynamics. These spiritual exercises produce healthy and happy individuals, families and groups. But ultimately worship enables individual Scientologists to discover themselves as spiritual beings in a spiritual universe that radically transcends the physical body and the material world.[7]

Usually the individual Scientologist is free to interpret God in whatever manner he or she wishes.[8] Basically there is no real view of God in Scientology. It's all about realizing that there is a thetan in you and you must restore free will in it, in order to be "free."

Scientologists have said (as previously stated) that they find their own concept of God – but this can't be true in light of this quote from L. Ron Hubbard:

"I have never said I didn't disbelieve in a big thetan, but there was certainly something very corny about Heaven, et. al."[9] This statement signifies what kind of "supreme being" is looked up to by Scientologists – frankly, it's the Scientologist who becomes the "supreme being."

In Scientology there is the "operating thetan three" which is an elite team of scientologists. Inspection of the activity of OT3 reveals that they cannot be functioning in the benign way they advertise. They have developed a set of disguised cognitive-procedural training actions to achieve: confusion of one's own thoughts, or the influence of others; and, strengthening their ability to smoothly control others by willpower.[10]

L. Ron Hubbard had once said: "The universe is a rough universe. It is a terrible and deadly universe. Only the strong survive it, only the ruthless can own it."[11]

Scientologists believe in this: "an aberrated state where one's energy is primarily absorbed attempting to straighten out personal problems, a person is unlikely to lift his gaze to the glories that could be his as a fully rehabilitated and able being, not just as homo sapiens."[12] L. Ron Hubbard once said: "Scientology is used to increase spiritual freedom, intelligence, ability, and to produce immortality."[13]

Marshall Applewhite (the founder of Heaven's Gate) invented the "Human Individual Metamorphosis" – the transformation into an "Evolutionary Level above Human."

In Anton LaVey's "Satanic Bible," there is a section called the "Book of Lucifer" in which it explains that the most important holiday in Satanism is one's own birthday, since it's the date of birth of one's own god. This is a reminder to a Satanist that they are the most important being in the universe, and they are to honor their own vital existence and life.[14]

THE SUPERMAN

Another form of worshipping one's self can be found in Hitler. Hitler was influenced by the writings of Friedrich Nietzsche. Nietzsche's idea of "the overman" (Übermensch) is one of the most significant concepts in his thinking. Even though it is mentioned only briefly in the prologue of *Thus Spoke Zarathustra*, it seems reasonable to believe that Nietzsche had something he believed about how a man should be more than just human – all-too-human, regardless if he was one or not. An overman is someone who can establish his own values, even as the world in which others live their lives are often unaware that those values were not pre-given. But more than this, he is an extraordinary person who is able to transcend the limits of traditional morality to live solely by his drive for power. This person is willing to risk all for the advancement of humanity, and can affect people's thinking through establishing their values. This means an overman will influence the lives of others, and this impact can last indefinitely.[15]

Thule society believed in "communication with a hierarchy of Supermen – The Secret Chiefs of the Third Order." The quality which would make these beings supermen was occultic spirituality. Further, they believed in Madame Blavatsky's secret doctrine, which taught that certain supermen had survived the destruction of Atlantis with their higher levels of consciousness intact. These supermen were Aryans. These two beliefs combined into one through the Thule Society and Hitler. It was this concept of Aryan supermen being inherently superior to other groups of people and occultic spirituality, which culminated in the Nazi death camps.[16]

FRIEDRICH NIETZSCHE

Nietzsche offered grounds for the reprehensible Nazi ideology of a superior race exercising its will to power as it saw fit. Hitler was living out what Nietzsche had envisioned, trying to prove himself to be the Übermensch (overman) and the precursor of the Master race. He despised weakness as much as Nietzsche did and wanted to reevaluate the current social values and change them into something that supported the aggressive instinct. He wanted to become, as Nietzsche called it, a "lord of the earth."[17]

Nietzsche wrote in *The Genealogy of Morals,* "The sick are the great danger of man, not the evil, not the 'beasts of prey.' They who are from the outset botched, oppressed, broken those are they, the weakest are they, who most undermine the life beneath the feet of man, who instill the most dangerous venom and skepticism into our trust in life, in man, in ourselves…Here teem the worms of revenge and vindictiveness; here the air reeks of things secret and unmentionable; here is ever spun the net of the most malignant conspiracy – the conspiracy of the sufferers against the sound and the victorious; here is the sight of the victorious hated."[18]

This hatred of the weak can also be found in Islam and evolution. The Quran says: "Against them make ready your strength to the utmost of your power, including steeds of war, to strike terror into [the hearts of] the enemies of God, and your enemies." (Quran 8:60) There is an Islamic verse that reads: "The Prophet, peace be upon him, said: Allah's Messenger said: 'The strong believer is better and more loved by Allah than the weak one, but they are both good.'"[19] According to a Muslim website: "Physical toughness, strength, absence of luxurious living are virtues that should be present in the Muslim."[20]

In Aleister Crowley's *The Book of The Law* it reads: "We have nothing with the outcast and the unfit: let them die in their misery. For they feel not. Compassion is the vice of kings: stamp down the wretched and the weak: this is the law of the strong: this is our law and the joy of the world."[21]

HERBERT SPENCER

In the case for evolution there are the works of Herbert Spencer. It was Spencer who actually coined the phrase "survival of the fittest" in *The Principles of Biology* (1864–1867), here he depicted a constant struggle amongst the species. [22] As a result of this continual struggle, the stronger species survived and multiplied while the weaker species perished. He left no room for doubt of his beliefs, declaring, "all imperfection must disappear." As such, he completely denounced charity; instead he extolled the purifying elimination of the "unfit." The unfit, he argued, were predestined by their nature to an existence of downwardly spiraling degradation.[23]

Spencer also wrote in *The Principles of Biology*, "The survival of the fittest which I have here sought to express in mechanical terms, is that which Mr.

Darwin has called 'natural selection,' or the preservation of favored races in the struggle for life."[24]

The subtitle of Darwin's *Origin of Species*, is "On the origin of species by means of natural selection or the preservation of favored races in the struggle for life."[25] Now we can confidently say to all those mole-faced, baby-killing teachers that drive (or drove) us nuts – evolution is nothing more than a theory that justifies the act of sadism. Think about it. Sadism is the act of putting pain on others. To inflict pain on the weak is sadistic. To choose one who is weak and eliminate them – is sadism! So, if the world would actually take evolution to its fullest extent, it would be justifiable to exterminate the weak ones amongst us – like women. Most women are a great deal weaker than men, therefore, under the provisions of evolution it would be permissible to eliminate them. Nazi Germany is a prime example of a nation that used evolution.

The ideology of evolution does a great job of degrading the human race. Evolutionists proclaim humans came from monkeys, Muslims claim monkeys are the descendants of Jews, and today the Christian belief of God creating man in His own image is scorned at. No longer is man seen as valuable, being created in the Image of God. Man has been relegated to just a random mutation; a meaningless conglomeration of cells and chemicals.[26] A worthless creation having evolved, but retaining the same attributes of an orangutan...hence having a hollow destiny, with no spiritual completion...and with no purpose.

This is not what is taught by our Savior in His Word, the Bible, or by our parents. This does not make sense when we remember the warmth of our first impulses of humanity. If we look at animals, with no souls or morals, who attack and overtake others of their own species, and then apply these characteristics to mankind, one can see it will lead to nothing but a thuggish life, carnage, and immorality.

Friedrich Nietzsche once wrote: "I teach you the overman. Man is something that shall be overcome. What have you done to overcome him? All beings so far have created something beyond themselves; and do you want to be the ebb of this great flood and even go back to the beasts rather than overcome man? What is the ape to man? A laughingstock or a painful embarrassment. And man shall be just that for the overman: a laughing-stock or a painful embarrassment."[27]

Nietzsche believed that everything alive is seeking to perfect itself and become stronger and in our present state, modern humans are just a mindless herd, more primitive than our ape ancestors and even the ances-tors of the apes. Modern man is just a shapeless mass, a monster but the superman forges his own destiny; he is at his highest intellectual and creative ability. "Man is to ape as Superman shall be to man. Man is a polluted stream which Christianity says must be rid of it's pollutants – yet the end result will leave hardly anything left. The best remedy for this problem, however, is the Superman, who is such a large sea that he can accommodate polluted streams without worry or hurt."[28]

EVOLUTION AND THE ANCIENT GREEKS

By 400 BC the Greek atomists were teaching that the sun, earth, life, humans, civilization, and society emerged over eons from the eternal and uncreated atoms colliding and vibrating in the void – all without divine intervention. In the epic poem *On the Nature of Things,* the Roman atomist Lucretius in about 60 B.C. described the stages of the living earth coming to be what it is. "The earth and sun formed from swirls of dust congregated from atoms colliding and vibrating in the void; early plants and animals sprang from the early earth's own substance because of the insistence of the atoms that formed the earth; the aging earth gave birth to a succession of animals including a series of progressively less brutish humans that made a succession of improved tools, laws, and civilizations with increasing complexity finally arriving at the current earth and life forms as they are." *(Wikipedia, Ancient Evolutionary Thought, On The Nature of Things By Lucretius)*

If an evolutionist tells you that we are not monkey's now – then he cannot be telling the truth. The theory of evolution has man being a descendent of an ape – so according to evolution, man is still a primate, because a gene can never die. Does a pencil lose its connection with a tree – or, can an American Italian lose his Italian ancestry? The Caterpillar still evolves into a butterfly, and the tadpole still changes into a frog. So, a question to an evolutionist is, what stopped the apes from continuing to evolve into humans? And if we came from algae – where did the algae come from? And from whatever it came from – where did that come from? You must keep asking these questions over and over again.

In fact, Darwin himself was a fanatic racist. Labeling Africans and Australians as apes and still-evolving. Stating that "At some future period, not very distant as measured by centuries, the civilized races of man will almost certainly exterminate, and replace the savage races throughout the world. At the same time the anthropomorphous apes...will no doubt be exterminated. The break between man and his nearest allies will then be wider, for it will intervene between man in a more civilized state, as we may hope, even than the Caucasian, and some ape as low as a baboon, instead of as now between the Negro or Australian and the gorilla."[29] He used his observations of indigenous people to prove his theory, calling them "the anthropomorphous apes." The word anthropomorphous signifies an animal which looks human but is not. I propose that we stop defining Darwin as a legitimate scientist and start labeling him for what he was – a philosopher whose baseless teachings played a major role in the influences of Hitler and the Nazi regime.

Then we have Emile Burnouf. Burnouf's work takes for granted a racial hierarchy that places Aryans as the master race at the top. Like Darwin, he uses "science" to define Semites (in his case, Jews), saying that "A real Semite has smooth hair with curly ends, a strongly hooked nose, fleshy, projecting lips, massive extremities, thin calves and flat feet...His growth is very rapid, and at fifteen or sixteen it is over. At that age the divisions of the skull which contain the organs of intelligence are already joined, and that in some cases even perfectly welded together. From that period the growth of the brain is arrested. In the Aryan races this phenomenon, or anything like it, never occurs, at any time of life, certainly not with people of normal development. The internal organ is permitted to continue its evolution and transformations up until the very last day of life by means of the never-changing flexibility of the skull bone."[30]

HOUSTON STEWART CHAMBERLAIN

Chamberlain was the author of the book, *The Foundations of The Nineteenth Century* which became one of the standards of racist and ideological anti-Semitism in early 20th century Germany. He was influenced (as was Hitler) by ideas of the Musician Richard Wagner, and he even married Wagner's daughter, Eva Wagner. He argued that when the Germanic tribes destroyed the Roman Empire, Jews and other non-Europeans already dominated it. The Germans, therefore, saved Western civilization from Semitic domination. He believed that the Aryan, or "noble" race was always in the process of creation as superior peoples supplanted inferior ones in evolutionary struggles for survival. Chamberlain used a now discredited notion of the ethnic make up of Galilee to argue that, while Jesus may have been Jewish by religion, he was not Jewish by race. During the Nazi period certain pro-Nazi theologians developed these ideas as part of the manufacture of an Aryan Jesus.[31]

Helen Blavatsky's teachings were instrumental to the creation of the Nazi Party as was the Darwinian drive to annihilate the "race polluters" and restore the Aryans with their "pure" religion of fire, sword, and swastika to their previous glory.[32]

Blavatsky outlined a map of evolution that went far beyond Darwin's theories to include vanished races from time immemorial through the present imperfect race of humans, then continuing on for races far into the future. Based on an idiosyncratic selection of various Asian scriptures – including a few she made up herself – the message of her book, *The Secret Doctrine's* would later be picked up by the German occultists, who welcomed the pseudoscientific prose of its author as the answer to a dream. Blavatsky took new scientific attitudes as they were popularly understood and gave them a mystical twist. Taking her cue from Darwin, she popularized the notion of a spiritual struggle between various "races," and the inherent superiority of the "Aryan" race, hypothetically the latest in the line of spiritual evolution. Blavatsky would borrow heavily from carefully chosen scientific authors in fields as diverse as archaeology and astronomy to bolster her arguments for the existence of Atlantis, extraterrestrial (or super terrestrial) life-forms, the creation of animals by humans (as opposed to the Darwinian line of succession), and many other conjectures.[33]

If you read Hitler's *Mein Kampf* you can identify the Darwinian influence, especially when it reads: "In the folkish state we will lift marriage out of race degradation in order to consecrate the image of the Lord and not the deformities of men who are half ape."[34]

Aleister Crowley once said (regarding the Jewish people): Human sacrifices are still practiced today by the Jews of Eastern Europe, as is set forth at length by the late Sir Richard Burton in the MS. The wealthy Jews of England have compassed heaven and earth to suppress this, evidenced by the ever-recurring attacks made by those who live among the degenerate Jews, who are at least not cannibals. (Equinox 1:8)

JEWS ARE MONKEYS

Jews depicted as monkeys is not only in Nazi ideology. In Quran 2: 64 it reads: "But you [Jews] went back on your word and were lost losers. So become apes, despised and hated. We made an example out of you."[35] Islam, like Satanism, considers anyone who is a Muslim to be superior to the rest of world.

The edicts regarding Jews in Nazi Germany and in Islam are almost identical:

the Omar Charter (adopted by Omar, Muhammad's successor in Islam) will reveal a true commonality:

Nazism: Jews need to wear a mark on their clothing to identify them as Jews. The Star of David for identification with the word (Jude) (must be) on the chest. A yellow banner is to be fixed around the shoulder or arm, as to be recognized as a Jew. They must live in the Jewish Ghettos.

Islam: Dhimmis (Jews and Christians) must wear identifiable clothing and live in clearly marked houses. For Jews, a yellow banner is to be fixed around the shoulder or arm, to identify them as being Jewish.

Nazism: Jews are not permitted to serve in the army or navy. They are not allowed to bear arms.

Islam: Jews must not own or ride a horse, or bear arms. They must yield the right-of-way to Muslims.

Nazism: Jews cannot hold public offices, whether national, state, or municipal, salaried or honorary. Jews cannot be Judges in criminal and disciplinary cases. Jews cannot serve on juries.

Islam: Dhimmis cannot be a witness in a legal court except in matters relating to other "Dhimmis," nor can they be a judge in a Muslim court.

Nazism: As compensation for the protection that Jews enjoy as aliens, they must pay double the taxes the Germans pay.

Islam: As compensation for the protection that Dhimmis enjoy, they must pay "Jizia," a special tax to be imposed on Dhimmis only.

Nazism: Marriage to Jews is prohibited. Adoption of Jews and by Jews is prohibited.

Islam: A Jew cannot be the guardian of a Muslim child, or the owner of a Muslim slave.

Nazism: Jews must live in Ghettos.

Islam: Jews may not build their houses in the neighborhood of Muslims.[36]

I can hear the argument: the Omar Pact was not part of the Quran or Muhammad (the Sunna). True, Omar was not the author; he derived his covenant from the highest of Islamic sources:

1. The killing of converts (after their three-day warning), came from Muhammad, the prophet of Islam: "Whoever changes his Islamic religion, kill him."

2. The Quran, 9:29, orders that non-Muslims must be fought until they believe in Islam or pay al-Jizia Tax. "Fight against such of those who have been given the Scripture and believe not in Allah nor the last day, and forbid not that which Allah hath forbidden by his messenger, and follow not the religion of truth, until they pay the tribute readily, being brought low."

3. Muhammad ordered: "Allah's Apostle said, 'I have been ordered to fight with the people till they say,' 'None has the right to be worshipped but Allah,' and whoever says, 'None has the right to be worshipped but Allah,' his life and property will be saved by me except for Islamic law, and his accounts will be with Allah, (either to punish him or to forgive him.)"[37]

4. Muhammad ordered that in a Muslim society, if a Muslim kills a non-Muslim, the Muslim is not put to death: "No Muslim should be killed for killing a Kafir (infidel)."[38]

5. A Muslim who kills a Muslim, and a non-Muslim who kills a Muslim, are both to be killed, Quran 2:178:

"O ye who believe! the law of equality is prescribed to you in cases of murder: the free for the free, the slave for the slave, the woman for the woman. But if any remission is made by the brother of the slain, then grant any reasonable demand, and compensate him with handsome gratitude, this is a concession and a mercy from your lord. After this whoever exceeds the limits shall be in grave penalty."

"Yahya related to me from Malik that he heard that Umar ibn Abd al-Aziz gave a decision that when a Jew or Christian was killed, his blood-money was half the blood-money of a free Muslim."[39]

6. Muhammad practiced and ordered ethnic cleansing by removing all Jews, Christians and pagans from the Arabian Peninsula. In fact, just before his death, he stated: "While we were in the Mosque, the Prophet came out and said, 'Let us go to the Jews.' We went out till we reached Bait-ul-Midras. He said to them, 'If you embrace Islam, you will be safe. You should know that the earth belongs to Allah and His

Apostle, and I want to expel you from this land. So, if anyone amongst you owns some property, he is permitted to sell it, otherwise you should know that the Earth belongs to Allah and His Apostle'"[40]

7. Muslims are ordered to push the non-Muslims to the narrowest part of the road when meeting them: "Do not initiate the greeting of salaam to a Jew or Christian, and if you meet them in the street, push them to the narrowest part of the road."[41]

In summary from the highest levels of authority in Islam, the Quran, Muhammad, and His apostles, Christians and Jews:

a. Cannot build any new houses of worship in their neighborhoods, and can't repair the ones that fall into ruin

b. Cannot evangelize, and yet they cannot forbid their kin from becoming Muslims

c. Cannot wear clothes that could make them look like Muslims, and they must wear distinguishing clothes

d. Cannot engrave Arabic inscription on their seals

e. Cannot do anything pertaining to their religion publicly (show their crosses or stars, be heard worshipping, etc.)

f. Cannot take slaves who have been allotted to Muslims (the reverse is possible)

g. Cannot build houses overtopping the houses of the Muslims, hatred has a long history. The Mufti of Jerusalem, Haj Amin Al-Husseini, the good friend of Adolf Hitler, was not original when he publicly stated:

"I declare a holy war, my Moslem brothers! Murder the Jews! Murder them all!"[42]

As we in the West describe terrorists, Muhammad and Haj Amin Al-Husseini cannot be labeled as hijackers of the faith, neither do we see much difference between Islamist goals and Nazi goals. Haj Amin was always in close contact with the Nazi Party. He had communications with

Heinrich Himmler, a close friend of Adolf Hitler, with whom he coordinated the final solution for the Jews on November 21, 1941.

ISLAM AND BLACKS

The case for African Americans can be found in this hadith: "I heard the Apostle say: 'Whoever wants to see Satan should look at Nabtal.' He was a black man with long flowing hair, inflamed eyes, and dark ruddy cheeks...Allah sent down concerning him: 'To those who annoy the Prophet there is a painful punishment.'"[43] And this Islamic verse as well: "Gabriel came to Muhammad and said, 'If a black man comes to you, his heart is more gross than a donkey's.'"[44]

MORMONISM AND BLACKS

The Book of Mormon teaches that black skin is a sign of God's curse, so that white-skinned people are considered morally and spiritually superior to black skinned people. In 2 Nephi 5:21 (from the book of Mormon) it reads: "And he had caused the cursing to come upon them, yea, even a sore cursing, because of their iniquity. For behold, they had hardened their hearts against him, that they had become like unto a flint; wherefore, as they were white, and exceedingly fair and delightsome, that they might not be enticing unto my people the Lord God did cause a skin of blackness to come upon them."[45] In contrast, the Bible teaches that God "made of one blood all nations of men" (Acts 17:26, KJV), that in Christ distinctions of ethnicity, gender and social class are erased (Galatians 3:28), and that God condemns favoritism (James 2:1).[46] In James 2:2-4 it reads: "For if there come unto your assembly a man with a gold ring, in goodly apparel, and there come in also a poor man in vile raiment, and you pay attention to the one wearing the fine clothes and say to him, 'You sit here in a good place,' and say to the poor man, 'You stand there,' or, 'Sit here at my footstool,' have you not shown partiality among yourselves, and become judges with evil thoughts?"

In Vienna, Hitler was also introduced to the social Darwinism subscribing to the idea that nations, people, cultures and individuals are subject to the same laws of natural selection as plants and animals. Life is a perpetual struggle between individuals and nations for existence, with the survival of the stronger and more brutal and the elimination of the weaker and less fit. In Mein Kampf, Hitler writes: "Humanity will be compelled, in consequence of the impossibility of making the fertility of the soil keep pace with the continuous increase of population, to halt the increase in human race...Nature has not reserved the soil for the future possession of any particular nation; but for the people that have the force to take it and the industry to cultivate it."[47] Hitler also wrote in Mein Kampf: "Either the world will be ruled according to the ideas of democracy, or the world will be dominated according to the natural law of force; in the latter case the people of brute force will be victorious."[48]

ANTON LAVEY

Anton LaVey was the founder of a cult called Satanism. Instead of encouraging "proliferation of the weak," LaVey feels it's imperative to isolate and foster the emerging new genetic strain of Satanists. With the debut of *The Compleat Witch* in 1970 (later, The Satanic Witch), LaVey presented his guide for selective breeding. In an August 16, 1971 article, "Evil, Anyone?," Newsweek captioned a picture of LaVey baptizing his daughter, Zeena, "...Building 'a better race.'" Anton quotes, describing his Satanic goal as, "the creation of a police state in which the weak are weeded out and the 'achievement-orientated leadership' is permitted to pursue the mysteries of black magic."[49]

In Herbert Spencer's 1884 *The Man Versus The State*, Spencer writes: "Thus by survival of the fittest, the militant type of society becomes characterized by profound faith in the governing power, joined with a loyalty causing submission to it in all matters whatever. And there must tend to be established among those who speculate about political affairs in a militant society, a theory giving form to the needful ideas and feelings; accompanied by assertions that the law-giver if not divine in nature is divinely directed, and that unlimited obedience to him is divinely ordered."[50]

According to Spencer, survival of the fittest, allows total militant control over the people. These type of situations can be viewed in Nazi Germany,

North Korea, and Islamic countries – like Somalia where it has established total Sharia law in the country; residents of a southern Somalia town who do not pray five times a day will be beheaded.[51]

Yet, in the West we have teachers who compare Americans who are fearful of Muslims to the Salem witch trials. What Spencer wrote could be connected with this Islamic verse: "Muhammad besieged them for twenty-five nights. When the siege became too severe for them, Allah terrorized them. Then they were told to submit."[52]

Anton LaVey also had a way to treat others who were inferior (i.e., not Satanist): "They have to be expected to come up to our standards rather than us lowering hurdles to suit them. If they can't, they should be told, probably for the first time in their lives, 'You know what? You're stupid! You're inferior!' instead of being protected from the effects of their incompetence. If a person is ethical, productive, sensitive, and knows how to conduct himself among human beings, fine; if he's an amoral parasite, he should be dealt with quickly and cruelly."

Islam can contrast to this with the way they should treat non-Muslims: "Fight and kill the disbelievers wherever you find them, take them captive, harass them, lie in wait and ambush them using every stratagem of war."[53] Also in the Book of Jihad it says: "Jihad is holy fighting in Allah's cause with full force of weaponry. It is given the utmost importance in Islam and is one of its Pillars. By jihad, Islam is established, Allah is made superior and he becomes the only god who may be worshipped. By jihad, Islam is propagated and made superior. By abandoning jihad, Islam is destroyed and Muslims fall into an inferior position. Their honor is lost, their lands are stolen, and Muslim rule and authority vanish. Jihad is an obligatory duty in Islam on every Muslim. He who tries to escape this duty dies as a hypocrite." This quote is very true – as my father was considered inferior and had his land taken away.

Sheikh Abu Hamza once said while lecturing to a group of Muslims, "If a kafir [nonbeliever – literally meaning a cow] is walking by and you catch him, he's booty – you can sell him in the market. Most of them are spies.

And even if they don't do anything, if Muslims cannot take them and sell them in the market, you just kill them. It's O.K."[54]

This Islamic 'police society' mentality can be seen in this quote made by an unidentified Muslim man in an Islamic demonstration:

> "One day, this very flag will fly over the parliament in London. We will see this flag fly over the White House, and we will see the Black House, the Kaaba, take over the whole world." [55]

Quran 9:29 reads:

> "Fight those who reject Allah or the final judgment or do not forbid what Allah forbids, or follow Islam, but spare those who are "people of the Book" [Jews and Christians] provided that they pay to the Muslims the annual Jizia (humiliation) tax in acknowledgment of the superiority of Muslims and their own abasement."

L. Ron Hubbard has made similar statements: "The law can be used very easily to harass...the purpose of the suit is to harass and discourage rather than to win" [56] and, "If possible, of course ruin him utterly" [57] also, "An enemy...may be injured by any means or tricked, sued, lied to or destroyed." [58]

Resources

1. What is Scientology, A description of Scientology, The parts of man.

2. Thelmapedia, The encyclopedia of Thelema and Maigick, Hadit.

3. Ibid

4. A Piece of Blue Sky, Scientology Dianetics & L. Ron Hubbard Exposed, By John Attack, Chapter Two: The Scientologist.

5. What Scientology won't tell you, an information pack, The Beliefs and Teachings of Scientology, Dianetics: The Modern Science of Mental Health, Science of Survival, A History of Man, Scientology 0-8, The Scientology Handbook.

6. Scientology today, Scientology press office, Answers to questions most commonly asked by media, Does Scientology have a concept of God?

7. Scientology as a Religion, Part Two, IV. An Analysis of Scientology as a Worshipping Community, The Object of Worship in Scientology, 32, By Professor Lonnie Kliever, Lonnie D. Kliever Department of Religious Studies Southern Methodist University Dallas, Texas.

8. News, Comments, and Insight from the Insight team Inside track, See the website Growth track.com, June 27th 2005, Tom Cruise: Evangelists, Hubbard, What Is Scientology? 200. Wallis (112n.) observes that God "does not figure greatly in either theory or practice."

9. Ron (and indeed everyone) has been to Heaven, Hubbard Communications Office, Saint Hill Manor, East Grinstead, Sussex, HCO Bulletin of May 11, AD13, Central Orgs, Franchise, Routine Three Heaven.

10. Essays on Scientology, A Scientific scrutiny of OT III, 1 Introduction, 1.1: Abstract (a brief resume of this paper), By Peter Forde, June 1996.

11. L Ron Hubbard and Jesus Christ, L. Ron Hubbard, Scientology: A History of Man, p.38.

12. Scientology, Auditing, The State of Operating Thetan.

13. Horrible Truths for Scientologists: Body Thetans, By Roland Rashleigh-Berry, Body Thetans.

14. Wikipedia, The Satanic Bible, The Book of Lucifer, XI, Religious Holidays.

15. Nietzsche's idea of an overman and life from his point of view, The Cambridge Companion to Nietzsche, ed. B.Magnus and K.M. Higgins, Cambridge University Press, 1990, Nietzsche, Life As Literature, Alexander Nehamas, Harvard University Press,1994, Nietzsche for Beginners, M.

Sautet, Writers and readers, 1990, Nietzsche:A Critical Reader, Philosophy II lecture handouts.

16. The Thule Society and NWO, Ravenscroft, p. 155, 173., Ibid, p. 166.

17. Court Tv, Crime Library, Criminal Minds and Methods, Nietzsche and Hitler.

18. Friedrich Nietzsche's Influence on Hitler's Mein Kampf, By Michael Kalish, June 2004, The Genealogy of Morals (III 14) By Friedrich Nietzsche.

19. Introduction to Islam, Some of The Human Qualities Allah Almighty Loves, Strength.

20. Islam's Green, Travels, thoughts, talks of Abdur-Raheem Green, The toughness of Shamyl

21. The Book of The Law, Liber AL vel Legis, sub figura CCXX, as delivered by XCIII = 418 to DCLXVI, Chapter II, line 21.

22. Herbert Spencer: Social Darwinism in Education, Foundations of Education, Ornstein & Levine, Educational Philosophy, Edward J. Power, Educational Ideologies, William F. O'Neill, Herbert Spencer on Education, Andreas M. Kazamias, Prepared by Julie Ann Keb.

23. Lewrockwell.com, Herbert Spencer: The Defamation Continues, By Roderick T. Long, Black, p. 12.

24. The Philosophy of Jack London, Herbert Spencer (1820 – 1903) English philosopher, Editor: Clarice Stasz, Professor of History, Sono ma State University, By Joseph Sciambra Sonoma State University.

25. Favored Races, Origin of Species, Charles Darwin.

26. Evolution and Genocide.

27. Nietzsche's Superman, By Anna Knowles, Towards the Übermensch, also Course Reading: Overman.

28. Nietzsche's Superman, By Anna Knowles, Consensus, Compromise.

29. Media Monitors Network, Darwin's Racism, By Harun Yahya, Charles Darwin, "The Descent of Man," 2nd edition, New York, A L. Burt Co., 1874, p. 178.

30. Wikipedia, Emile Burnouf, The Science of Religions, p. 190.

31. Wikipedia, Houston Stewart Chamberlain, Early Life, Works, Houston Stewart Chamberlain – a website devoted to him., Theodore Roosevelts review of The Foundation of the 19th Century.

32. Freemasonry Watch, The Nazi Party, The Thule Society, the Occult, and Freemasonry, Helen Blavatsky, Unholy Alliance A History of Nazi Involvement with the Occult, Peter Levenda, Avon Books, 1995

33. Ibid

34. Prophet of Doom, By Craig Winn, POD, Mein Kampf, Hitler and Muhammad Find Religion, Excerpt from Prophet of Doom, Chapter 21 – Blood & Booty, (pages 545-560), Mein Kampf:606

35. Prophet of Doom, By Craig Winn, POD, Mein Kampf, Hitler and Muhammad Find Religion, Excerpt from Prophet of Doom, Chapter 21 – Blood & Booty, (pages 545-560), Qur'an 2.64.

36. Faqeeh Al-Muluk, Omar Charter, vol. 2, pages 124-136

37. Sahih Al-Bukhari, 9:57

38. Ibid

39. Malik, Book 43, #43.15.8b.

40. Al-Bukhari, 4:392

41. Narrated by a Muslim, 2167

42. Leonard J. Davis, and M. Decter, Myths and Facts – a Concise Record of the Arab-Israeli Conflict, Washington DC: Near East Report, 1982, p. 199)

43. Prophet of Doom, By Craig Winn, POD, Mein Kampf, Hitler and Muhammad Find Religion, Excerpt from Prophet of Doom, Chapter 21 – Blood & Booty, (pages 545-560), "The Anti-Semite" chapter, Ishaq:243.

44. Prophet of Doom, By Craig Winn, POD, Mein Kampf, Hitler and Muhammad Find Religion, Excerpt from Prophet of Doom, Chapter 21 – Blood & Booty, (pages 545-560), "The Anti-Semite," Surah 9:61.

45. LDS.org, The Scriptures, The Second Book of Nephi, Chapter 5, Verse 21.

46. Mormon In Transition, Sponsored By The Institute of Religious Research, Contradictions Between the Book of Mormon and the Bible. See also Mormon Quotes, John Taylor, Source: Journal of Discourses, Volume: 23, Page: 36.

47. Favored Races, Origin of Species, Charles Darwin.

48. Holocaust Understanding and Prevention, Hitler and The Jews, Written by Alexander Kimel – Holocaust Survivor.

49. Elitism and Satanism, Description, Justification, Philosophies, Satanism index page, 6. Building a Master Race, a Police State, "Secret life of a Satanist," by Blanche Barton pp. 215-216, By Vexen Crabtree, 2002 Jan 19.

50. The Man Versus The State, Postscript, By Herbert Spencer, 1884.

51. Anti-Dhimmi, Pray or Die, By Freedom.

52. Prophet of Doom, Muhammad's Own Words, Terrorism, Ishaq: 461.

53. Prophet of Doom, Muhammad's Own Words, Qur'an 9:5.

54. Documentary of Obsession, by Waynne Coping

55. CNN.com, Transcripts, Will New War Plan Succeed?; Elton John Calls for End to Organized Religion; California College Bans Pledge of Allegiance

56. L. Ron Hubbard, The Scientologist – A Manual on the Dissemination of Material, reprinted in The Technical Bulletins of Dianetics and Scientology volume 2, pp.151-171, 1979 printing.

57. L.Ron Hubbard, Magazine articles on Level O Checksheet, American Saint Hill Organization 1968.

58. L. Ron Hubbard, HCO Policy Letter, 18 Oct 67 and HCO Policy Letter, Attacks on Scientology (Additional Pol Ltr), 25 Feb 66.

Chapter Ten – Devilution

THE EVOLUTION OF THE HOLOCAUST

I believe that Evolution, not as I learned in school – that life came into existence from primal organisms evolving to more complex – but that spiritual
entropy, disorder, and decline has taken us to the holocaust and now all
the way to killing the unborn. Allow me to prove my case.

SELECTIVE BREEDING

The Nazis didn't envision the Holocaust without the help of Charles
Darwin and others like him who advanced the concept of *Selective
Breeding*. Darwin went even further with his theory of how life came
about, to suggest government institutions for a special selection of the
human race. Darwin's theories were nothing new, but an old idea from the
time of Plato, just re-packaged. Plato believed that human reproduction
should be controlled by the government. This idea, as recorded by Plato in
The Republic, is exactly what was suggested by the Nazis: "The best men
must have intercourse with the best women as frequently as possible, and
the opposite is true of the very inferior." Plato proposed that the process
be concealed from the public via a form of lottery.[1]

But it is Darwin's book, *The Descent of Man*, which could very well have
been read in Nazi Germany: "With savages, the weak in body and mind are
soon eliminated; and those that survive commonly exhibit a vigorous state
of health. We civilized men, on the other hand, do our utmost to check the
process of elimination; we build asylums for the imbecile, the maimed and
the sick; we institute poor laws; and our medical men exert their utmost
skill to save the life of everyone to the last moment. There is reason to

believe that vaccination has preserved thousands who, from a weak constitution, would formerly have succumbed to smallpox. Thus, the weak members of civilized society propagate their kind. No one who has attended to the breeding of domestic animals will doubt that this must be highly injurious to the race of man. It is surprising how soon a want of care, or care wrongly directed, leads to the degeneration of a domestic race; but, excepting in the case of man himself, hardly anyone is so ignorant as to allow his worst animals to breed."[2]

Anton LeVay had once stated: "Now it is the higher man's role to produce the children of the future. Quality is now more important than quantity. One cherished child who can create will be more important than ten who can produce – or fifty who can believe!"[3]

Other ancient examples include the city of Sparta's purported practice of leaving weaker babies outside of the city boundaries to die. However, it was also reported they would leave all babies outside for a period of time, and those that survived were considered stronger, while many "weaker" babies perished.[4]

EMPEDOCLES

Empedocles (Greek philosopher, 495-435 BC), quoted by Aristotle, gave a hypothetical description of evolution that is surprisingly similar to natural selection: "Why should not nature work...of necessity?...(some) things survived, being organized spontaneously in a fitting way; whereas those which grew otherwise perished and continue to perish." *(Wikipedia, Evolutionism, Ancient Evolutionary Thought)*

During the 1860s and 1870s, Sir Francis Galton systematically arranged these ideas and practices according to new knowledge about the evolution of man and animals provided by the theory of his cousin Charles Darwin. After reading Darwin's *Origin of Species*, Galton became familiar with an interpretation of Darwin's work whereby the mechanisms of natural selection were potentially thwarted by human civilization. He reasoned that, since many human societies sought to protect the underprivileged and weak, those societies were at odds with the natural selection which was responsible for the extinction of the weakest. Galton believed that only by changing these social policies, could society be saved from a "reversion towards mediocrity," a phrase that he first coined in statistics, but later changed to the now common "regression towards the mean."[5]

In his book, *Hereditary Genius*, it reads:

> "I propose to show in this book that a man's natural abilities are derived by inheritance, under exactly the same limitations as are the form and physical features of the whole organic world. Consequently, as it is easy, notwithstanding those limitations, to obtain by careful selection a permanent breed of dogs or horses gifted with peculiar powers of running, or of doing anything else, so it would be quite practicable to produce a highly-gifted race of men by judicious marriages during several consecutive generations. I shall show that social agencies of an ordinary character, whose influences are little suspected, are at this moment working towards the degradation of human nature, and that others are working towards its improvement. I conclude that each generation has enormous power over the natural gifts of those that follow, and maintain that it is a duty we owe to humanity to investigate the range of that power, and to exercise it in a way that, without being unwise towards ourselves, shall be most advantageous to future inhabitants of the earth..."[6]

This quote contrasts with a quote from Plato: "The best men must have intercourse with the best women as frequently as possible, and the opposite is true of the very inferior."

EUGENICS

Phrases such as "survival of the fittest" and "struggle for existence" came into use at the end of the 19th century when eugenic societies were created throughout the world to popularize genetic science. "Negative eugenic" initiatives included marriage restriction, sterilization, or custodial commitment of those thought to have unwanted characteristics.

"Positive eugenic" programs tried to encourage the population, who was perceived as the "best and brightest" to have more offspring.[7]

Nicholas Agar compares the terms "authoritarian eugenics" where the state defines and controls the definition of a good human life, and "liberal eugenics" where the state encourages a broad range of enhancement technologies. These two concepts are very close to what Plato espoused – that human reproduction should be controlled by government.

Plato recommended in his book, *The Republic* that the ruling class should be carefully protected by a secret program of selective breeding in which seemingly random orgies would be staged in order to breed desirable qualities. Strangely, the concept of this program tends to be left out of high school history books.[8] Yet, why not include in our school textbooks how Nazi Germany ran state-owned Aryan Breeding Farms where blond, blue-eyed Aryan SS men were bred to young single "Aryan" women to produce "Super Race" babies to be raised by the state?[9]

This is what Galton said, regarding the case for the definition of Eugenics:...with questions bearing on what is termed in Greek *eugenes* namely, good in stock, and hereditarily endowed with noble qualities. This, and the allied words, eugeneia, etc., are equally applicable to men, brutes, and plants. We greatly want a brief word to express the science of improving stock, which is by no means confined to questions of judicious mating, but which, especially in the case of man, takes cognizance of all influences that tend in however remote a degree to give to the more suitable races or strains of blood a better chance of prevailing speedily over the less suitable than they otherwise would have had. The word eugenics would sufficiently express the idea; it is at least a neater word and a more generalized one than viticulture which I once ventured to use.[10] In 1904 he clarified his definition of eugenics as "the science which deals with all influences that improve the inborn qualities of a race; also with those that develop them to the utmost advantage."[11] Compare this with the subtitle to Darwin's "Origin of Species:" On the origin of species by means of natural selection or the preservation of favored races in the struggle for life.

WORLD EUGENICS AND ITS' RELATIONSHIP WITH NAZI GERMANY – CONNECTING THE DOTS

Eugenics in Sweden

Eugenic ideology spread like wildfire throughout many countries. For over 40 years, young socially inferior working class women in Sweden faced the danger of forced sterilization. This was carried out under laws which were intended to purify the Swedish race, prevent the mentally ill from reproducing and stamp out social activities considered to be deviant.[12]

Eugenics in the United States

The American Eugenics Society had received funds for research from such philanthropic organizations as the Carnegie Institute and the W. K. Kellogg Foundation.[13] It didn't take long before the political, academic, and medical mainstream began assimilating more of the eugenicists' principles. Politicians, including President Theodore Roosevelt, embraced the ideals behind eugenics. Professors at high profile universities such as Harvard, Columbia and Cornell taught more than 375 separate eugenics courses. Biology textbooks included chapters on eugenics, complete with diagrams showing how "defects" pass from one generation to the next. Fairs were organized hosting "Fitter Family" exhibits, giving awards to those who had "strong family trees."[14]

In 1921, Alexander Graham Bell was the honorary president of the Second International Congress of Eugenics held under the auspices of the American Museum of Natural History in New York. Organizations such as these advocated passing laws (with success in some states) that established the compulsory sterilization of people deemed to be, as Bell called them, a "defective variety of the human race."[15]

Many of his thoughts about people he considered to be defective centered on the deaf because of his long contact with them in relation to his work in deaf education. In addition to advocating sterilization of the deaf, Bell wished to prohibit deaf teachers from being allowed to teach in schools for the deaf. He worked to outlaw the marriage of deaf individuals to one another, and was an ardent supporter of oralism over manualism. His avowed goal was to eradicate the language and culture of the deaf so as to force them to integrate into the hearing culture for their own long-term benefit and for the benefit of society at large. Although this attitude is widely seen as paternalistic and arrogant today, it was accepted in that era. He was a personal and longtime friend of Helen Keller, and a sad irony is, his wife Mabel, a former student of his, was deaf.[16]

Like many other early eugenicists, he proposed controlling immigration for the purpose of eugenics and warned that boarding schools for the deaf could possibly be considered as breeding places of a deaf human race.[17]

The second largest eugenics movement was in the United States and began in Connecticut in 1896. Many states enacted marriage laws using eugenic criteria, prohibiting anyone who was "epileptic, imbecile or feeble-minded" from marrying.[18]

The German program began in January 1934. But in the U.S., the State of Indiana passed a forced sterilization law for mental defectives twenty-seven years earlier in 1907 (when Adolf Hitler was 18 years old). Before the German program even began, at least seventeen U.S. states (including California) had 'forced sterilization' laws. Before 1930 there were 200-600 forced sterilizations per year in the U.S., but in the 1930s the rate jumped to 2,000-4,000 per year.[19]

Eugenic Sterilizations in the U.S.

Some states sterilized "imbeciles" throughout much of the 20th century. The U.S. Supreme Court ruled in the 1927 Buck v. Bell case, that the state of Virginia could sterilize those it thought unfit. (Dr. James H. Bell was the Superintendent at the Virginia State Colony for Epileptics and Feeble-Minded.) The most significant era of eugenic sterilization in the U.S. was between 1907 and 1963, when over 64,000 individuals were forcibly sterilized under eugenic legislation.[20]

Hitler's Germany adopted Virginia's sterilization law in 1933, calling it the "Law for the Prevention of Defective Progeny." Nazi doctors went on to forcibly sterilize an estimated 350,000 to 400,000 people. This effort to "cleanse" the Aryan race targeted Germans with every kind of "defect or disability." This project started several years before Hitler embarked on his "final solution" to eliminate the Jewish race.[21]

A favorable report on the results of sterilization in California (the state with the most sterilizations), was published in book form by the biologist Paul Popenoe and was widely cited by the Nazi government as evidence that wide-reaching sterilization programs were not only feasible, but humane. When Nazi administrators went on trial for war crimes in Nuremberg after World War II, they justified the mass sterilizations (over 450,000 in less than a decade) by citing the United States as their inspiration.[22]

The leaders of the sterilization movement in Germany stated repeatedly that their legislation was formulated after careful study of the California experiment as reported by Mr. Gosney and Dr. [Paul] Popenoe. It would have been impossible, they say, to undertake such a venture involving some 1 million people without drawing heavily upon previous experience elsewhere.[23]

PAUL POPENOE

"It is conservatively estimated that there are approximately five million people in the United States who will at some time be committed to state hospitals as insane and that there are approximately five million more who are so deficient intellectually (with less than 70% of average intelligence) as to be, in many cases, liabilities rather than assets to the race. The situation will grow worse instead of better if steps are not taken to control the reproduction of the mentally handicapped. Eugenic sterilization represents one such step that is practicable, humanitarian, and certain in its results."[24] – Paul Popenoe

Harry H. Laughlin, a biologist who was the most forceful advocate for compulsory sterilization in the United States, wrote the law on which both the Virginia and German eugenics statutes were based. Laughlin spent most of his career campaigning for sterilization of what he called the "most worthless one-tenth of our present population."

In 1922 Laughlin, acting as Eugenics agent of the U.S. House of Representatives, published the Model Eugenical Sterilization law which defined who would be subjected to mandatory sterilization. This became the model that later would be seen as the direct link between the U.S. authorities' eugenics program and the Nazi regimes' sterilization program. Prominent supporters of eugenics in the U.S. included Alexander Graham Bell (inventor), John Maynard Keynes (economist), Harry H. Laughlin (biologist) and Planned Parenthood founder Margaret Sanger.[25]

Laughlin was also the architect of the notorious Immigration Restriction Act of 1924 that ended the greatest era of immigration in U.S. history. He successfully argued before Congress that the American gene pool was being polluted by intellectually and morally defective immigrants from Europe. The act, which wasn't repealed until 1965, targeted Italians and Eastern European Jews. In 1936, Laughlin received an honorary medical degree from the Nazi-controlled University of Heidelberg for his contributions to the "science of race cleansing."[26]

In *The Science and Politics of Racial Research* (pp. 126-127), Rutger's psychology professor William H. Tucker discloses:

The American eugenicists such as Margaret Sanger even made their own modest contribution to the plight of Jews in the Reich. In the late 1930s there were last-ditch attempts to waive some of the restrictions in the 1924 Immigration Act in order to grant asylum to a few eventual victims of the Holocaust. These efforts were vigorously opposed by eugenicists, especially by Harry Hamilton Laughlin, who submitted a new report, Immigration and Conquest, reiterating the biological warnings against the "human dross" that would produce a "breakdown in race purity of the...superior stocks." While almost one thousand German Jews seeking to immigrate waited hopefully in a ship off the coast of Florida, Laughlin's report singled them out as a group "slow to assimilate to the American pattern of life," and he recommended a 60 percent reduction in quotas, together with procedures to denationalize and deport some immigrants who had already attained citizenship. For the eugenicists, Nordic purity was as important in the United States as it was in Germany. The ship was sent back to Germany.[27]

Sanger asked for no relief for Jews fleeing Germany. But how many Jewish refugees were accepted by the U.S. during World War II? David S. Wyman writes in *The Abandonment of the Jews: America and the Holocaust 1941-1945*, that during the WWII the United States admitted only 21,000 Jewish refugees, and describes how Britain did all it could to prevent Jews fleeing the Holocaust from settling in Palestine [ISRAEL].[28] Sanger also advocated that Congress set up a special 'Department of Population' with 7 goals as its objective, one of which was: "to keep the doors of immigration closed to the entrance of certain aliens whose condition is known to be detrimental to the stamina of the race, such as feeble-minded, idiots, morons, insane, syphilitic, epileptic, criminal, professional prostitutes, and others in this class barred by immigration laws of 1924." – Margaret Sanger[29]

By the late 1930s about half the states in the U.S. had eugenics laws, with the law in California being used as a model for eugenics laws in Nazi Germany.[30]

A book titled *Civic Biology from 1930's* written by G. W. Hunter, describes popular opinion during that time: "Hundreds of families... exist today, spreading disease, immorality and crime to all parts of this country. The cost to society of such families is very severe. Just as certain animals or plants become parasitic on other plants or animals, these families have become parasitic on society. They not only do harm to others by corrupting, stealing or spreading disease, but they are actually protected and cared for by the state out of public money. Largely for them the poorhouse and the asylum exist. They are true parasites. If such people were lower animals, we would probably kill them off to prevent them spreading. Humanity will not allow this, but we do have the remedy of separating the sexes in asylums or other places and in various ways preventing intermarriage and the possibilities of perpetrating such a low and degenerate race."[31] This may relate with what Anton LaVey said: if he's an amoral parasite, he should be dealt with quickly and cruelly.

Eugenics in Nazi Germany

Hitler not only described Jews as parasites, but also as bacteria and viruses. Nazi ideology was constructed based on the fantasy of Germany being a "living organism" containing the Jew as a disease that threatened to cause the death of the nation.[32]

In Nazi Germany there was the Euthanasia Program. The "Sterilization Law" explained the importance of weeding out so-called genetic defects from the total German gene pool. Since the National Revolution, public opinion had become increasingly preoccupied with questions of demographic policy and the continuing decline in the birthrate. However, it was not only the decline in population which was a cause for serious concern, but equally important, the increasingly evident genetic composition of their people. Whereas the hereditarily healthy families had for the most part adopted a policy of having only one or two children, countless numbers of inferiors and those suffering from hereditary conditions were reproducing unrestrained, while their sick and asocial offspring were a burden to the community.[33]

The Nazi government was praised for being the "first of the world's major nations to enact a modern sterilization law." The German law reads almost like Harry Laughlin's "American model sterilization law," and along with the American statutes, was expected to "constitute a milestone" (sic) in the movement to control human reproduction.[34] Ten years after Virginia passed its 1924 Sterilization Act, Joseph Dejarnette, superintendent of Virginia's Western State Hospital, complained in the Richmond Times-Dispatch: "The Germans are beating us at our own game."

It's not surprising the work on "selective breeding" caught the attention of Adolph Hitler, who was just rising to power in Germany. The relationship between German and American eugenicists had been strong before Hitler, but strengthened under his command. The Rockefeller Foundation funded construction of the Kaiser Wilhelm Institute of Anthropology, Human Genetics, and Eugenics in Berlin. Joseph Mengele was one of the institute's eugenics students. Harry Laughlin's contributions earned him an honorary degree from the University of Heidelberg.[35]

In the spring and summer months of 1939, a number of planners – led by Philipp Bouhler, the director of Hitler's private chancellery, and Karl Brandt, Hitler's attending physician – began to organize a secret killing operation targeting disabled children. Beginning in October 1939, children with disabilities, brought to a number of specially designated pediatric clinics throughout Germany and Austria, were murdered by lethal overdoses of medication or by starvation. Some 5,000 disabled German infants, toddlers, and juveniles are estimated to have been killed by war's end.[36]

Euthanasia planners quickly envisioned extending the killing program to adult disabled patients living in institutional settings. In the autumn of 1939, Hitler signed a secret authorization in order to protect participating physicians, medical staff, and administrators from prosecution; this authorization was backdated to September 1, 1939, to suggest that the effort was related to wartime measures. The secret operation was code-named T-4, in reference to the street address (Tiergartenstrasse 4) of the program's coordinating office in Berlin. Six gassing installations for adults were eventually established as part of the Euthanasia Program: Bernburg, Brandenburg, Grafeneck, Hadamar, Hartheim, and Sonnenstein.[37]

Euthanasia was not limited to Germans. Frenchmen Alexis Carrel advocated the use of gas chambers to rid humanity of "inferior stock," thus endorsing the scientific racism discourse. His endorsement of this idea came in the mid-1930s, prior to the Nazi implementation of such practices in Germany. In the 1936 publication of Carrel's book, *L'Homme, cet inconnu* (Man, This Unknown) the publishers requested this introduction to the German translation of the book. He added the following praise of the Nazi regime, which did not appear in the editions in other languages: "the German government has taken energetic measures against the propagation of the defective, the mentally diseased, and the criminal. The ideal solution would be the suppression of each of these individuals as soon as he has proven himself to be dangerous." In doing so, he applauded the Nazi T-4 Euthanasia Program.[38]

Moreover, in August 1942 the killings resumed, although more carefully concealed than before. Victims were no longer murdered in centralized gassing installations, but rather, killed by lethal injection or drug overdose at a number of clinics throughout Germany and Austria. Many of these institutions also systematically starved adult and child victims. The Euthanasia Program continued until the last days of World War II, expanding to include an ever widening range of victims, including geriatric patients, bombing victims, and foreign forced laborers. Historians estimate that the Euthanasia Program, in all its phases, claimed the lives of 200,000 individuals.[39]

By 1945, almost 300,000 "pure blood Aryan" Germans had been killed. By then, these doctors had so lowered the value of human life, they were killing bed wetters, children with misshapen ears, and those with learning disabilities.[40]

MORMONS KILLED BABIES

The Mormon Prophet Warren Jeffs was the leader of the FLDS, Fundamentalist Church of Jesus Christ of Latter Day Saints. It was Jeffs who committed the murder of a deformed baby. Here is an excerpt from a video interview of Warren Jeff's sister, Elaine Jeffs: "I personally know of a woman who had a child – the baby was deformed – and he (Warren) drowned it…This was condoned by the FLDS leadership.[41]

MARGARET SANGER

The American eugenics has also contributed to murders as well. It's something that today we call abortion and certain types of birth control.

Margaret Sanger was a pioneer of legalized abortion and the founder of Planned Parenthood, the largest provider of abortions in the U.S. Sanger was also a well-known eugenicist, whose writings make clear the historic connection between abortion on demand and eugenic thinking.[42] Here's a passage from Mary Senander, of the Minneapolis Star Tribune: Contemporary liberal social planners have elevated Sanger to sainthood, protesting that her birth control campaign was nothing more than a vehicle for economic betterment and health for the masses. But Sanger's own well-documented words, publications and associations indicate a deeper and darker motivation. Sanger began publishing the Birth Control Review in 1917 and served as its editor until 1938. The May 1919 Review proclaimed, "More children for the fit, less for the unfit." By unfit, Sanger meant the mentally retarded or physically handicapped; later her definition expanded.[43]

A careful examination of the history of the abortion rights movement would shock even the most ardent defender of a woman's right to choose. The founders of the movement were in fact racists, who despised the poor and were searching for a way to prevent races of color from reproducing. Rather than defending the rights of the poorest of the poor, which is the tradition of liberalism, the founders advocated abortion as a means of eliminating the poor; especially Blacks, Jews, Slavs, and Italians. Rather than a desire to help the poor through welfare programs, they wanted to eliminate all charities and government aid.[44]

Many Americans are unaware of other programs Sanger initiated. In 1939, she created the program called the "Negro Project."[45] In fact, she was so grounded in her ideology, that she was the guest speaker at a Ku Klux Klan rally in Silverlake, N.J. in 1926. Not only did she associate herself with these racist views, her own writings leave little doubt as to her sympathies. The "Negro Project" she implemented was designed to sterilize Blacks and reduce the number of Black children being born in the South. Sanger wrote: "[We propose to] hire three or four colored ministers, preferably with social-service backgrounds, and with engaging personalities. The most successful educational approach to the Negro is through a religious appeal. And we do not want word to go out that we want to exterminate the Negro population, and the minister is the man who can straighten out that idea if it ever occurs to any of their more rebellious members."[46]

Joseph Smith once said, "Had I anything to do with the Negro, I would confine them by strict law to their own species and put them on a national equalization."[47]

JOSEPH FIELDING SMITH
Joseph Fielding Smith – the tenth prophet said, "Not only was Cain called upon to suffer, but because of his wickedness he became the father of an inferior race."[48]

Some Pre-Adamite theorists maintain that Cain left his family to master an inferior tribe depicted as "non-white Mongols," "Black Races," or "beasts of the field." They further contend that Cain took a wife from one of the inferior "pre-Adamite" people. The idea that Cain's 'mark' was blackness began in eighteenth century Europe, and was made popular in 19th century America by the founder of Mormonism – Joseph Smith. (Haynes, 2002, p. 15.)

THE EVILS OF PLANNED PARENTHOOD

As we have already discussed, Margaret Sanger was also strongly anti-Semitic. She started a birth control organization with a man named Henry Pratt Fairchild. Fairchild wrote *The Melting Pot Mistake*, in which he accused "the Jews" of diluting the true American stock. In his book, *Race and Nationality*, (1947), Fairchild blamed anti-Semitism and the holocaust, in part, on "the Jews."[49]

Margaret Sanger aligned herself with the eugenicists whose ideology prevailed in the early 20th century. Eugenicists strongly espoused racial supremacy and "purity," particularly of the "Aryan" race. Eugenicists hoped to purify the bloodlines and improve the race by encouraging the "fit" to reproduce and restrict reproduction of the "unfit." They sought to contain the "inferior" races through segregation, sterilization, birth control and abortion.[50]

Sanger embraced Malthusian eugenics. Thomas Robert Malthus, a 19th century cleric and professor of political economy, believed a population time-bomb threatened the existence of the human race. He viewed social problems such as poverty, deprivation and hunger as evidence of this "population crisis." According to writer George Grant, Malthus condemned charities and other forms of benevolence, because he believed they only exacerbated the problems. His answer was to restrict the population growth of certain groups of people. His theories about population growth and economic stability became the basis for national and international social policy. Grant quotes from Malthus' magnum opus, *An Essay on the Principle of Population*, published in six editions from 1798 to 1826:

All children born, beyond what would be required to keep up the population to a desired level, must necessarily perish, unless room is made for them by the deaths of grown persons. We should facilitate, instead of foolishly and vainly endeavoring to impede, the operations of nature in producing this mortality.[51]

Malthus' disciples believed if Western civilization was to survive, the physically unfit, the materially poor, the spiritually diseased, the racially inferior, and the mentally incompetent had to be suppressed and isolated – or even, perhaps, eliminated. His disciples felt the subtler and more "scientific" approaches of education, contraception, sterilization and abortion were more "practical and acceptable ways" to ease the pressures of the alleged overpopulation.[52] Another solution for population growth-control by Malthus was for the poor and working classes to stop, or postpone, their multiplying activities by marrying late in life and abstaining from sex until then. He believed certain 'positive checks' would help prevent excessive population growth. These included war, famine, infanticide, diseases and homosexuality. (Environmentalists help Uranium's price, By James Finch)

Here are a few quotes from Sanger on the case of abortion, sterilization, and birth control:

"The most merciful thing that a family does to one of its infant members is to kill it."[53]

"Eugenic sterilization is an urgent need...We must prevent multiplication of this bad stock."[54]

"Birth control itself, often denounced as a violation of natural law, is nothing more or less than the facilitation of the process of weeding out the unfit, of preventing the birth of defectives or of those who will become defectives."[55]

"Eugenics is...the most adequate and thorough avenue to the solution of racial, political and social problems."[56]

"The unbalance between the birth rate of the 'unfit' and the 'fit,' [is] the greatest present menace to civilization...the most urgent problem today is how to limit and discourage the over-fertility of the mentally and physically defective."[57]

"Our failure to segregate morons who are increasing and multiplying...a dead weight of human waste...an ever-increasing, unceasingly spawning class of human beings who never should have been born at all."[58]

"The undeniably feeble-minded should, indeed, not only be discouraged but prevented from propagating their kind."[59]

"The procreation of [the diseased, the feeble-minded and paupers] should be stopped."[60] "[Mandatory] sterilization for [the insane and feeble-minded] is the answer."[61]

"[Our objective is] unlimited sexual gratification without the burden of unwanted children..."[62]

"The marriage bed is the most degenerative influence in the social order..."[63]

"The campaign for birth control is not merely of eugenic value, but is practically identical with the final aims of eugenics."[64]

Margaret Sanger, Founder of Planned Parenthood, proposed the Population Congress with the aim, "...to give certain dysgenic groups in our population their choice of segregation or sterilization."[65] Sanger built the work of the ABCL, and, ultimately, Planned Parenthood, on the ideas and resources of the eugenics movement. Grant reported that "virtually all of the organization's board members were eugenicists." Eugenicists financed the early projects, from the opening of birth control clinics to the publishing of "revolutionary" literature. Eugenicists comprised the speakers at conferences, authors of literature and the providers of services "almost without exception." And Planned Parenthood's international work was originally housed in the offices of the Eugenics Society. The two organizations were intertwined for years.[66] Among its founding board members were Margaret Sanger, Lothrup Stoddard, and C. C. Little.

Margaret Sanger appointed Lothrup Stoddard as a board member of the Birth Control League (the forerunner of Planned Parenthood). What did Stoddard think about Nazi eugenics? Author Stefan Kuhl writes: When the Nazis came to power, argued Stoddard, they started to increase "both the size and the quality of the population." They coupled initiatives designed to encourage "sound" citizens to reproduce with a "drastic curb of the defective elements." Stoddard personally witnessed how the Nazis were "weeding out the worst strains in the Germanic stock in a scientific and truly humanitarian way."[67]

It is no secret that Adolf Hitler and the Nazis wanted Jews to be subject to induced abortions and sterilizations more than other groups. Stefan Kuhl writes (pp. 61-62): He [Lothrup Stoddard] even met personally with Adolf Hitler. William L. Shirer, an American colleague who had been in Germany since 1934, complained that the Reich minister for propaganda [Joseph Goebbels] gave special preference to Stoddard because his writings on racial subject were "featured in Nazi school textbooks."[68]

Kuhl continues: In 1940, Stoddard claimed that the "Jew problem" is "already settled in principle and soon to be settled in fact by the physical elimination of the Jews themselves from the Third Reich."[69]

The ABCL became a legal entity on April 22, 1922, in New York. Prior to that, Sanger illegally started a birth control clinic in October 1916, in the Brownsville section of Brooklyn, NY, which eventually closed. The clinic serviced the poor immigrants who heavily populated the area – those deemed "unfit" to reproduce.[70]

Sanger's early writings clearly reflected Malthus' influence. She writes: "Organized charity itself is the symptom of a malignant social disease. Those vast, complex, interrelated organizations aiming to control and to diminish the spread of misery and destitution and all the menacing evils that spring out of this sinisterly fertile soil, are the surest sign that our civilization has bred, is breeding and perpetuating constantly, increasing numbers of defectives, delinquents and dependents."[71]

Nazi propaganda for their compulsory "euthanasia" program: "This person suffering from hereditary defects costs the community 60,000 Reichsmark during his lifetime. Fellow Germans, that is your money, too."[72]

In 1934 one of Hitler's staff members wrote to Leon Whitney of the American Eugenics Society and asked in the name of the Fuhrer for a copy of Whitney's recently published book, *The Case for Sterilization*. Whitney complied immediately, and shortly thereafter received a personal letter of thanks from Adolf Hitler. In his unpublished autobiography, Whitney reported a conversation he had with Madison Grant about the letter from the Fuhrer. Because he thought Grant might be interested in Hitler's letter he showed it to him during their next meeting. Grant only smiled, reached for a folder on his desk, and gave Whitney a letter from Hitler to read. In this, Hitler thanked Grant for writing *The Passing of the Great Race* and said that "the book was his Bible." Whitney concluded that, following Hitler's actions, one could believe it.[73]

Madison Grant was the author of the book, *The Passing of the Great Race* and the subtitle of the book was 'The Racial Basis of European History.'[74] It was reported that Grant was involved in many debates over the discipline of anthropology with the anthropologist Franz Boas, whom he reputably would not shake hands since the latter was Jewish, even though they both served (along with others) on the National Research Council Committee on Anthropology after the First World War.[75]

Grant's book was well-received by 1920's American society. Grant instantly became an icon of popular culture, and the superiority of the Nordic Race became ingrained in the minds of both the scientific establishment and in society in general. Nordicist theory, however, had fallen out of favor in the United States by the mid 1930s. In Germany, on the other hand, it was at the peak of its power during the '30s due to the Nazis' obsession with the blonde, blue-eyed Aryan ideal. At the postwar Nuremberg trials, Grant's *Passing of the Great Race* was introduced into evidence by the defense of Karl Brandt, in order to justify the population policies of the Third Reich, or at least indicate that they were not ideologically unique to Nazi Germany, although it seemed to have had little effect, as Brandt was sentenced to death.[76]

A passage in Grant's book reads:

> "[Sterilization could] be applied to an ever widening circle of social discards, beginning always with the criminal, the diseased and the insane, and extending gradually to types which may be called weaklings rather than defectives, and perhaps ultimately to worthless race types...Indiscriminate efforts to preserve babies among the lower classes often results in serious injury to the race...Mistaken regard for what are believed to be divine laws and sentimental belief in the sanctity of human life tend to prevent both the elimination of defective infants and the sterilization of such adults as are themselves of no value to the community."[77]

This extract reminds us of something Charles Darwin wrote in his *The Descent of Man*, "Thus the weak members of civilized society propagate their kind. No one who has attended to the breeding of domestic animals will doubt that this must be highly injurious to the race of man. It is surprising how soon a want of care, or care wrongly directed, leads to the degeneration of a domestic race; but, excepting in the case of man himself, hardly anyone is so ignorant as to allow his worst animals to breed."[78]

In this section I'll explain how many of these Satanic organizations use deceiving propaganda – such as not being honest; reversing what they really mean and making it seem their agenda can benefit society.

Notice what happens when you wipe out absolutes and replace them with relativism. In 1933, when the Nazi's came to power, the law was changed to legalize abortion and make the decision a matter for a medical review board. The development of Germany's abortion policy was left to the country's most outspoken abortion advocacy group, the Berlin Chamber of Physicians. This group, which advocated abortion on demand, determined that "The health of the mother – considered from all angles – is the decisive factor." At that time, just as now, the health of the mother criterion was loosely understood to mean any economic or psychological affect on the woman's total well being.[79] But the absolute issue is that you are killing a human baby and the relativism of it is – it's healthy for the mother.

There were approximately 500,000 abortions performed annually in Germany (a country of 60 to 70 million people) under the Third Reich. In Nazi Germany, racial stock was considered an aspect of the health of the mother. If she was from an "unhealthy" race, such as Polish, Czech or Jewish, she was often forced to have an abortion against her will.[80]

Replacing absolutes with relativism can be seen in international and American eugenics.

In the late 1950s, a leader of the British eugenics movement proposed an interesting idea. Dr. Carlos Paton Blacker had been an officer in the Eugenics Society since 1931; he had been Secretary, General Secretary, Director, and then Chairman. His proposal to the ES was that the Society should pursue eugenic ends by less obvious means, that is, by a policy of crypto-eugenics, which was apparently proving successful in the U.S. Eugenics Society.[81] From Blacker's proposal, we can see several things. Leaders of the eugenics movement were concerned about their public image, but were continuing at least some of their work. One of their tools was the International Planned Parenthood Federation, which promoted access to birth control. Eugenicists were still interested in biology, or some part of biology. And there was something like "crypto-eugenics" in the United States, a success story which the British wanted to imitate.[82]

The dominant figure in American eugenics after World War II was a complex individual, Frederick Osborn (1889-1981). He is credited with reforming eugenics, removing the taint of racism and putting the field back on a firm scientific footing. However, during his "reform," from 1947 until 1956, he was president of the Pioneer Fund, a secretive white supremacist group. Apparently he did not oppose racism, he opposed 'open' racism. His reform of eugenics, then, was to disguise, not remove, the taint of racism.[83]

In 1956, Osborn traveled across the Atlantic to give the annual Galton Lecture at a meeting of the Eugenics Society.[84] Here are the major points of his speech: People simply are not willing to accept an idea that the genetic base on which their character is formed is inferior and should not be repeated in the next generation. We have asked whole groups of people to accept this idea and we have asked individuals to accept it. They have constantly refused, and we have all but killed the eugenic movement...They won't accept the idea that they are, in general, second rate. We must rely on other motivations...Let's stop telling anyone that they have a generally inferior genetic quality, for they will never agree. Let's base our proposals on the desirability of having children born in homes where they will get affectionate and responsible care, then perhaps our proposals will be accepted.[85]

Let's not forget what Margaret Sanger said, "[We propose to] hire three or four colored ministers, preferably with social-service backgrounds, and with engaging personalities. The most successful educational approach to the Negro is through a religious appeal. And we do not want word to go out that we want to exterminate the Negro population, and the minister is the man who can straighten out that idea if it ever occurs to any of their more rebellious members."

In 1929, 10 years before Sanger created the Negro Project, the ABCL laid the groundwork for a clinic in Harlem, a largely Black section of New York City. It was the dawn of the Great Depression, and for Blacks that meant double the misery. They faced harsher conditions of desperation and deprivation because of widespread racial prejudice and discrimination. From the ABCL's perspective, Harlem was the ideal place for this "experimental clinic," which officially opened on November 21, 1930. Many Blacks looked to escape their adverse circumstances and therefore did not recognize the eugenic undercurrent of the clinic. The clinic relied on the generosity of private foundations to remain in business. In addition to being thought of as "inferior" and disproportionately represented in the underclass, according to the clinic's own files used to justify its "work," Blacks in Harlem:

- were segregated in an over-populated area (224,760 of 330,000 of greater New York's Black population lived in Harlem during the late 1920s and 1930s);

- comprised 12 percent of New York City's population, but accounted for 18.4 percent of New York City's unemployment;

- had an infant mortality rate of 101 per 1000 births, compared to 56 among whites;

- had a death rate from tuberculosis – 237 per 100,000 – which was the highest in central Harlem, out of all of New York City.[86]

All these factors were used by Sanger and her organization to deceive the African American community. Instead of encouraging charity or other ways to help the Black community – she simply used these figures to further her agenda – which was to simply cut them off from producing more offspring.

Sanger did such a good job of convincing the community that Harlem's largest Black church, the Abyssinian Baptist Church, held a mass multi-church meeting featuring Sanger as the speaker. But that event received criticism. At least one "very prominent minister of a denomination other than Baptist" spoke out against Sanger. Dr. Adam Clayton Powell, Sr., pastor of Abyssinian Baptist, "received adverse criticism" from the (unnamed) minister who was "surprised that he'd allow that awful woman in his church."[87] So I guess not all the sheep went astray.

Sanger had selected Dr. Clarence J. Gamble (of Procter and Gamble) to be the BCFA Regional Director in the South. In November 1938, Gamble wrote a memorandum entitled "Suggestions for the Negro Project." In it, he suggested that "Black leaders might regard birth control as an extermination plot," and recommended Black leaders be placed in positions where it would appear they were in charge. From Sanger's reply one can get a sense as to Gamble's uncertainty about having Blacks in authoritative positions:

> "I note that you doubt it worthwhile to employ a full-time Negro physician. It seems to me from my experience...that, while the

colored Negroes have great respect for white doctors, they can get closer to their own members and more or less lay their cards on the table, which means their ignorance, superstitions and doubts. They do not do this with white people and if we can train the Negro doctor at the clinic, he can go among them with enthusiasm and...knowledge, which...will have far-reaching results among the colored people."[88]

Margaret Sanger wrote an article, decisively titled: *A Plan for Peace.* In this article she presents some points:

- to keep the doors of immigration closed to the entrance of certain aliens whose condition is known to be detrimental to the stamina of the race, such as feeble-minded, idiots, morons, insane, syphilitic, epileptic, criminal, professional prostitutes, and others in this class barred by the immigration laws of 1924.[89]

- to apply a stern and rigid policy of sterilization and segregation to that grade of population whose progeny is tainted, or whose inheritance is such that objectionable traits may be transmitted to offspring.[90]

- to insure the country against future burdens of maintenance for numerous offspring as may be born of feeble-minded parents, by pensioning all persons with transmissible disease who voluntarily consent to sterilization.[91]

- to give certain dysgenic groups in our population their choice of segregation or sterilization.[92] Further in the article she wrote:

    "Having corralled this enormous part of our population and placed it on a basis of health instead of punishment, it is safe to say that fifteen or twenty million of our population would then be organized into soldiers of defense – defending the unborn against their own disabilities."[93]

Near the end of the article it states:

    "The third step would be to give special attention to the mothers' health, to see that women who are suffering from tuberculosis, heart or kidney disease, toxic goiter, gonorrhea, or any disease where the condition of pregnancy disturbs their health, are placed under public health nurses to instruct them in practical, scientific methods of contraception in order to safeguard their lives – thus reducing maternal mortality."[94]

"The above steps may seem to place emphasis on a health program instead of on tariffs, moratoriums and debts, but I believe that national health is the first essential factor in any program for universal peace."[95]

Treating the sick and weakest among us the way she advocated, sounds very much like Nazi Germany.

EVIL IS USUALLY CLOAKED WITH PEACE

With the future citizen safeguarded from hereditary taints, with five million mental and moral degenerates segregated, with ten million women and ten million children receiving adequate care, we could then turn our attention to the basic needs for international peace.[96]

Then the last statement reads: "In the meantime we should organize and join an International League of Low Birth Rate Nations to secure and maintain World Peace."[97]

The article's title is *The Plan for Peace*. I don't know about you, but I don't see peace. The whole thing sounds more like world domination with some sinister agenda; especially the part when she says: "we should organize and join an International League of Low Birth Rate Nations to secure and maintain World Peace" – not with all the garbage she was writing about, will we maintain world peace.

TODAY'S BABY KILLING

The baby-killing that we are enduring now, is from the famous Roe v. Wade decision in 1973 – in which the Supreme Court of the United States ruled that a woman has a constitutional right to abort her baby during the first six months of pregnancy.

Prior to the Court's ruling, a majority of states prohibited abortion, although most allowed an exception when the pregnancy threatened the woman's life. But then the Court ruled that states could only restrict abortions during the final three months of pregnancy, a stage when medical experts consider the fetus capable of "meaningful life" outside the womb (I'll discuss that later). The decision was strongly endorsed by many women's rights groups that had long sought to guarantee a woman's right to choose an abortion.[98]

Norma McCorvey, a pregnant woman from Dallas, Texas, was the first to challenge the constitutionality of the Texas abortion law at that time. Using the pseudonym "Jane Roe," McCorvey sued Dallas County district attorney Henry Wade to be allowed to have an abortion. Roe's pregnancy did not threaten her life, but as a poor, single woman she did not want to bear a child she could not afford to raise. Roe and her attorneys asked the federal district court to declare that the Texas abortion statute violated her rights under the Constitution of the United States. They also asked the court to forbid the district attorney from prosecuting anyone else under the Texas abortion law in the future. The court ruled that the 9th Amendment and the 14th Amendment of the Constitution guaranteed privacy rights that were broad enough to protect a woman's choice to have an abortion.[99]

The Supreme Court heard arguments for Roe v. Wade in December 1971. After the justices intensely debated the issues, Chief Justice Warren Burger recommended that the case be reargued, stating, "These cases...are not as simple for me as they appear to be for the [other justices]." The Court then ordered a second round of arguments, which it then heard in October 1972. Finally, in January 1973 the Court yielded a 7-2 decision in favor of Roe.[100]

Justice Harry A. Blackman wrote the Court's majority opinion, the written document which announces the Court's decision and explains its reasoning. At the outset of his opinion, Blackman noted 'the sensitive and emotional nature of the abortion controversy' and the 'vigorous opposing views' held by many Americans. He observed that "one's philosophy, one's experiences, one's exposure to the raw edges of human existence, one's religious training, one's attitudes toward life and family and their values, and the moral standards one establishes and seeks to observe, are all likely to influence and to color one's thinking and conclusions about abortion." But having noted these difficulties, Blackman stressed the need to resolve the issue of abortion based on their interpretation of the Constitution.[101]

Blackman then considered an argument that the state had a responsibility to protect the fetus. He agreed this was so, but stated that this responsibility had to be balanced against the concerns of the pregnant woman. Among those concerns was the woman's right of privacy. Blackman also noted that 'the Constitution does not explicitly mention any right of privacy,' but he wrote that since at least 1891 the Supreme Court had 'recognized that a right of personal privacy, or a guarantee of certain areas or zones of privacy, does exist under the Constitution.' He then mentioned many cases in which the Court had upheld the right of personal privacy in marriage, family relationships, contraception, childbirth, child rearing, and education. He also noted the Constitutional protections which guarantee that the government not intrude into the privacy of the home without a legal cause and a warrant.[102]

HARRY A. BLACKMAN

Blackman flatly rejected the idea put forth by the state of Texas that a fetus was a person protected by the 14th Amendment to the Constitution. (The 14th Amendment says that no state can 'deprive any person of life, liberty, or property, without due process of law.') Blackman pointed out that all references to a person in the Constitution assume that the person is already born, rather than a fetus.[103]

Since the Roe decision, the Supreme Court has heard more than a dozen cases involving attempts by states or the national government to restrict abortion. In deciding these cases, the Court has modified its decision in Roe v. Wade by allowing states to regulate abortion in many additional ways. However, the Court has always maintained that, at least in the first trimester, a woman has the right to choose whether or not to continue a pregnancy.[104]

Sadly, there have been more than 40 million abortions in the twenty six years since the U.S. Supreme Court legalized unrestricted abortion on January 22, 1973.[105]

On December 7, 1995, the United States Senate passed the Partial-Birth Abortion Ban Act by a margin of 54-44, which would end partial-birth abortions (those performed during the 3rd trimester of pregnancy). House members voted 2-to-1 in favor of the ban, 288-139 [Republicans 215-15; Democrats 73-123; Independents 0-1]. When it reached the desk of President Bill Clinton on April 10, 1996, he vetoed the Act, thereby allowing the brutally barbaric procedure to continue with no restrictions.[106] Now look at Clinton's Veto Message and his excuse for his action: "I do so because the bill does not allow women to protect themselves from serious threats to their health. By refusing to permit women, in reliance on their doctors' best medical judgment, to use their [sic] procedure when their lives are threatened or when their health is put in serious jeopardy, the Congress has fashioned a bill that is consistent neither with the Constitution nor with sound public policy."[107] Clinton continued to state: "I cannot sign H.R. 1833, as passed, because it fails to protect women in such dire circumstances – because by treating doctors who perform the procedure in these tragic cases as criminals, the bill poses a danger of serious harm to women.[108] What about the baby? What about the civil rights for the baby? Forget women's lib!! How about infants lib?! Oh! I'm sorry for offending the non-thinking women's lib advocates. After all, Sanger did say: A woman's right to control her body is the foundation of her human rights. And women are entitled to sexual pleasure and fulfill-ment.[109] If only fetuses could talk.

He continued further, "There are, however, rare and tragic situations that can occur in a woman's pregnancy in which, in a doctor's medical judg-ment, the use of this procedure may be necessary to save a woman's life or to protect her against serious injury to her health.[110] Rare is true! The risk of maternal death during childbirth in developed nations is comparatively low; only about 1 in 1800 mothers die in childbirth (only 1 in 3700 in North America). This means the rest of the abortions are performed because of the mother's own choice.

Anyway – thanks to Clinton's actions, Dr. Martin Haskell of Dayton, Ohio has performed over 1,000 partial-birth abortions [and counting]. In a tape-recorded interview, Dr. Haskell told American Medical News, "I'll be quite frank: most of my abortions are elective in that 20-24 week range...In my particular case, probably 20% are for genetic reasons. And the other 80% are purely elective." One of Haskell's nurses, Brenda Pratt Shafer glimpsed a partial birth abortion committed by Haskell. Here is Shafer's reaction to the abortion: "...Dr. Haskell delivered the baby's head. He cut the umbilical cord and delivered the placenta. He threw that baby in a pan, along with the placenta and the instruments he had used. I saw the baby move in the pan. I asked another nurse and she said it was just 'reflexes.'"[111]

GEORGE TILLER

Then there is the notorious Dr. George Tiller from Kansas. The process can take several days. On the first day, Tiller inserts laminaria into the woman's cervix. Laminaria are thin sticks of seaweed material that absorb moisture and expand. The process dilates (opens) the cervix to prepare for the abortion. Tiller replaces the laminaria each day using more sticks each time. During this time, Tiller kills the baby by injecting a drug called Digoxin into its heart. He guides a long needle through the mother's abdomen into the baby's beating heart. After the baby is dead and the cervix is fully dilated, Tiller delivers the dead baby while the mother is under a twilight anesthesia.[112]

Tiller's website contains some disturbing options that women may wish to do after the abortion has taken place. This is from his website: Many patients request a remembrance of their baby to take home with them. The following lists items and services that some of our previous patients have found helpful in their emotional recovery. Everyone approaches this experience with their own unique emotional, spiritual, and cultural background. There is no right way or wrong way, just "your way." Once the process of healing has begun, you may want to consider a token of the precious time you and your baby had together. All of these features of our program will be discussed with you while you are with us:

- Viewing your baby after delivery

- Holding your baby after delivery

- Photographs of your baby

- Baptism of your baby, with or without a certificate

- Footprints and handprints of your baby

- Certificate of premature miscarriage

- Cremation

- An urn for ashes

- Arrangement of burial in either Wichita or your home state

- Arrangement of amniocentesis/autopsy

- Medical photographs and x-rays for your health care professional[113]

Proving what Tiller is doing is murder, Tiller says this: When you and your family arrive, you will meet other families who find themselves in a similar situation – having to make a difficult decision about the babies they love.[114]

Here's an excerpt from a recording made by Tiller: "You will be controlled. You will be subjugated. You will be marginalized. And when subjugation walks in, freedom walks out. Now what do I mean? That means gone will be equal opportunity in the work force. Gone will be equal education. Gone will be equal pay for equal work. Gone will be health care benefits. Gone will be retirement benefits. Your freedoms will be gone. Because this is not about babies. Again, it's about subjugation of women by male dominated societies. It's no more; it's no less."[115]

And this excerpt as well: "In our organization we have made the decision that in situations of fetal abnormality, the woman is the patient and the fetus is the problem."[116]

This is an excerpt from a video in which Tiller talks openly about the reasons women come to Wichita for late-term abortions which include "occupational issues" and "financial issues:" "Your presence here this morning means that something is going dramatically wrong in your life. You may be here to end a pregnancy early because of fetal abnormality – to save your unwell, unborn child from a lifetime of pain, suffering, disability, and hardship."[117]

Abortion is murder, it's no more, it's no less. So let's stop all this nonsense about saving the turtle eggs in Panama.

A MODERN DAY EUGENICIST: PETER SINGER

The very controversial Princeton University professor of practical ethics, Peter Singer said he supports the infanticide of children who are born ill or who have older siblings, ill and in need of the infant's body parts. An interviewer questioned him: "What about parents conceiving and giving birth to a child specifically to kill him, take his organs, and transplant them into their sick, older children?" Singer replied, "It's difficult to warm to parents who can take such a detached view, [but] they're not doing something really wrong in itself." "Is there anything wrong with a society in which children are bred for spare parts on a massive scale?" "No." Replied Singer. *(World Magazine, Blue-State Philosopher, By Marvin Olasky)*

He also reaffirmed that it would be ethically O.K. to kill 1-year-olds with physical or mental disabilities, although ideally the question of infanticide would be "raised as soon as possible after birth." (Ibid) Interestingly, Singer has a strong Jewish background but believes in a system that almost wiped out that background.

PROVING ABORTION IS MURDER

In the schools I attended, every biology teacher was pro-abortion, yet in these same schools I learned the seven characteristics that define life:

1. Living things obtain and use energy. A baby in the womb obtains food through the mother's umbilical cord and uses energy to move around, so this can't provide a reason for an abortion, especially since there are sick people in hospitals getting their nourishment from tubes and IV's – and we don't kill them, do we?

2. Living things grow and develop. Babies grow larger and larger in and out of the womb – there's no arguing that. In the fifth week of pregnancy the very tiny embryo has three layers; the neural tube will form and develop into the nervous system, the middle layer will develop into the heart and circulatory system, bones, muscles, kidneys and reproductive organs, and the inner layer will develop into the intestines, liver, pancreas and bladder. Shortly after the beginning of the third trimester, babies are fully viable – able to survive and grow outside of the womb. So, how can we justify killing a baby in the womb, yet protect it the moment it's outside the womb?

3. Living things reproduce. Babies in their wombs cannot reproduce – but neither can three-year old children – but they can later on. So, are we going to kill those darling three-year old toddlers, too?

4. Living things respond to their environment. Pregnant women are very careful about the foods and medicines they ingest. Why? because their unborn babies respond to their maternal environment. They respond to soothing sounds and by 24 weeks gestation, human fetuses respond to loud noises.[118]

5. Living things are made of cells.[119] Within 24-hours after fertilization, the egg begins dividing rapidly into many cells. The fertilized egg (called a zygote) continues to divide as it passes slowly through the fallopian tube to the uterus where its next job is to attach to the endometrium (a process called implantation). First the zygote becomes a solid ball of cells, then it becomes a hollow ball of cells called a blastocyst.[120]

6. Living things adapt to their environment. Embryos adapt to its surroundings, so that it can carry out the other necessary functions for life to occur.

7. Living things have DNA. The first sperm that penetrates fully into the egg donates its genetic material (DNA).[121] The 23 chromosomes of the paternal sperm (male pronucleus) fuses with the 23 chromosomes of the maternal oocyte (egg or female pronucleus) at fertilization to create a single cell embryo or zygote containing 46 chromosomes. The fertilization process takes about 24 hours.[122]

In light of these facts, it's difficult to make a case that abortion isn't murder. To claim that abortion should be legal so that women won't die from unclean surgical instruments in an illegal clinic makes as much sense as saying we should legalize murder (it's going to happen anyway) so that we can protect the murderers from any weapons the potential victims might have. So, isn't it time to stop all of this "its my body" nonsense, since the baby is the father's child as well?

CONCLUSION

We can see Satan's footprints throughout history – hatred for the weak – the so called "lower" class of the earth – and hatred especially for God's chosen people, the Jews. This hatred has been evident against the undesirable to the weak, to the very weak, to the unborn. But it's not enough to know about the hate, we need to understand why the devil hates children and people with mental disorders. In Matthew 18:3-4 Jesus says: "Verily I say unto you, except you be converted, and become as little children, you shall not enter into the kingdom of heaven. Whosoever therefore shall humble himself as this little child, the same is greatest in the kingdom of heaven." Is it possible Satan wants to destroy those who are the most innocent – babies, young children, the simple minded or mentally challenged – because they are the very ones Jesus said we must become like before we can enter His heavenly kingdom? We can see that the greatest in heaven's kingdom will be those who are as humble as a little child. We know how Satan, the deceiver, takes truths from the Bible and creates his own principles which are completely opposite to those in the Bible. However, the Bible says: "But God has chosen the foolish things of the world to put to shame the wise, and God has chosen the weak things of the world to put to shame the things which are mighty." (First Corinthians 1:27)

Resources

1. Eugenics, History, Pre-Galton Eugenics

2. Creation Ministries International, Darwin Versus Compassion, Charles Darwin, The Descent of Man, 2nd Ed., pp. 133–134, 1887.

3. Elitism and Satanism, Description, Justification, Philosophies, 6. Building a Master Race, a Police State, Burton H Wolfe, "Interview with Anton LaVey" Fling (July 1978), By Vexen Crabtree.

4. Eugenics, History, Pre-Galton Eugenics.

5. Eugenics, History, See Chapter 3 in Donald A. MacKenzie, Statistics in Britain, 1865-1930: The social construction of scientific knowledge (Edinburgh: Edinburgh University Press, 1981).

6. Hereditary Genius, By Francis Galton, 1869, (Second Edition, 1892).

7. Scope Note 28, Eugenics, Introduction, V, Ludmerer, 1978, p. 459.

8. Rotten, Eugenics.

9. Fascism: Neo-Nazism Reimmerges from its Roots, Zenith Harris Merrill.

10. Eugenics, Galton's Theory, Francis Galton, Inquiries into human faculty and its development (London, Macmillan, 1883): 17, fn1.

11. Wikipedia, Eugenics, Galton's Theory, Francis Galton, "Eugenics: Its definition, scope, and aims," The American Journal of Sociology 10:1 (July 1904).

12. World Socialist website, Sweden continued eugenics policy until 1976, Social Democrats implemented measures to forcibly sterilize 62,000 people.

13. The eugenics apologies: How a pair of disability rights advocates scored the first state apology for eugenics, and what they have planned next., By Dave Reynolds, Nov./Dec. 2003.

14. Ibid

15. Alexander Graham Bell from Wikipedia, Eugenics.

16. Ibid.

17. Wikipedia, Eugenics, History, Eugenics and The State, 1890's – 1945.

18. Ibid.

19. Why was a ship with German Jews sent back to Nazi Germany from the U.S.A.?, [article in the Public Domain], The Surgical Solution, Philip R. Reilly.

20. Wikipedia, Eugenics, History, Eugenics and the State, 1890's – 1945, Paul Lombardo, "Eugenic Sterilization Laws."

21. The eugenics apologies: How a pair of disability rights advocates scored the first state apology for eugenics, and what they have planned next., By Dave Reynolds, Nov./Dec. 2003.

22. Alexander Graham Bell from Wikipedia, Eugenics.

23. Life Advocate, January/February, 1998 Volume XII Number 10, Margaret Sanger's Eugenics, By Mike Richmond, Who 'Inspired' the architects of the German Sterilization law?, "Legal and Medical Aspects of Eugenic Sterilization in Germany," American Sociological Review, Marie E. Kopp, 1936:763.

24. Life Advocate, January/February, 1998 Volume XII Number 10, Margaret Sanger's Eugenics, 1924: A year of infamy, By Mike Richmond, Written By Robert N. Proctor ("A Plan for Peace," Birth Control Review, April 1932).

25. Poor Magazine Online, Poor News Network, A Simple Act of Mothering, By Ana Morrow.

26. Ibid

27. Why was a ship with German Jews sent back to Nazi Germany from the U.S.A.?, Who is Margaret Sanger?, In The Science and Politics of Racial Research (pp. 126-127), Said by Rutger's psychology professor William H. Tucker.

28. Life Advocate, January/February, 1998 Volume XII Number 10, Margaret Sanger's Eugenics, 1924: A year of infamy, By Mike Richmond, "A Plan for Peace," Birth Control Review, April 1932.

29. Ibid.

30. Wikipedia, Alexander Graham Bell, Eugenics.

31. Poor Magazine Online, Poor News Network, A Simple Act of Mothering, By Ana Morrow.

32. The AnthroGlobe Journal, Why Do Ideologies Exist: The Psychological Function of Culture, By Richard Koenigsberg, Library of Social Science, What Do Ideologies Do?, "The Jewish Parasite" By Alexander Bein.

33. Jewish Virtual Library, Nazi Persecution of the Mentally and Physically Disabled, Forced Sterilizations.

34. Barry Mehler, "Eliminating the Inferior: American and Nazi Sterilization Programs," Science for the People (Nov-Dec 1987) pp. 14-18.

35. The eugenics apologies: How a pair of disability rights advocates scored the first state apology for eugenics, and what they have planned next., By Dave Reynolds, Nov./Dec. 2003.

36. Holocaust Encyclopedia, Euthanasia Program.

37. Ibid

38. Wikipedia, Alexis Carrel, Relation to eugenics and fascism, Quoted in Reggiani, p. 339.

39. Holocaust Encyclopedia, Euthanasia Program.

40. Why Can't We Love Them Both? By Dr. and Mrs. J.C. Wilke, Chapter 25, Euthanasia, Wertham, The German Euthanasia Program, Hayes Publishing Co., Cinn, 1977, p. 47.

41. Youtube, Polygamy traitor, Banking on Heaven.

42. Abortion and Eugenics, The Eugenics root of the pro-abortion movement.

43. Abortion and Eugenics, The Eugenics root of the pro-abortion movement, Eugenics part of Sanger Legacy, Mary Senander, the Minneapolis Star Tribune.

44. Abortion – A Liberal cause?, By Jefferis Kent Peterson.

45. The Negro Project, Margaret Sanger's Eugenic plan for Black Americans, By Tanya L. Green.

46. Abortion – A Liberal cause?, By Jefferis Kent Peterson, Emily Taft Douglas, Margaret Sanger; Pioneer of the Future, Holt, Rinehart & Winston, N.Y., 1970, p. 192., Margaret Sanger, letter to Clarence Gamble, Oct. 19,1939. – Sanger manuscripts, Sophia Smith Collection, Smith College.

47. Not White not Delightsome, The curse of the Negroes.

48. Ibid

49. The Negro Project, Margaret Sanger's Eugenic plan for Black Americans, By Tanya L. Green, Malthusian Eugenics.

50. Ibid

51. Ibid

52. American Death Camps, The Holocaust, Meet Margaret Sanger Founder of Planned Parenthood.

53. Ibid

54. Ibid

55. Ibid

56. Ibid

57. Ibid

58. Ibid

59. Ibid

60. Ibid

61. Ibid

62. Ibid

63. Ibid

64. Ibid

65. The Ethical Spectacle, Margaret Sanger, Sterilization, and the Swastika, by Mike Richmond, The Planned Parenthood connection – Who is Lothrup Stoddard? The Nazi Connection (Eugenics, American Racism, And German National Socialism), Stefan Kuhl, Oxford University Press, 1994, p. 62. The Nazi Connection, p. 85. Into The Darkness: Nazi Germany Today, Lothrup Stoddard, 1940, pp. 190-191.

66. The Ethical Spectacle, Margaret Sanger, Sterilization, and the Swastika, by Mike Richmond, Lothrup Stoddard and the "Jews Problem," Berlin Diary: The Journal of a Foreign Correspondent, William L. Shire (New York: Alfred Knopf, 1941):257.

67. Life Advocate, January/February, 1998 Volume XII Number 10, Margaret Sanger's Eugenics, By Mike Richmond, Who 'Inspired' the architects of the German Sterilization law?, "Legal and Medical Aspects of Eugenic Sterilization in Germany," American Sociological Review, Marie E. Kopp, 1936:763.

68. The Negro Project, Margaret Sanger's Eugenic plan for Black Americans, By Tanya L. Green, Malthusian Eugenics.

69. Ibid

70. Eugenics, History, Eugenics and The State, 1890's – 1945.

71. Margaret Sanger, Sterilization, and The Swastika, By Mike Richmond, High Praise from Adolf Hitler, unpublished autobiography of Leon F. Whitney, written in 1971, Whitney Papers, APS, 204-5., The Nazi Connection, p. 85.

72. Wikipedia, The Passing of the Great Race, Nordic theory.

73. Ibid

74. Wikipedia, The Passing of the Great Race, Reception and Influence.

75. Life Advocate, Flowers of Evil, March/April, 1998 Volume XII Number 11, The Question history tries to answer, Madison Grant's The Passing of the Great Race 1916.

76. Creation Ministries International, Darwin Versus Compassion, Charles Darwin, The Descent of Man, 2nd Ed., pp. 133–134, 1887.

77. American Death Camps, The Holocaust, Hitler was Pro-Choice.

78. Ibid

79. Chapter 10: Eugenics after World War II, C. P. Blacker and "Crypto-Eugenics."

80. Ibid.

81. Chapter 10: Eugenics after World War II, The Fraudulent Reform.

82. Ibid

83. Life Advocate, Flowers of Evil, March/April, 1998 Volume XII Number 11, Different Tactics, Eugenics Review (volume 48, number 1, April 1956).

84. The Negro Project, Margaret Sanger's Eugenic Plan for Black Americans, By Tanya L. Green, posted at Concerned Women of America, The Harlem Clinic, Letter from Nathan W. Levin, comptroller for the Julius Rosenwald Fund, responding to Sanger's request for funds, which opens with, "I am pleased to enclose our check in the amount of $2,500, representing the balance of our appropriation to the Harlem Birth Control Clinic for 1930." 5 January 1931, MSCLC., The Harlem Clinic 1929 file, MSCLC.

85. The Negro Project, Margaret Sanger's Eugenic Plan for Black Americans, By Tanya L. Green

86. Ibid

87. Ibid

88. A Plan for Peace*, By Margaret Sanger, *Summary of address before the New History Society, January 17th, New York City.

89. Ibid

90. Ibid

91. Ibid

92. Ibid

93. Ibid

94. Ibid

95. Ibid

96. MSN Encarta, Roe v. Wade, Encyclopedia Article, I Introduction.

97. MSN Encarta, Roe v. Wade, Encyclopedia Article, III The Challenge of Roe V. Wade.

98. MSN Encarta, Roe v. Wade, Encyclopedia Article, IV The Supreme Court's Decision.

99. MSN Encarta, Roe v. Wade, Encyclopedia Article, D Trimester Guidelines

100. Online Encyclopedia, Roe vs. Wade, 2006

101. MSN Encarta, Roe v. Wade, Encyclopedia Article, D Trimester Guidelines.

102. MSN Encarta, Roe v. Wade, Encyclopedia Article, V Aftermath.

103. National Right to Life, Over 40 Million Abortions, in U.S. since 1973

104. Jeremiah Project, Partial Birth Abortion.

105. Partial Birth Abortion: President Clinton's Veto Message, The White House, April 10, 1996., Written May, 1996. Posted 25 Jan 2001.

106. Ibid

107. Wikipedia, Childbirth, Complications and Risks during Childbirth.

108. Partial Birth Abortion: President Clinton's Veto Message, The White House, April 10, 1996., Written May, 1996. Posted 25 Jan 2001.

109. Planned Parenthood, Margaret Sanger, Planned Parenthood Founder.

110. Why Are Partial-Birth Abortions Performed?

111. BP News, Baby's 'angelic' face haunts former abortion nurse, Nov 6, 2003, By Michael Foust, Baptist Press.

112. www.tillerthekiller.com, What Methods Does Tiller Use To Kill Babies?

113. Women's Health Care Services, P.A. , Specialist in 2nd Trimester Elective and 2nd/3rd trimester Therapeutic Abortion Care, Late Abortion Care for Fetal Anomaly, Remembrances and Special Requests.

114. http://www.drtiller.com, see also www.tillerthekiller.com, In Their Own Words., From an interview Tiller gave to "Alligator Cowgirl Productions" at the proabortion "March for Women's Lives" in Washington, DC in 2004.

115. Women's Health Care Services, P.A. , Specialist in 2nd Trimester Elective and 2nd/3rd trimester Therapeutic Abortion Care, Late Abortion Care for Fetal Anomaly, Remembrances and Special Requests.

116. www.tillerthekiller.com, In Their Own Words., From an interview Tiller gave to "Alligator Cowgirl Productions" at the proabortion "March for Women's Lives" in Washington, DC in 2004.

117. Bamford Lahey Children's Foundation, Harriet Klein, Ph.D. New York University Nelson Moses Long Island University, Abstract 2: Third Trimester Auditory Stimulation Selectively Enhances Language Development.

118. Characteristics of Living Thing, Updated June 15, 2000 by: Glen Westbrook.

119. WebMD, Pregnancy: Understanding Conception, Implantation, Springfield Technical Learning College. The Merck Manual.

120. The 7 Characteristics of Life, 4. Have DNA.

121. Prenatal development, Human prenatal development, Fertilization and embryo genesis, "MedlinePlus Medical Encyclopedia," Moore, Keith L. The Developing Human: 3rd Edition. W.B. Saunders Company, Philadelphia PA., Wilcox AJ, Baird DD, Weinberg CR. Time of implantation of the conceptus and loss of pregnancy. 1999 N Engl J Med. 340(23):1796-9. PMID 10362823., Ljunger, E, Cnattingius, S, Lundin, C, & Annerén, G. 2005 Chromosomal anomalies in first-trimester miscarriages. Acta Obstetricia et Gynecologica Scandinavica 84(11):1103-1107. PMID 10362823.

122. Life Begins at Conception!, Medical Aspects, Life in The Womb.

Chapter Eleven – The Devilution of Death

THE ORIGINS OF THE CULTURE OF DEATH
Suicide

Suicides in cult-cultures are quite common. Mostly, they are committed out of misery – their motive is to escape the world and their own self-hate, and enter into an astral place or some celestial heaven. However, some suicides are committed with the intention of killing others – as has been seen from the Muslim world.

This second motivation is evident in every video clip of suicide (or better called, homicide) martyrs, every statement made by Muslim clerics regarding suicide, and the volumes written in the Hadith interpretation of Allah's edicts regarding Jihad. The "shaheed," Fida'e sacrificial lamb, in Islam, is a warrior who sacrifices himself for a religious holy war (Jihad) or national cause.

Seeking to transport oneself instantly to heaven is one of the most important elements of Islamic Fundamentalism which can be defined as:

Religious conditioning taught to Muslim masses, by using allusions of misery, historic manipulation, and the illusion of virtues from a distant past by continually reflecting on glory days of long ago, in order to convert masses into angry, pride-filled, remorseless killers and seekers of salvation by death. The goal is to intimidate non-Muslims by fear and threats, in order to re-establish a utopian theocratic world order in which Islam and Muslims are dominant and all non-Muslims are subservient, living under Sharia law. This conditioning becomes the sole focus of both the spiritual leaders, and the followers in every aspect of their daily lives.

This is what Islamic fundamentalism is all about, and you will find that everything in this dangerous movement fits within this definition. It's crucial to keep this definition in mind. It will help you when watching news media coverage, if you are able to understand their mindset.

For Muslims, self-destruction for the goal of heaven is to deny the crucifixion of Jesus Christ. But Jesus already atoned for our sins. Why should we try to atone ourselves? Through the cult's self blood atonement – death becomes glorious.

There is also the action that is second to suicide which is self-affliction. Every year, Shiite Muslims cut themselves in remembrance to Muhammad's nephew Ali and the death of other Imams – like Imam Hussein. This event is called Qama Zani or "hitting of swords." Here is what Al-Imam al-Sheikh Abdul Kareem al-Ha'ery (The Founder of the current Hawzah in the holy city of Qum) said about the hitting of swords:

"The hitting of swords on the heads (causing bleeding) is allowed provided there is no harm to the person doing this. Furthermore no one has the right to prohibit this (hitting the head with sword). In fact all kinds of TA'ZIAH – mourning – for SEYYED AL-SHUHADA' – Imam Hussein – may our souls be sacrificed for him, are MUSTAHAB – desirable deeds."[1]

A quote from Al-Imam al-Sheikh Muhammad Hussein al-Naa'ini (The teacher of the Maraje' of the holy city of Najaf):

"There is no doubt as to the permissibility of the beating of the chest and the face with the hands to the point of redness or blackness (of the chest or the face). This is also extended to the lashing of the shoulders and the back with chains to the extent mentioned (above), and even if this led to bleeding. As for causing the bleeding of the head by sword beating, this is also allowed provided it does not lead to endangering harm, such as unstoppable bleeding or harm to the skull, etc., as it is known amongst the experts in doing this (hitting on the head)."[2]

SELF AFFLICTION REJECTED IN THE BIBLE

The ritual of Qama Zani reminds me of what happened with Elijah in First Kings 18:26-28. Speaking of the worshippers of Baal: "And they took the bullock which was given them, and they dressed [it], and called on the name of Baal from morning even until noon, saying, O Baal, hear us. But [there was] no voice, nor any that answered. And they leaped upon the altar which was made. And it came to pass at noon, that Elijah mocked them, and said, Cry aloud: for he [is] a god; either he is talking, or he is pursuing, or he is in a journey, [or] peradventure he sleepeth, and must be awakened. And they cried aloud, and cut themselves after their manner with knives and lancets, till the blood gushed out upon them." The Scriptures also tell us of a possessed man in Mark 5:5 – Jesus meets a possessed man who "night and day, he was in the mountains, and in the tombs, crying, and cutting himself with stones." In Deuteronomy 14:1 we find: "You [are] the children of the Lord your God: you shall not cut yourselves, nor make any baldness between your eyes for the dead." These verses are totally opposite to the Shia who cut themselves in remembrance of a dead nephew of Muhammad – Ali.

SELF AFFLICTION IN THE MORMON CULT

Self-afflicted pain can be seen in Mormonism. The men were stripped, washed, anointed, and then, as in the Masonic ceremony, dressed in special "garments." The Masonic square and compass were cut into the garment on the breast and a slash was made across the knee. In the beginning, the cut across the knee was apparently deep enough to penetrate the flesh and leave a scar. This act was banned because of a protest by the Mormon women.[3] There was also castration: "The subjects of eunuchs came up...Brigham Young said the day would come when thousands would be made eunuchs in order for them to be saved in the kingdom of god."[4]

SELF AFFLICTION BY THE SHAKERS

The Shakers are a Protestant religious denomination officially called the United Society of Believers in Christ's Second Appearing. They originated in Manchester, England in 1772, but moved to New York in 1775. It was the Shakers who castrated all their males,[5] and danced naked at their night-time meetings.

SELF AFFLICTION IN HEAVEN'S GATE

When Heaven's Gate leader Marshall Applewhite was castrated, five other cult members eagerly followed and "couldn't stop smiling and giggling" about the procedure. This was stated by a former member of the cult, Rio Diangelo.[6]

SELF AFFLICTION IN CYBELE CULT

In the Cybele cult (writings place them in ancient Asia Minor), the pagan goddess Cybele's most ecstatic followers were males who ritually castrated themselves, after which they were given women's clothing and assumed "female" identities.[7] This custom gave rise to Satanic homosexuality in the Cybele cult.

SELF AFFLICTION IN THE MAYAN CULT

The Mayans also took part in these types of rituals. Within the Mayan empire the rulers performed bloodletting ceremonies using obsidian knives or stingray spines to cut their penis, allowing the blood to fall onto paper held in a bowl. The Kings' wives also took part in this ritual by pulling a rope with thorns attached through their tongues, or ear lobes. Interestingly, a recently discovered Queen's tomb in the Classical Mayan site of Waka, formerly known as El Peru, had a Ceremonial Stingray spine placed in her genital area, suggesting that women also perform bloodletting in their genitalia.[8]

SELF AFFLICTION WITH DRUG ADDICTS

This act of self-inflicted pain can be also found with the use of drugs like PCP, etc. Here are some situations which have occurred numerous times because of drug use: "Person gouges out own eyes," "Person sits engulfed in flames, unable to perceive danger," "Person pulls out own teeth with pliers," "Person amputates a body part: nose, breast or penis," "Motorcyclist points vehicle head-on into a Trailway bus (or tree)."[9]

The Quran states: "The believers fight in Allah's cause, they slay and are slain, kill and are killed" (Q9:111) "For those who fought and were killed in my cause, I shall blot out their sins and admit them indeed into Paradise." (Q3:195)

> Allah's Apostle said: "Allah has undertaken to look after the affairs of one who goes out to fight in his way believing in him and affirming the truth of his apostle. He is committed that he will either admit him to Paradise or bring him back to his home with a reward, or his share of booty. By the being in whose hand is the life of Muhammad, if a person gets wounded in Allah's cause he will arrive on the day of judgment with his wound in the same condition as it was when it was first inflicted; its color will be blood but its smell will be musk perfume. If it were not too hard on Muslims I would not lag behind any raid going out to fight in the cause of Allah. But I do not have abundant means to provide them (the mujahids [Islamic terrorists]) with riding beasts, nor have they all the means (to provide themselves with the weapons of Jihad). I love to fight in the way of Allah and be killed, to fight and again be killed and to fight and be killed."[10]

> "Before the battle of Uhud a Muslim asked, 'Messenger, where shall I be if I am killed?' He replied, 'In Paradise.' The man fought until he was killed."[11]

> "Let those fight in the way of Allah who sell the life of this world for the other. Whoso fighteth in the way of Allah, be he slain or be he victorious, on him we shall bestow a vast reward. (Q4:74)

Here's an excerpt from a video with Palestinian-Kuwaiti Sheikh Ahmad Qattan on Allah's Rewards to a Martyr:

"The Mujahid, the warrior on the frontier, the preacher, the faithful, the martyr, the martyrdom seeker...These heroes who stand in line and await their turn, not for bread and potatoes, but to sacrifice themselves for the sake of their god's religion and to exalt his words. They seek the most ideal life, the longest life in the heavens. They want to join their brothers, the martyrs, and to reap martyr's rewards. A martyr gets six rewards from Allah: 1) His sins are forgiven with the first drop of his blood, and he sees his place in heaven; 2) He is spared the torments of the grave; 3) He is safe from the great horror; 4) The crown of honor is placed on his head – with a jewel finer than this world and what is in it; 5) He is married off to 72 black-eyed women; and 6) He may plead for 70 of his relatives. This reminds me of the mujahideen and martyrdom seekers who stand in line in Palestine: men and women, adults and children, awaiting their turn to sign, with their blood and their broken bones, their pledge of faith in Allah.[12]

What Qattan said relates to what Brigham Young once said:

"Now take a person in this congregation who has knowledge with regard to being saved in the kingdom of our god and our father, and being exalted, one who knows and understands the principles of eternal life, and sees the beauty and excellency of the eternities before him compared with the vain and foolish things of the world, and suppose that he is overtaken in a gross fault, that he has committed a sin that he knows will deprive him of that exaltation which he desires, and that he cannot attain to it without the shedding of his blood, and also knows that by having his blood shed he will atone for that sin, and be saved and exalted with the gods, is there a man of woman in this house but what would say, 'shed my blood that I may be saved and exalted with the gods?'"[13]

Similarly, L. Ron Hubbard also spoke about mankind being their own Jesus Christ. Hubbard stated: "Every man is then shown to have been crucified so don't think that it's an accident that this crucifixion, they found out that this applied. Somebody somewhere on this planet, back about 600 BC, found some pieces of R6, and I don't know how they found it, either by watching madmen or something, but since that time they have used it and it became what is known as Christianity. The man on the Cross. There was no Christ, but the man on the cross is shown as Every man." (The Hubbard Quotes Collection, Class VIII course lecture #10 on the ship Apollo, October 3, 1968)

He has also stated: "Man is basically good but he could not attain expression of this until now. Nobody but the individual could die for his own sins – to arrange things otherwise was to keep man in chains." ("What is Scientology?" 1992) He also believed that "Christ died for his own sins." (L Ron Hubbard and Jesus Christ, Peik J. Strômsholm)

MUHAMMAD BOUYERI

Muhammad Bouyeri, the one who killed the film director Theo Van Gogh by shooting him with eight bullets from a HS 2000. Van Gogh died on the spot. Bouyeri then slit Van Gogh's throat, and stabbed him in the chest. Muhammad Bouyeri was arrested on November 2, 2004, shortly after the death of Theo Van Gogh, close to the scene of the crime, after an exchange of gunfire with the police in which he was shot in the leg.[14]

When arrested, Bouyeri had on him a farewell poem which was labeled "Baptized in Blood" – a lyrical poem which signified his assumed plan for martyrdom and encouraging others to do the same. Here's the poem:

So this is my final word...Riddled with bullets...
Baptized in blood...As I had hoped.
I am leaving a message...For you...the fighter...
The tree of Tawheed is waiting...Yearning for your blood...
Enter the bargain...And Allah opens the way...
He gives you the garden...Instead of the earthly rubble.
To the enemy I say...You will surely die...
Wherever in the world you go...
Death is waiting for you...

Chased by the knights of death...
Who paint the streets with Red.
For the hypocrites I have one final word...
Wish death or hold your tongue and...sit.
Dear brothers and sisters, my end is nigh...
But this does not end the story.

A picture of Karim Mufarja, who was responsible for perpetrating a number of terrorist attacks. The inscription above his head reads, "The shaheeds are in the company of their Sovereign, [from whom] they receive their reward and from whom light radiates." (To the right) The Islamic Block emblem. It depicts the Quran, the globe, a raised assault rifle upon which is the jihad flag and a map of "Palestine" in the background.[15]

The above poster commemorates two shaheeds (martyrs). On the right is Ramez Fahmi Izz al-Din (Abu Salim) al-Rantisi, a member of the Izz al-Din al-Qassam, who carried out the suicide bombing attack at the Hillel Café in Jerusalem. On the left is Ihab 'Abd al-Qader Mahmud al-Rantisi, who carried out the suicide bombing attack at Tserifin. In the center is a picture of Sheikh Ahmad Yassin, the Hamas leader, above the Hamas emblem. The inscription at the top of the poster is a "suicide bombers'" Quran verse, one of the most frequently quoted on posters of this kind. The motto of Hamas (emphasizing Izz al-Din al-Qassam) appears at the bottom of the poster, and reads, "This is indeed a jihad [holy war], [leading to] victory or death for the sake of Allah [istishhad]."[16]

Linguistically the word tawheed means unification (to make something one). However, in Islam it is in reference to Allah being singled out alone, in all that is particular to him. The opposite of tawheed is 'shirk' which is to associate partners with Allah by giving that which belongs to him, to others. Muslims say that, "The division of tawheed does not divide Allah up into three separate parts (as does trinity), but rather it helps us to understand how our Creator is unique and alone in being singled out for worship and reverence. Unfortunately there are some Christians today who seem to forget this fact and continue to spread lies about the meaning of the tawheed of Allah."[17]

As you can tell, Muslims are extremely anti-Trinity. There is no Jesus, therefore they have no salvation – which becomes another incentive for their self-destructive tendencies. A Muslim martyr has the ability to bring seventy of his relatives into paradise – thus he becomes their personal savior.

This encouragement for suicide is especially found in Islamic music – which is called "anasheed" or "nasheed." – devotional songs. In an Iranian video identified as "A Bridegroom Turns into a Suicide Bomber in an Iranian TV Music Video," the young man stops the car, steps out, lifts the hood of the trunk and sets the hidden bomb inside. He ties the red sash around his forehead, inscribed with the words "Jerusalem is ours." The young man starts out again on his journey, while his mother is shown with tears running down her cheeks. The young man accelerates the car. Israeli soldiers turn to see the car approaching their base, but are unable to stop the car with gunfire. The singer sings: "Hurry, brother. Hurry. It's time for my martyrdom. It's time for self-sacrifice. It's time to save the homeland." The young man crashes his car into the base, and there is a huge explosion. The singer then chants: "The stone is my weapon. It shatters the night. My cry is an axe ripping out the root of the night." The Israeli flag is shown burning.[18]

In an Al-Aqsa animated music-video for children, it rhythms these words:

Enemies harm us
Oh children, cry Allah Akbar
You are the aim and the concern,
let your stone pour out blood
Your land is your honor and is what matters
It is your promise and your friend
My book has turned into a stone.
With it I repel the treacherous
My book has turned into a stone
With it I repel the treacherous
It is small like (the boy)
But its effect is great.
Purify yourself,
Pray and set out
Your blood perfumes that soil of your land
Your name will be engraved on heaven's door
I swear my loyalty to you, Al Aqsa
I swear my loyalty to you, Jerusalem
I may miss a lesson
But my love for you itself is a lesson
Come out of every tunnel, window and door
Join your stone to mine.
Shooting doesn't scare us
[child gets shot by Israeli shoulder and falls to the ground]
The dear (child) has fulfilled his desire,
Achieving the honor of Martyrdom,
He is not considered dead
He who dies for his country[19]

But, have there been instances of suicide-bombings that were not Islamic? Indeed there have been.

WOO BUM-KON

A police officer, Woo Bum-Kon, carried out the worst incident of a killing spree in known history, killing 58 (including himself), and wounding 35 in

Gyeongsangnam-do, South Korea. After an argument with his live-in girlfriend he left the house and went to the police armory, where he began consuming large amounts of whiskey. He became moderately drunk, raided the police armory of its weapons and put together a personal arsenal. Bum-Kon then stole a single high-powered rifle and some grenades as he left the armory. He walked from house to house, abusing his position as a police officer to make people feel safe and gain entry into the home. Then he shot the victims, or killed the entire family with a grenade. He continued this pattern for the next eight hours, into the early morning hours of April 27. When Bum-Kon had shot numerous people in his village, he ran to another village and started killing there, too. Eventually, he had reeked havoc through five villages in Uiryeong county. In the early hours of April 27, Bum-Kon took his last two grenades and strapped them to his body. He grabbed three people as he set the fuse of the grenades. They became his final victims as he blew himself up, killing the three he had taken hostage, thus ending the world's worst killing spree.[20]

SEPPUKU

Seppuku, the Japanese formal language term for ritual suicide (commonly known as *Hara-kiri* [Har-rah-kee-ree]), was an integral ritual of feudal Japan (1192-1868).[21] It developed as part of the code of bushido and the discipline of the samurai warrior class. The early history of Japan reveals quite clearly that the Japanese were far more interested in living the good life than in dying a painful death. It was not until well after the introduction of Buddhism, with its theme of the transitory nature of life and the glory of death, that such a practice became possible. Honor for the samurai was dearer than life, and in many cases, self destruction was regarded not simply as the right course of action, but as the only course of action. Disgrace and defeat were atoned for by committing hara-kiri or seppuku.[22])

Stephen Turnbull who holds a PhD from Leeds University for his work on Japanese religious history, wrote: "In the world of the warrior, seppuku was a deed of bravery that was admirable in a samurai who knew he was defeated, disgraced, or mortally wounded. It meant that he could end his days with his transgressions wiped away and with his reputation not merely intact but actually enhanced. The cutting of the abdomen released the samurai's spirit in the most dramatic fashion, but it was an extremely painful and unpleasant way to die, and sometimes the samurai who was performing the act asked a loyal comrade to cut off his head at the moment of agony."[23]

SEN NO RIKYÛ

Okakura Kakuzo, a Japanese scholar and author, wrote in his book, *The Book of Tea*, about the most influential Japanese Tea Master, Sen no Rikyû. Rikyû's last act was to hold an exquisite tea ceremony. He presented each of his guests with a piece of the equipment as a souvenir, with the exception of the bowl, which he shattered, uttering "Never again shall this cup, polluted by the lips of misfortune, be used by man." As the guests departed, one remained to serve as witness to Rikyû's death. Rikyû's last words, which he wrote down as a death poem, were in verse, addressed to the dagger with which he took his own life:

Welcome to thee,
O sword of eternity!
Through Buddha
And through Daruma alike
Thou hast cleft thy way.[24]

HÔJÔ UJIMASA

Japanese commander, Hôjô Ujimasa, commanded in many battles, until he retired in 1590. His son Hojo Ujinao took over as head of the clan and lord of Odawara. However, later that year he (and his clan) failed to hold Odawara against the forces of Toyotomi Hideyoshi. Ujimasa was forced to commit suicide along with his brother Ujiteru.[25]

In the shame of his son's miserable defeat; Hôjô Ujimasa wrote a death poem:

Autumn wind of eve
Blow away the clouds that mass
O'er the moon's pure light.
And the mists that cloud our mind
Do thou sweep away as well.
Now we disappear
Well, what must we think of it?
From the sky we came
Now we may go back again
That's at least one point of view.[26]

SALLEKHANA

A Nishidhi-stone is a memorial erected in the memory of someone who gives up their life by fasting (suicide) while meditating. We see numerous instances of such suicides in India.[27]

While in Hinduism and Jainism suicide is condemned, the concept of starving yourself to death when one is near death due to illness or old age is acceptable. "Sallekhana" or "santhara" is the ritual one can choose to "calmly withdraw from worldly preoccupations" by abstaining from food and water. Prior to this practice, one must take a special vow to ensure that they will leave the world without fear – in complete peace and harmony of mind and soul. The purpose is to free one from old karmas and prevent new ones. It is viewed that suicide involves harm and negativity, while sallekhana is considered peaceful and tranquil.[28]

In Jainism, they believe that each and every action (including eating) may or may not become karma. Jains are strictly vegetarian. A tree is alive, thereby it has organisms, so taking a piece of it, vegetable, fruit, or leaf, hurts it – thereby adding negative karma. They are so sensitive to karma activity, that even drinking water adds to their karma, since water contains microscopic organisms.[29]

Its interesting how most people look at Hinduism and Jainism as religions of pure peace. The religion might teach self-control and inner peace, but what about the other things it promotes? In India, the Hindus might possess more inner peace than Muslims, but they are not allowed to eat cows, since cows are worshipped. They are not allowed to kill rats – since rat worship takes place in India. What happens to the vegetables and grains? The animals eat them, and through that comes starvation. More importantly, through rats, comes disease. Yet rat worship can be found in the Indian temple of Karni Mata, (a Hindu goddess) where it is believed the souls of followers are in rats, making them holy.[30] So holy are the rats, that where food or drinking water has been previously sampled by a rat is considered to be supremely blessed[31] It is estimated that twenty thousand rats inhabit, and are woshipped in, northwestern India's Karni Mata Temple.[32]

MESOAMERICAN HUMAN SACRIFICE

Human sacrifice was a common ritual in the ancient Mesoamerican cultures. It possessed a great religious and political significance. The sacrifice symbolized the renewal of the divine cosmic energy. The gods had given life to mankind by sacrificing parts of their own bodies, and the Mesoamericans believed that humans should give their lives in order to maintain order in the universe. As in many cultures, blood signifies life, and human blood was the liquid that satisfied the thirst of the gods, in this case the sun god. They believed that human blood was partially made up of blood from the gods to whom, through sacrifice, it was being returned. This "sacrificial blood" would not only revitalize the gods, but also the earth, the plants – in particular the maize or corn harvest – and the animals, for example, the jaguar and the eagle. Blood was considered to be as necessary for life as water, both in the terrestrial world and the spiritual world.[33]

TONATIUH

In Aztec mythology, Tonatiuh was the Aztec sun god. He was in charge of the Aztec Heaven called Tollan. Only dead warriors and women who died in childbirth could be received into Tollan. Tonatiuh was responsible for supporting the universe. It was believed that this god demanded human sacrifice, or he would refuse to move through the sky. To prevent the end of the world, Aztecs believed it was essential to maintain the strength of the sun god by offering human sacrifices to him.[34] It is estimated that 20,000 people were sacrificed each year to Tonatiuh and other gods.

THE MESOAMERICAN BALLGAME

Mesoamerican "ballgame" – sounds rather sporting, doesn't it? But it was actually more of a ritual than a sport. The "sporting" point of the game was to get a large rubber ball inside of a ring. But the real point of the game was death. From depictions on ancient stone panels we see that the losers of the games were either decapitated, or had their hearts cut out. Yet another form of sacrifice to the gods. Even though this is what some historians say – this is not what I learned during my visit to Chitzinitza; I was told that is was the victorious team who would gain the 'privilege' to let themselves be sacrificed to their gods. An interesting sidenote, many of the "balls" found had human skulls in the center with rubber wrapped all around them.

MURDER

The Spanish chronicler, Juan de Castellanos, reported that when the Tainos of Anasco, Puerto Rico, began their rebellion, they captured a young Spaniard named Juan Suarez. The cacique (local chieftain) ordered that Suarez be tied up and that a ball game be played in which the winners were to be granted the privilege of killing the young Christian. Suarez was saved at the last minute by a Spanish soldier, Diego de Salazar, who reported the natives to be, "almost stuptified in the preparations for the sacrifice."[35]

TZOMPANTLI

Tzompantli, otherwise known as the "wall of skulls" at Chichen Itza, Mexico. Here there was a sacrifice platform where the Mayans displayed the heads of their dead enemies, showing the glory of their military conquest, and also serving as a warning to potential invaders. There are many indications here that ritual human sacrifices were carried out at this site.[36]

The "Wall of Skulls" strongly reminds me of a song, a fanatic yet mesmerizing anasheed (Islamic song):

> We are those who built our forts
> Out of skulls
> Which we brought from the land of Choseros
> By force and on top of the booty.
> Our messenger is the one who made us
> Noble builders of Glory.
> Our Messenger is the sun of truth
> Who lit the face of the world.[37]

CALLOUS KILLING

Talk of beheadings and killings is not unusual in class discussions, or even casual conversations within Muslim circles. One could find hundreds of examples of beheadings in Muslim writings, which are currently being used in school textbooks, news media, poetry, and even street graffiti. One example which comes from Islamic history goes as follows:

Abu Musa said: "I came to the Prophet along with two men of Ash'ariyin, one on my right and the other on my left, while Allah's Apostle was brushing his teeth. Both men asked him for employment. The Prophet said, you with the Truth, these two men did not tell me what was in their hearts and I did not feel (realize) that they were seeking employment." As if I were looking now at his Siwak (toothbrush) being drawn to a corner under his lips, he said, "We never appoint for our affairs anyone who seeks to be employed. But O Abu Musa, go to Yemen." The Prophet then sent Mu'adh bin Jabal after him and when Mu'adh reached him, he spread out a cushion for him and requested him to get down (and sit on the cushion). Behold, there was a fettered man beside Abu Musa. Mu'adh asked, "Who is this (man)?"

Abu Musa said: "He was a Jew and became a Muslim, and then reverted back to Judaism." Then Abu Musa requested Mu'adh to sit down, but Mu'adh said, "I will not sit down till he has been killed."

This is the judgment of Allah and his apostle [for such cases] and he repeated it three times. Then Abu Musa ordered that the man be killed, and he was killed. Abu Musa added that they discussed the night prayers and one of them said, "I pray and sleep, and I hope that Allah will reward me for my sleep as well as for my prayers."

The historic regaling of the fettered Jew is told to make believers callous. After beheading the Jew, the two men sat and had a silly discussion about prayers and sleep. Usually, and in most acts of jihad killing, one sees the jihadists smirk and smile, adding a sense of joy and pleasure to the process of killing and/or torturing. The Quran has many other orders for beheadings and killings:

"Strike terror (into the hearts of) the enemies of Allah and your enemies." (Sura 8:60)

"Fight (kill) them (non-Muslims), and Allah will punish (torment) them by your hands, cover them with shame." (Sura 9:14)

"I will instill terror into the hearts of the unbelievers, smite ye above their necks and smite all their finger-tips off them. It is not ye who slew them; it was Allah." (Sura 8:12, 17)

"When ye encounter the infidels, strike off their heads till ye have made a great slaughter among them." (Sura 47:3)

When we look at Mormonism, we find similar stories. The following is from the autobiography "Brigham's Destroying Angel" by William Adams Hickman. It explains the killing of a fellow Mormon, Richard Yates, who was killed for selling ammunition to government soldiers, thus being considered a spy:

"Supper was brought to us, and Yates soon went to sleep on his blankets. Flack and Meacham spread their blankets and soon went to sleep also. I told them to do it, as I would guard the prisoner until I called them...when Col. Jones and two others, Hosea Stout and another man whose name I do not recollect, came to my camp-fire and asked if Yates was asleep. I told them he was, upon which his brains were knocked out with an ax...Our horses were immediately sent for, and we were off before daylight; went to the next station, found my brother, got breakfast, and arrived at Salt Lake that day."[38]

Here is another story of a callous killing from within Mormonism we need to mention. It is a memoir written by the wife of Jesse Hartley who was murdered by William Adams Hickman (or Wild Bill Hickman):

"I married Jesse Hartley, knowing he was a Gentile in fact, though he passed for a Mormon; but that made no difference with me, because he was a noble man, who had sought only the right. By being my husband he was brought into closer contact with the heads of the Church, and thus was soon enabled to learn of many things he did not approve, and of which I was ignorant, though brought up among the Saints, and which if known to the Gentiles, would have greatly damaged us. I do not understand all he discovered or all he did; but they found he had written against the Church, and he was cut off, and the Prophet required as an atonement for his sins, that he should lay down his life; that he should be sacrificed in the endowment rooms, where such atonement is made. This I never knew until my husband told me; but it is true. They kill those there who have committed sins too great to be atoned for in any other way. The Prophet says if they submit to this, he can save them; otherwise they are lost. Oh! that is horrible. But my husband refused to be sacrificed, and so set out alone for the United States, thinking there might be at least a hope of success. I told him when he left me, and left his child, that he would be killed; and so he was. William Hickman and another Danite shot him in the Cañons; and I have often since been obliged to cook for this man, when he passed this way, knowing all the while he had killed my husband. My child soon followed its father, and I hope to die also; for why should I live? They have brought me here, where I wish to remain rather than to return to Salt Lake, where the murderers of my husband curse the earth, and roll in affluence unpunished."[39]

In 1858, an extremely grotesque double murder was committed. Henry Jones and his mother were both put to death. These murders were obviously the direct result of Brigham Young's doctrine of "blood atonement." Two months before Henry Jones was actually murdered, he was viciously attacked. Hosea Stout, a very dedicated Mormon defender, wrote the following regarding the first attack on Jones: "Saturday 27 Feb 1858. This evening several persons disguised as Indians entered Henry Jones" house and dragged him out of bed with a whore and castrated him by a square & close amputation."[40]

On April 19, 1859, the newspaper Valley Tan printed an affidavit by Nathaniel Case which contained a statement implicating a bishop and other Mormons who lived in Payson: "Nathaniel Case being sworn, says: that he has resided in the Territory of Utah since the year 1850; lived with Bishop Hancock (Charles Hancock) in the town of Payson, at the time Henry Jones and his mother were murdered...The night prior to the murder a secret council meeting was held in the upper room of Bishop Hancock's house; [Nathaniel] saw Charles Hancock, George W. Hancock, Daniel Rawson, James Bracken, George Patten and Price Nelson go into that meeting that night...About 8 o'clock in the evening of the murder the company gathered at Bishop Hancock's...They said they were going to guard a corral where Henry Jones was going to come that night and steal horses; they had guns. "I had a good mini rifle and Bishop Hancock wanted to borrow it; I refused to lend it to him. The above persons all went away together...Next morning I heard that Henry Jones and his mother had been killed. I went down to the dug-out where they lived...The old woman was laying on the ground in the dugout on a little straw, in the clothes in which she was killed. She had a bullet hole through her head...In about 15 or 20 minutes Henry Jones was brought there and laid by her side; they then threw some old bed clothes over them and an old feather bed and then pulled the dug-out on top of them..."[41]

In 1834, Joseph Smith and Sidney Rigdon reportedly advocated decapitation or throat-cutting for various crimes and sins.[42]

Porter Rockwell was one of the most vicious Danites (Soldier of the "Army of Zion"). Stewart Durham writes, "The most notorious Danite was (Orrin) Porter Rockwell, the so-called "Destroying Angel," who served occasionally as bodyguard for Joseph Smith...and for Brigham Young. Though he was never convicted, Rockwell was implicated in several murders, including the 1850 decapitation in Utah of a Missourian who was said to be a member of the mob that killed Joseph Smith."[43]

MORE MUSLIM MURDERS

Before I present more stories of Islamic murders, here's a quote that comes from the founder of Islam, Muhammad: "The sword is the key of heaven and hell."[44] This recorded murder comes from the Hadith:

> "One of the Meccans recognized me and shouted, 'That is Amr!' They rushed after us, saying, 'By Allah, Amr has not come here for any good purpose! He has come for some evil reason.' Amr had been a cutthroat and a desperado before accepting Islam.

Amr said, 'Let's wait here until the cry has died down. They are sure to hunt for us tonight and tomorrow.' I was still in the cave when Uthman bin Malik came riding proudly on his horse. He reached the entrance to our cave and I said to my Ansar companion, 'If he sees us, he will tell everyone in Mecca.' So I went out and stabbed him with my dagger. He gave a shout and the Meccans came to him while I went back to my hiding place. Finding him at the point of death, they said, 'By Allah we knew that Amr came for no good purpose.' The death of their companion impeded their search for us, for they carried him away. I went into a cave with my bow and arrows. While I was in it, a one-eyed man from the Banu Bakr came in driving some sheep. He said, 'Who's there?' I said [lied], 'I'm a Banu Bakr.' 'So am I.' Then he laid down next to me, and raised his voice in song: 'I will not believe in the faith of the Muslims.' I said, 'You will soon see!' Before long the Bedouin went to sleep and started snoring. So I killed him in the most dreadful way that anybody has ever killed. I leant over him, struck the end of my bow into his good eye, and thrust it down until it came out the back of his neck. After that I rushed out like a wild beast and took flight. I came to the village of Naqi and recognized two Meccan spies. I called for them to surrender. They said no so I shot an arrow and killed one, and then I tied the other up and took him to Muhammad."[45]

In the Quran, Sura 9:30, it reads: "And the Jews say: Uzair is the son of Allah; and the Christians say: The Messiah is the son of Allah; these are the words of their mouths; they imitate the saying of those who disbelieved before; may Allah destroy them; how they are turned away!"[46]

Bat Ye'or has recorded a sinister story that happened on Bacon Island, Indonesia, wherein "a whole village was captured and told they would be released if they gave up their village elders and church leaders. The elders and leaders surrendered themselves and were beheaded. The rest of the villagers, both men and women, were forcibly circumcised. Any who refused were killed." If this story sounds familiar, maybe it's because it parallels a story of The Mountain Meadow massacre, which is never mentioned in American History school textbooks. On September 7th, 1857, approximately forty families from Arkansas (called the Fancher party) were traveling to California, stopping at Salt Lake City, where they were attacked by a group of Native American Paiutes and Mormon militiamen dressed as Native Americans. The Fancher party defended itself by encircling and lowering their wagons, wheels chained together, along with digging shallow trenches and throwing dirt both below and into the wagons, which made a stronger barrier. Seven emigrants were killed during the opening attack and were buried somewhere within the wagon encirclement. Sixteen more were wounded. The attack continued for five days, during which time the besieged families had little or no access to fresh water, food or game and their ammunition was depleted.[47]

On Friday, September 11 two Mormon militiamen approached the Fancher party wagons with a white flag and were soon followed by an Indian agent and militia officer John D. Lee. Lee told the battle weary emigrants he had negotiated a truce with the Paiutes, whereby they would be escorted safely to Cedar City under Mormon protection in exchange for leaving all their livestock and supplies to the Native Americans. Accepting this, they were split into three groups. Seventeen of the youngest children along with a few mothers and the wounded were put into wagons, which were followed by all the women and older children walking in a second group. Bringing up the rear were the adult males of the Fancher party, each walking with an armed Mormon militiaman at his right. Making their way back northeast towards Cedar City, the three groups gradually became strung out and visually separated by shrubs and a shallow hill. After about 2 kilometers, all of the men, women, older children and wounded were massacred by Mormon militia and Paiutes who had hidden nearby. A few who escaped the initial slaughter were quickly chased down and killed. Two teenaged girls, Rachel and Ruth Dunlap, managed to climb down the side of a steep gully and hide among a clump of oak trees for several minutes. They were spotted by a Paiute chief from Parowan, who took them to Lee. 18 year old Ruth Dunlap reportedly fell to her knees and pleaded, "Spare me, and I will love you all my life!" (Lee denied this). 50 years later, a Mormon woman who was a child at the time of the massacre recalled hearing LDS women in St. George say both girls were raped before they were killed.[48]

It is said that the survivors of the Mountain Meadows Massacre were spared because they were young with innocent blood, which would put them under the age of eight at the time. There were approximately seventeen survivors.

Similarly, in Islamic history, the Jews of Banu Qurayza suffered a similar fate:

"Huyai Ibn Akhtab, the chief of the Bani Nadeer and Safiyah's father, was captured in this siege and brought to the Prophet with his hands tied to his neck with a rope. In an audacious defiance he rejected Muhammad and preferred to be beheaded than submitting to his religion by force. He was ordered to sit down and was beheaded on the spot.

"To separate men from the boys, the youngsters were examined and if they had grown any pubic hair, it was enough to behead them."[49]

THE APOCLYPSE
SHOKO ASAHARA

Shoko Asahara was the founder of the cult called Aum Shinrikyo, which translates into "supreme truth." The group is now labeled as "Aleph." It is a Japanese religious cult obsessed with the apocalypse whose teachings are based on tenets borrowed from Hinduism and Buddhism. Their more benign activities include yoga, meditation, and breathing exercises.

The previously obscure group became infamous in 1995 when some of its members released deadly sarin nerve gas into the Tokyo subway system, killing twelve people and sending more than 5,000 others to hospitals.[50]

Millennial visions and apocalyptic scenarios dominate the group's doctrine, as is evidenced by the prominent role of Nostradamus as a prophet in Aum Shinrikyo teaching. Asahara has, on many occasions, claimed to be the reincarnated Jesus Christ, as well as the first "enlightened one" since Buddha. He has frequently preached about a coming Armageddon, which he describes as a global conflict that would, among other things, destroy Japan with nuclear, biological, and chemical weapons. According to Asahara, only the followers of Aum Shinrikyo will survive this conflagration.[51]

JEFFREY LUNDGREN, THE COMMUNITY OF CHRIST

This was a destructive, doomsday cult founded and led by Jeffrey Lundgren. He was the leader of a small group of about one-to two-dozen members who broke away from the Reorganized Church of Jesus Christ of Latter Day Saints (RLDS), now called the Community of Christ. The RLDS Church has a membership of about 250,000, and is centered in Independence, MO. The much larger Church of Jesus Christ of Latter-day Saints split from the RLDS when the former moved to Utah. (The split with this church is reminiscent of the split within Islam which left two sects, Shia and Sunni.)

From the beginning, Jeff Lundgren had promised his followers he would take them to see God. To make the journey, he said, the cult first had to seize the Kirtland Temple and kill anyone who tried to stop them. However, as time went on, Lundgren claimed to have a vision and began to revise this plan.

Lundgren proclaimed he had received a call from God to move to Kirtland, Ohio, a small town near Cleveland which is the historic center of the RLDS. According to Lundgren, he was told by God that he and his supporters would soon witness the second coming of Christ if they moved to Kirtland.[52]

In 1984, Lundgren, his family, and his followers moved to Ohio. In Kirtland, Lundgren received a job as a tour guide at the Kirtland Temple, the first Mormon Temple of early Latter-day Saints (Mormons), deserted in 1837, and now primarily a tourist museum preserved by the RLDS church.[53] The Averys were one of the families to follow Lundgren. The Avery family father, Dennis, sold his Missouri house in order to move his family to Ohio. Avery decided to set aside a relatively small amount of money for his family's use and put it into a bank account. Lungren considered this a sin, because he wanted all of his followers' money to be given entirely to him.[54]

Lundgren split from the RLDS in 1987 because of its liberal tendencies, i.e., allowing women to be ordained as priests. They (Lundgren and his group) engaged in strange sexual rituals, and para-military training. Also in 1987, Lundgren was dismissed as a lay minister by the RLDS.[55]

As time went by, seven of Lundgren's 12 followers had moved into the Lundgren family home. The remaining five were the members of the Avery family. Lundgren felt that the Averys were committing a sin by not living in his house. Dennis Avery was beginning to question Lundgren's teachings during class. Lundgren felt Cheryl Avery was being headstrong, and that she allowed her children to behave unruly. The Averys opposed some of Lundgren's rulings and no one ever questioned his word. Others in the group couldn't understand why the Averys didn't comprehend the potentially lethal ramifications of their actions. The group agreed with Lundgren that the behavior of the Avery family was extremely sinful.[56]

Lundgren had a vision that told him to sacrifice the Avery family. On April 17, 1989, Jeff and the group moved all of the Averys' belongings to the farm and rented a room for them at a nearby motel. Everyone in the house, except the Averys, knew that this would be their last meal as the group sat down for dinner at 6:30 p.m. that night. The mood in the group was solemn. Most had come to accept that the Averys had to pay for their sins.[57] They were executed and buried on the group's ranch. Lundgren referred to the killings of the parents and their three daughters as: "pruning the vineyard."[58]

To get through the gruesome details, I'll praphrase the murders: Mr. Avery was shot twice in the chest, Mrs. Avery was shot three times, twice in the breasts and once in the abdomen. The Averys' 15-year-old daughter was shot twice in the head the first shot which missed, but the second killed her instantly. Thirteen year old Becky Avery was shot twice and left to die, while six-year-old Karen Avery was shot in the chest and head.[59]

After the murders Lundgren decided the group would head for West Virginia, collect their thoughts and await a sign from God that would instruct him on where to find the "golden sword," which some thought to be the "sword of Laban" spoken of in the Book of Mormon. Lundgren believed that the sword would rest with the golden plates from which Joseph Smith is believed to have translated the Book of Mormon.[60]

In Mosiah 1: 16 of the Book of Mormon it reads: "And moreover, he also gave him charge concerning the records which were engraven on the plates of brass; and also the plates of Nephi; and also, the sword of Laban, and the ball or director, which led our fathers through the wilderness, which was prepared by the hand of the Lord that thereby they might be led, every one according to the heed and diligence which they gave unto him."[61]

MAHMOUD AHMADINEJAD

Both sects of Islam believe in the coming of the Mahdi (prophesied Islamic Messiah). Ahmadinejad is part of a secret Shi'a society called the Hojjatieh which is governed by the conviction that the 12th Imam's return will be hastened by the creation of chaos on earth.[62] Shi'a believe in the future coming of the Mahdi; Jaf'ar Al-Sadiq, the sixth Imam, stated regarding the appearance of the Mahdi:

> "Before the coming of the one who will rise (al-qa'im), peace be on him, the people will be chided for their acts of disobedience by a fire which will appear in the sky and a redness which will cover the sky. It will swallow up Baghdad, it will swallow up Kufa (one of three religiously important cities in Islam). There blood will be shed and houses destroyed. Death (fana) will occur amid their people and a fear will come over the people of Iraq from which they shall have no rest."[63]

Shi'a revolutionists are creating havoc in Iraq in an effort to usher the coming of the Mahdi by this self-fulfilling prophecy.

Similarly, Crowley's messenger taught that the old Age of Osiris would soon end followed by the new Age of Horus. But first Earth must bathe in blood. There should be a World War.[64]

CHARLES MANSON AND THE FAMILY

Three months after the "Tate-LaBianca Murders," police arrested a group of cult members for these murders who were known as "The Family" (a.k.a. the Manson Family, the devoted followers of Charles Manson). The Family seemed obsessively fixated upon their leader's dark vision of a coming apocalypse. It is believed that Charles Manson envisioned the Tate-LaBianca murders as a pivotal point in a coming apocalyptic drama. Through these deaths Manson hoped a race war would begin that would engulf society and thus initiate the fulfillment of his prophetic view.[65] A murderous rampage against blacks by frightened whites would have been exploited by the Black Muslims to trigger a war of mutual near-extermination between racist and non-racist whites over the treatment of Blacks. The Black Muslims would arise to finish off sneakily the few whites they would know to have survived. In this epic sequence of events...the Family had little to fear; they would wait out the war in a secret city that was underneath California's Death Valley which they would reach through a hole in the ground. As the actual remaining whites upon the war's true conclusion, they would emerge from underground to rule the now-satisfied blacks, who, as the vision went, would be incapable of running the world. Manson "would scratch [the black man's] fuzzy head and kick him in the butt and tell him to go pick the cotton and go be a good nigger."[66]

———— Resources ————

1. On the movement of Imam Hussein alayhis-salam, Ashura, Fatawa of Imam Shirazi and other most eminent Maraje' on Hussaini Sha'a'er including "TATBIR" or "Qama-Zani," Al-Imam al-Sheikh Abdul Kareem al-Ha'ery The Founder of the current Hawzah in the holy city of Qum.

2. On the movement of Imam Hussein alayhis-salam, Ashura, Fatawa of Imam Shirazi and other most eminent Maraje' on Hussaini Sha'a'er including "TATBIR" or "Qama-Zani," Al-Imam al-Sheikh Muhammad Hussein al-Naa'ini, The teacher of the Maraje' of the holy city of Najaf.

3. No Man Knows My History, The Life of Joseph Smith, By Fawn M. Brodie, First published in 1945 – revised in 1970, Chapter XIX Mysteries of the Kingdom.

4. Mormon Blood Atonemnt: Fact or Fantacy, By Jerald & Sandra Tanner, (This article originally appeared in The Salt Lake City Messenger, Issue No. 92, April, 1997), Wilford Woodruff's Diary, June 2, 1857, Vol. 5, pages 54-55.

5. City of Springdale History On-Line, Springdale Home Page, Chapter two, Certainty in an uncertain world.

6. Heavens Gate Members 'Giggly' After Castration, The Associated Press, The Inevitable Apocalypso, Home to Positive Atheism, April 6, 1997, New York.

7. Wikipedia, Cybele, Burkert, Walter, 1982., Greek Religion (Cambridge:Harvard University Press), especially section III., 3.4 Roller, Lynn E., 1999., In Search of God the Mother: the cult of Anatolian Cybele (U. of California Press) pp.230-231 Mark Munn, "Kybele as Kubaba in a Lydo-Phrygian Context": Emory University cross-cultural conference "Hittites, Greeks and Their Neighbors in Central Anatolia," 2004 (Abstracts) Virgil., The Aeneid trans from Latin by West, David (Penguin Putnam Inc. 2003) p.189-190 ISBN 0-14-044932-9 .

8. Wikipedia, Mesoamerica, Human Sacrifice, Carmack, Robert; et. al. (1996). The legacy of Mesoamerica: history and culture of a Native American civilization. New Jersey: Prentice Hall. ISBN 0-13-337445-9.

9. The Dusting of America, John P. Morgan, M.D. & Doreen Kagan, M.S. From the Journal of Psychedelic Drugs 12(3-4), Jul-Dec 1980, Gay, B. 1978. The evils of angel dust and other " a P P P drugs.," Sepia VOL 27: 17-19., Koper, P. 1978. Angel death. New Times March 20., Table III, Popular Horror Tales of PCP Users.

10. Prophet of Doom, By Craig Winn, 25 Prophet of Doom, Muslim:C28B20N4626.

11. Prophet of Doom, By Craig Winn, 17 Good Muslims Kill, Muslim:B20N4678.

12. MEMRI TV, 1/3/2005, Clip No. 463, Palestinian-Kuwaiti Sheikh Ahmad Qattan on Allah's Rewards to a Martyr.

13. Mormon Quotes, Brigham Young, Journal of Discourses, Volume: 4, Page: 219.

14. Intelligence and Terrorism Information Center at the Center for Special Studies (C.S.S), Special Information Bulletin, 2004, Student timetable commemorating a Hamas suicide bomber.

15. Intelligence and Terrorism Information Center at the Center for Special Studies (C.S.S), Special Information Bulletin, 2003, Appendix A: Posters and a leaflet commemorating the two students who carried out the suicide bombing attack at the Hillel Café in Jerusalem (September 9, 2003) and in Ramla [i.e., Tserifin].

16. Wikipedia, Mohammad Bouyeri, Arrest.

17. Thetruereligion.org, Author: Admin, Invitation to Islam, Issue 1, May 1997.

18. MEMRI The Middle East Media Research Institute, TV Monitor Project, 10/28/2005, Clip No. 917, A Bridegroom Turns into a Suicide Bomber in an Iranian TV Music Video.

19. Palestinian Media Watch, Condoleezza Rice, By Itamar Marcus and Barbara Crook – July 30, 2006, Palestinians Love to Hate, 1. Cartoons brainwashing children to die as Shahids (Martyrs for Allah).

20. Wikipedia, Woo Bum-Kon, April 26, 1982, Village to village, Suicide.

21. Wikipedia, Seppuko, Artist: Yoshitoshi Tsukioka, created about 1890., Title: Akashi Gidayu, No 83 100 Aspects of the Moon Series

22. Seppuko – Ritual Suicide

23. Wikipedia, Sepukko, Overview, The Samurai Way of Death, Samurai: The World of the Warrior (ch.4), Dr. Stephen Turnbull.

24. Wikipedia, Sen no Rikyû.

25. Opentopia, Hojo Ujimasa, Turnbull, Stephen (1998). 'The Samurai Sourcebook.' London: Cassell & Co.

26. Ibid.

27. Historical Artifacts, Death by Sallekhana, An Example of Nishidhi Stone.

28. Wikipedia, Sallekhana, 5 Violations of the Vow of Santhara, Jainworld.com Pratikraman.

29. Wikipedia, Santhara, Why not eat?

30. Wikipeida, Karni Mata.

31. National Geographic News, Rats Rule at Indian Temple, Page 1.

32. National Geographic News, Rats Rule at Indian Temple, Page 1, Photograph by Pat Hankinson.

33. Wikipedia, Mesoamerica, Human Sacrifice, Carmack, Robert; et. al. (1996). The legacy of Mesoamerica: history and culture of a Native American civilization. New Jersey: Prentice Hall. ISBN 0-13-337445-9.

34. Windows to The Universe, Tonatiuh.

35. The Origin of Ball Games, By Gerald Singer.

36. Mexico, Press Room, Mexico From A to Z, Ancient Civilizations of Mexico, W – Wall of Skulls.

37. The Manhattan Raids, Islamic Nasheed.

38. Brigham's Destroying Angel, Of The Notorious Bill Hickman, Written by Himself, with Explanatory Notes by J. H. Beadle ESQ. of Salt Lake City., 1904 Edition, Chapter V., A Chapter of Horrors, Page 125.

39. Brigham's Destroying Angel, Appendix C.

40. Mormon Blood Atonement, Fact or Fantasy?, By Jerald & Sandra Tanner, This article originally appeared in The Salt Lake City Messenger, Issue No. 92, April, 1997, On the Mormon Frontier; The Diary of Hosea Stout, Vol. 2, page 653.

41. Mormon Blood Atonement, Fact or Fantasy?, By Jerald & Sandra Tanner, This article originally appeared in The Salt Lake City Messenger, Issue No. 92, April, 1997, Nathaniel Case., "Sworn to and signed before me this 9th day of April, 1859.

42. Mormon History – A Chronology, 1843.

43. Wikipedia, Porter Rockwell, Biography, Durham, 331-332.

44. The Great Divide, By Alvin J. Schmidt, Chapter 1, Jesus and Muhammad: Polar Opposites, Page 24, Cited in Arthur Gilman, The Story of the Saracens: From the Earliest Times to the Fall of Baghdad (New York: G.P. Putnam's Sons, 1896), 143.

45. Prophet of Doom, By Craig Winn, Muhammad's Own Words, Murder, Tabari VII:148 – Tabari VII:149.

46. The Koran, Browse the Koran, Sura 9:30.

47. Wikipedia, Mountain Meadows Massacre, Mountain Meadows, Shirts, (1994) Paragraph 8.

48. Wikipedia, Mountain Meadows Massacre, Mountain Meadows, Lee was a scribe for the Council of 50 and a friend of both Joseph Smith, Jr. and Brigham Young, Shirts, (1994) Paragraph 9, Gibbs (1910) p. 36., St. George is about 15 miles from the Mountain Meadows., Gibbs (1910), Part 3 under heading "The Massacre," paragraphs 16-19.

49. Book 38, Number 4390, Narrated Atiyyah al-Qurazi

50. Wikipedia, Xenu, Summary, Jon Atack, A Piece Of Blue Sky (Kensington Publishing Corporation, New York, 1990; ISBN 0-8184-0499-X)

51. Ron (and indeed everyone) has been to Heaven, Hubbard Communications Office, Saint Hill Manor, East Grinstead, Sussex, HCO Bulletin of May 11, AD13, Central Orgs, Franchise, Routine 3 Heaven.

52. Prophet of Doom, By Craig Winn, 72: The Jinn, Maududi's Qur'an commentary.

53. Commemorating the prophet's rapture and ascension to his lord, III. The Collated Hadith of Isra' and Mi`raj

54. Wikipedia, Genie, Jinn in Islam

55. Prophet of Doom, By Craig Winn, 72: The Jinn, Maududi's Qur'an commentary.

56. Commemorating the prophet's rapture and ascension to his lord, III. The Collated Hadith of Isra' and Mi`raj

57. Muhammadanism, The Occult in the Qur'an, Muhammad's Fear of the Occult, In Sura al-Falaq 113:1-5.

58. Prophet of Doom, By Craig Winn, 72: The Jinn, Maududi's Qur'an commentary.

59. Bukhari 7/527 and Abu Daud 3722

60. Wikipedia, Cult Suicide, Solar Temple

61. Encyclopedia Mythica, Tecciztecatl, By Micha F. Lindemans

62. Masonic Symbols and the LDS Temple, By Sandra Tanner, Morals and Dogma of the Ancient and Accepted Scottish Rite of Freemasonry, discusses the various Masonic symbols and their meaning.

63. Wikipedia, The Book of Lies (Crowley), Crowley, Aleister (1979), The Confessions of Aleister Crowley, London; Boston: Routledge & Kegan Paul Crowley, Aleister (1978), The Book of Lies, New York, NY: S. Weiser.

64. Joseph Smith: America's Hermetic Prophet, By Lance S. Owens, Dean C. Jessee, ed., The Papers of Joseph Smith, Vol. 1 (Salt Lake City: Deseret Book Co., 1989), 6. For a detailed examination of Joseph Smith's early years, see

Richard L. Bushman, Joseph Smith and the Beginnings of Mormonism (Urbana: University of Illinois Press, 1984). Despite many interpretive limitations, Smith's best over-all biography remains Fawn M. Brodie, No Man Knows My History (New York: Alfred A. Knopf, 1945, 2nd ed. 1971).

65. Cult Education and Recovery, Sponsored by the Rick A. Ross Institute, The Changing Face of Cults, The Tate-LaBianca Murders and The Manson Family, September 1999, By Rick Ross, "Manson's legacy of fear lives on 30 years later" Reuters, August 9, 1999 By Michael Miller "30 years later, Manson cult thrives" Associated Press, August 9, 1999 By Linda Deutsch "A look at key figures in the Tate-LaBiannca murders 30 years ago" The Associated Press, August 8, 1999.

66. Wikipedia, Charles Manson, Possible Motives, 7.

Chapter Twelve – Entertaining Devils

In this section I'll be showing you how Joseph Smith, Lucy Mack Smith, the jinn, Allah, etc., are all connected to dark magic.

For example: jinn are believed to have the power to transform into other animals and humans, but they are known to prefer the form of a snake.[1]

ABRAXAS

The demon of Abraxas has the feet of snakes. In *The Book of The Law*, Hadit describes himself in this way: "I am the Secret Serpent coiled about to spring: in my coiling there is joy. If I lift up my head, I and my Nuit are one. If I droop down mine head, and shoot forth venom, then is rapture of the earth, and I and the earth are one. There is great danger in me..."[2]

There was a serpent that was an ancient Near Eastern and Aegean god of wisdom, who was always, quite naturally, an earth symbol.[3]

The worship of the serpent can be seen in Latin America. The Mexican century was represented by a circle, having the sun in the center, surrounded by the symbols of the years. The circumference was a serpent twisted into four knots at the cardinal points.[4]

The Mexican month was divided into twenty days; the serpent and dragon symbolized two of them. In Mexico there was also a temple dedicated to "the god of the air;" and the door of it was formed so as to resemble a serpent's mouth.[5]

MAYA VISION SERPENT

The serpent was a very important social and religious symbol, revered by the Mayans. Maya mythology describes serpents as being the vehicles by which celestial bodies, such as the sun and stars, cross the heavens. The shedding of their skin made them a symbol of rebirth and renewal. The Vision Serpent is thought to be the most important of the Mayan serpents. "It was usually bearded and had a rounded snout. It was also often depicted as having two heads, or with the spirit of a god or ancestor emerging from its jaws." During Mayan bloodletting rituals, participants would experience visions in which they communicated with the ancestors or gods. These visions took the form of a giant serpent "which served as a gateway to the spirit realm.[6]

In the Book of Genesis the snake is viewed as Satan: "Now the serpent was more crafty than any of the wild animals the Lord God had made. He said to the woman, "Did God really say, 'You must not eat from any tree in the garden?'" (Genesis 3:1)

VISIONS FROM THE DEVIL

There are also factual stories that prove visions from the devil and/or fear of being possessed:

Here is Muhammad explaining one of his dreams: "When I thought I was nearly dead I said, 'What shall I read;' only to deliver myself from him, lest he should do the same thing to me again. He said, 'Read in the name of your lord who created man of blood coagulated. Read! Your lord taught by the pen.' So I read it, and he departed from me. I awoke from my sleep. These words were written on my heart. None of Allah's creatures was more hateful to me than an ecstatic poet or a man possessed.' I thought, 'Woe is me, I'm a possessed poet.'"[7]

"The Prophet said, 'A good dream is from Allah, and a bad dream is from Satan.'" – Bukhari: V9B87N113[8]

"Magic was worked on Allah's Apostle and he was bewitched so that he began to imagine doing things which in fact, he had not done." (Bukhari: V7B71N661)

Joseph Smith even admitted to once having a revelation from Satan. David Whitmer (one of Three Witnesses to the Book of Mormon's Golden Plates) writes: "Joseph looked into the hat in which he placed the stone, and received a revelation that some of the brethren should go to Toronto, Canada, and that they would sell the copyright of the Book of Mormon. Hiram Page and Oliver Cowdery went to Toronto on this mission, but they failed entirely to sell the copyright, returning without any money. Joseph was at my father's house when they returned. I was there also, and am an eye witness to these facts. Jacob Whitmer and John Whitmer were also present when Hiram Page and Oliver Cowdery returned from Canada. Well, we were all in great trouble; and we asked Joseph how it was that he had received a revelation from the lord for some brethren to go to Toronto and sell the copyright, and the brethren had utterly failed in their undertaking. Joseph did not know how it was, so he enquired of the lord about it, and behold the following revelation came through the stone: some revelations are of God; some revelations are of man; and some revelations are of the devil. So we see that the revelation to go to Toronto and sell the copyright was not of God, but was of the devil or the heart of man. I will say here that I could tell you other false revelations that came through Brother Joseph as a mouthpiece, (not through the stone) but this will suffice. Many of Brother Joseph's revelations were never printed. The revelation to go to Canada was written down on paper, but was never printed."[9]

These "accidental" situations from the devil are nothing new.

When the messenger of god (Muhammad) saw how his tribe turned their backs on him and was grieved to see them shunning the message he had brought to them from god, he longed in his soul for something to come to him from god which would reconcile him with his tribe. With his love for his tribe and his eagerness for their welfare it would have delighted him if some of the difficulties which they made for him could have been smoothed out, and he debated with himself and fervently desired such an outcome. Then god revealed: "By the Star when it sets, your comrade does not err, nor is he deceived; nor does he speak out of (his own) desire..." When he came upon these words: "Have you thought upon al-Lat and al-Uzza and Manat, the third, the other?" Satan cast on his tongue, because of his inner debates and what he desired to bring to his people, the words: "These are the high flying cranes; verily their intercession is accepted with approval." When Quraysh heard this, they rejoiced and were happy and delighted at the way in which he spoke of their gods, and they listened to him, while the Muslims, having complete trust in their prophet in respect of the messages which he brought from god, did not suspect him of error, illusion, or mistake. Referenced in the Hadith and Quran. Later Muslims, ashamed that their self declared prophet spoke Satan's words, denied the event occurred.[10]

Muslim authorities admit that Muhammad was at one time inspired by Satan to put some verses into the Quran. Some time later, upon receiving further revelation from Jibril, that those verses were not from god, but interjected by Satan, they were removed again. The Quran reports about it in Sura 22:52: "Never sent we a messenger or a prophet before thee but when He recited (the message) Satan proposed (opposition) in respect of that which he recited thereof. But Allah abolished that which Satan proposed. Then Allah established his revelations. Allah is knower, wise;"[11]

■ ■ ■ ■ ■

When Hitler was fifteen years old he was confident that he was going to be the one that would lead humanity into a brand new world.

He had just finished listening to Wagner's Rienzie play with his childhood friend, Gustl Kubizek. Kubizek watched with horror as a being began speaking out of Hitler's mouth in a most unusual voice. This voice began speaking visions of how Hitler was going to change European history, that one day, he would receive a Mandate from his people to lead them "from servitude to the heights of freedom, a special mission which would one day be entrusted to him."[12]

■ ■ ■ ■ ■

William Stafford, a neighbor of Joseph Smith, swore that Smith told him there was buried money on his property, but that it could not be secured until a black sheep was taken to the spot, and "led around a circle" bleeding, with its throat cut. This ritual was necessary to appease the evil spirit guarding the treasure. "To gratify my curiosity," Stafford acknowledged, "I let them have a large fat sheep. Afterwards they informed me that the sheep was killed pursuant to commandment; but as there was some mistake in the process, it did not have the desired effect. This, I believe, is the only time they ever made money-digging a profitable business."

THE SEER STONE

In the Latter Day Saint movement, the use of seer stones has been a form of divination which played a significant role in shaping the movement's history and theology. Seer stones of particular importance to the movement include a "chocolate-colored" stone that Joseph Smith, Jr. found while digging a neighbor's well, and a pair of crystals joined in the form of a large pair of spectacles referred to as the Urim and Thummim or Interpreters. Prior to founding the Latter Day Saint movement, Smith used seer stones to find buried treasure. He also used the stones to discover the

One of several magical parchments in the possession of the Joseph Smith family. This one is called the "Holiness to the Lord" parchment.

words of the Book of Mormon. Seer stones are also mentioned several times in the Book of Mormon and in other Latter Day Saint scripture.[13] "For behold, the language which ye shall write I have confounded; wherefore I will cause in my own due time that these stones shall magnify to the eyes of men these things which ye shall write."[14] from The Book of Mormon, Ether 3: 24.

Using seer stones (or sometimes called "peep" stones), is the act of "scrying" or "crystal gazing." Scrying has been used in many cultures as a means of seeing the past, present, or future; in this sense scrying constitutes a form of divination or fortune-telling.[15] From the Book of Mormon:

"But a seer can know of things which are past, and also of things which are to come, and by them shall all things be revealed, or, rather, shall secret things be made manifest, and hidden things shall come to light, and things which are not known shall be made known by them, and also things shall be made known by them which otherwise could not be known."[16]

When one stares into the media for a long period of time, he may receive visions of various nature. Some believe that scrying is a form of divination, while others believe that the visions merely comes from the subconscious.[17]

The most common media used for scrying are:

- Flat, polished portions of Obsidian

- Crystal balls, crystals, precious stones, polished quartz, or another transparent body, this is called crystallomancy. Sometimes "crystal gazing" refers specifically to crystallomancy. Crystal balls are also called shew stones. A stone or crystal is also called a seer stone or peep stone.

- Water or another liquid, this is called hydromancy.

- Mirrors, this is called catoptromancy, also known as captromancy, enoptromancy, or mirror gazing.[18]

Specific objects that have been used for scrying include:

- A pool of ink in the hand (Egypt)

- The liver of an animal (tribes of the North-West Indian frontier)

- A hole filled with water (Polynesia)

- Quartz crystals (Apaches and the Euahlayi tribe of New South Wales)

- A smooth slab of polished black stone (the Huille-che of South America)

- Water in a vessel (Zulus and Siberians)

- A crystal (the Incas)

- A mirror (classical Greece and the Middle Ages)

- A fingernail

- A sword blade

- A ring-stone

- A glass of sherry

- The burning of a poppy flower bud on hot coals[19]

Around 2,000 BC, Greece, as well as "early" Britain and its subsequent Celtic population, was practicing many forms of scrying. The media often used were beryl, crystal, black glass, polished quartz, water, and other transparent or light-catching bodies.[20]

The Shahnameh, a semi-historical epic work written in the late 10th century, gives a description of what was called the Cup of Jamshid or Jaam-e Jam, used in pre-Islamic Persia. The cup was used by wizards and practitioners of the esoteric sciences for observing all the seven layers of the universe. The cup also contained an elixir of immortality.[21]

Joseph Smith utilized a seer stone. Beginning in his late-adolescent years, Joseph was first recognized by others to have paranormal abilities, and between 1822 and 1827 he was enlisted to act as "seer" (which is why Mormons call him a "seer") for several groups engaged in treasure digging. Not only did he possess a "seer stone" into which he could gaze and locate things lost or hidden in the earth, but it recently became evident this same stone was probably the "Urim and Thummim" later used to "translate" portions of the Book of Mormon.[22]

David Whitmer wrote: "Joseph Smith would put the seer stone into a hat, and put his face in the hat, drawing it closely around his face to exclude the light; and in the darkness the spiritual light would shine. A piece of something resembling parchment would appear, and on that appeared the writing. One character at a time would appear, and under it was the interpretation in English. Brother Joseph would read off the English to Oliver Cowdery, who was his principal scribe, and when it was written down and repeated to Brother Joseph to see if it was correct, then it would disappear, and another character with the interpretation would appear.

Thus, the Book of Mormon was translated by the gift and power of god, and not by any power of man."[23]

It is likely Joseph Smith was cognizant of at least the rudiments of ceremonial magic during his adolescent years. A possible occult mentor to the young Smith has also been identified – a physician named Dr. Luman Walter. Walter was a distant cousin of Smith's future wife and a member of the circle associated with Smith's early treasure quests. By contemporary reports he was not only a physician, but a magician and mesmerist who had traveled extensively in Europe to obtain "profound learning" – probably including knowledge of alchemy, paracelcian medicine, and hermetic lore.[24]

According to the majority of Islamic scholars, the Quran states that the devil was not an angel (which is believed by Christians), but a jinn who was given a higher honor and rank than angels. In fact, it is mentioned in the Quran that Prophet Muhammad was sent as a prophet to both "humanity and the jinn." In fact, according to some hadith, the great-grandson of Iblis, or the devil (who was born before mankind), converted to Islam during the time of Muhammad.[25]

Then there is Abraxas who was somehow used by Lucy Mack Smith. This subject is further explored in LaMar Petersen's new book, The Creation of the Book of Mormon. "Lucy [Joseph Smith's mother] provided an even more revealing glimpse into the Smith family's involvement in magical abracadabra and other aspects of folk magic: 'Let not the reader suppose that because I shall pursue another topic for a season that we stopped our labor and went at trying to win the faculty of Abrac [Abraxas], drawing magic circles or soothsaying [sic] to the neglect of all kinds of business. [We] never during our lives suffered one important interest to swallow up every other obligation but whilst we worked with our hands we endeavored to remember [sic] the service of and the welfare of our souls.'"[26]

The Basilidian sect of the Gnostics of the second century claimed Abraxas as their supreme god, and said that Jesus Christ was only a phantom sent to earth by him.[27] Finally, Lucy mentions the "faculty of Abrac," which refs to the deity regarded by the second-century Basilidians as the "chief of the 365 genies ruling the days of the year."[28]

In Muhammad's day, 365 idols were worshipped at the Kaaba, standing in the great courtyard. One of those deities was called Allah and was the god of the Quarish tribe, of which Muhammad was a member. Allah was the main exalted god of the 365 that were worshipped. When the Muslims took control of Mecca, all the idols except Allah, the idol of their tribe, were destroyed.[29]

Now to Hitler. As you may already know, many people accuse Hitler and his Nazi regime of being Christian, therefore blaming Christianity for the Holocaust. From my research, this accusation cannot possibly be true. In fact, let's get this out of the way – Hitler was not a Christian. I will show you why...

FÖRSTER-NIETZSCHE

In 1930, Förster-Nietzsche, sister of philosopher Friedrich Nietzsche, (her full name, Therese Elisabeth Alexandra Förster-Nietzsche) was a German nationalist and anti-Semite, and became a supporter of the Nazi Party. After Hitler and the Nazis came to power in 1933, the Nietzsche Archive received financial support and publicity from the government, in return for which Förster-Nietzsche bestowed her brother's considerable prestige on the régime. Förster-Nietzsche's funeral in 1935 was attended by Hitler and several high-ranking Nazi officials.[30]

Friedrich Nietzsche once wrote:

"Against 'meaninglessness' on the one hand, against moral value judgments on the other: to what extent has all science and philosophy so far been influenced by moral judgments? and won't this net us the hostility of science? Or an anti-scientific mentality? Critique of Spinozism. Residues of Christian value judgments are found everywhere in socialistic and positivistic systems. A critique of Christian morality is still Lacking."[31]

THE THETAN AND AL-JINN

In Scientology they are thetans and in Islam they are Jinns. When a Scientologist escalates himself/herself to the high level of OT 3 (operating thetan three) they are told that they are full of the thetans (or souls) of murdered space-aliens. Roughly 2,500 of them. And they have to talk to them telepathically to make them go away.[32]

In Islam, it is said that all Muslims are possessed: "Allah's Messenger said: 'Everyone has an attaché from amongst the jinn (devils).' The Prophet's companions asked Allah's Messenger, is there one with you too.' He said: 'Yes, but Allah helps me so I am safe from his hand and he does not command me but for good.'"[33] This reminds me of what the Mormons believe. The Church teaches that we existed in heaven with god (our literal father) as spirits before we became human.[34]

MUHAMMAD FOUND NOTHING NEW

Before Muhammad saw this angel of light, Muhammad was engaged in what was known in Arabia as tahannuth (religious devotion to pagan idols):

"The Apostle would pray in seclusion on Hira every year for a month to practice tahannuth as was the custom of the Quraysh in the heathen days. (In other words, Muhammad was a heathen and the Islamic Pillar requiring Ramadhan fasting was pagan.) After praying in seclusion, he would walk around the Kaaba seven times."[38]

This is similar to the Islam that is practiced today; tahannuth included self-justification, and meditation during the pagan holy month of Ramadhan.[39] There was nothing new, simply the names switched from tahannuth to Islam.

There is an array of evidence that black stones were commonly worshipped in the Arab world. In 190 A.D. Clement of Alexandria mentioned that "the Arabs worship stone." He was alluding to the black stone of Dusares at Petra. In the 2nd century, Maximus Tyrius wrote, "The Arabians pay homage to what god I know not, which they represent by a quadrangular stone." Maximus was speaking of the Kaaba (Ka'ba) that contains the Black Stone.[40]

THE DIRTY CLEANSING

Since there is no salvation offered by many cults, they present physical washing as a form of fulfilling spiritual cleansing and completion. L. Ron Hubbard, in his book *Clear Body, Clear Mind* purports to "flush" poisons from the body's fat-stores using an intensive regimen of jogging, oil ingestion, sauna, and high doses of vitamins, particularly niacin.[41]

Similarly, in Islam the Hadith states: "Truly, Allah loves those who turn unto Him in repentance and loves those who purify themselves (by taking a bath and cleaning and washing thoroughly their private parts, bodies, for their prayers etc.)." (Al Baqarah 2:222) And then there is this verse as well:

"The Messenger of Allah (peace and blessings be upon him) said: Cleanliness is half of faith and Alhamdulillah (Praise be to Allah) fills the scale, and Subhan Allah (Glory be to Allah) and Alhamdulillah (Praise be to Allah) fill up what is between the heavens and the earth, and prayer is a light, and charity is proof (of one's faith) and endurance is a brightness and the Quran is a proof on your behalf, or against you. All men go out early in the morning and sell themselves, thereby setting themselves free or destroying themselves."[42] One of the types of cleanliness in Islam is "to cleanse one's body, dress or place from an impurity of filth."[43]

Mormons follow a strict health code called the "word of wisdom," which prohibits wine, tobacco, tea, coffee, and any type of hot drinks. In Doctrine and Covenants it reads:

"And all saints who remember to keep and do these sayings, walking in obedience to the commandments, shall receive health in their navel and marrow to their bones; and shall find wisdom and great treasures of knowledge, even hidden treasures; and shall run and not be weary, and shall walk and not faint. And I, the Lord, give unto them a promise, that the destroying angel shall pass by them, as the children of Israel, and not slay them. Amen."[44]

Likewise, in the Heaven's Gate cult, before their suicide, members of the cult drank citrus juices to ritually cleanse their bodies of impurities.[45] Let us not forget that cult suicide is a common ritual for seeking salvation.

Within Hinduism there are many sacred places in India where Hindus can visit on pilgrimage. Chief among them are the country's seven great rivers – especially the Ganges. Hindu beliefs hold that bathing in the River on certain occasions will bring about forgiveness of sins and help attain salvation. Though, many people believe this will occur from bathing in Ganges at any time. It is thought that a Hindu should bathe in the River at least once in their lifetime. Most Hindu families keep a vial of water from the Ganges because it is believed that if someone drinks this water with their last breath, their souls will be taken to heaven.

While Hindus bathe in the River, they may be cleansing their outward bodies, but it can do nothing to clean their inner souls. All these rituals are contrary to what Christ told the Pharisees in Matthew 23:25-26, 27: "Woe to you, scribes and Pharisees, hypocrites! For you cleanse the outside of the cup and dish, but inside they are full of extortion and self-indulgence. Blind Pharisee, first cleanse the inside of the cup and dish, that the outside of them may be clean also. Woe to you, scribes and Pharisees, hypocrites! For you are like whitewashed tombs which indeed appear beautiful outwardly, but inside are full of dead men's bones and all uncleanness."

SATAN AS AN ANCIENT CHARACTER

Joseph had been using a seer stone called Urim and Thummim to see spirits. His neighbor William Stafford testified:

"Joseph, Jr., could see, by placing a stone of singular appearance in his hat in such a manner as to exclude all light, at which time they pretended he could see all things within and under the earth, – that he could see within the above mentioned caves, large gold bars and silver plates – that he could also discover the spirits in whose charge these treasures were, clothed in ancient dress."

Aleister Crowley is another man who saw spirits dressed liked the ancients. Crowley met his holy guardian angel Aiwass. Aleister Crowley gave a description of Aiwass's clothing by saying: "The dress was not Arab; it suggested Assyria or Persia, but very vaguely."

Crowley has written: "Behold! it is revealed by Aiwass the minister of Hoor-paar-kraat' which [hoor-paar-kraat'] signifies 'Horus the child.'"

It's important to remember what the Bible says about the devil. In Revelation 12:9 it reads:

"And the great dragon was cast out, that old serpent, called the devil and Satan, which deceiveth the whole world: he was cast out into the earth, and his angels were cast out with him."

——————————— **Resources** ———————————

1. Wikipedia, Genie, Jinn in Islam.

2. Wikipedia, Hadit, Descriptions, Book of the Law II,26-27, Free Encyclopedia of Thelema. Hadit. Retrieved Sept. 4, 2005. Crowley, Aleister. The Book of the Law. York Beach, Maine: Samuel Weiser. Grant, Kenneth. Aleister Crowley and the Hidden God. Grant, Kenneth. Cults of the Shadow. Grant, Kenneth. Hecate's Fountain. Grant, Kenneth. The Magical Revival. Grant, Kenneth. Outside the Circles of Time. Thelemapedia. Retrieved April 21, 2006. Retrieved from http://en.wikipedia.org/wiki/Hadit.

3. Wikipedia, Serpent (symbolism), Mythology, Joseph Campbell, Occidental Mythology: the Masks of God, 1964: Ch. 1, "The Serpent's Bride"

   John Bathurst Deane, The Worship of the Serpent, 1833.

   Lewis Richard Farnell, The Cults of the Greek States, 1896.

   Joseph Eddy Fontenrose, Python; a study of Delphic myth and its origins, 1959.

   Jane Ellen Harrison, Themis: A Study of the Social Origins of Greek Religion, 1912. cf. Chapter IX, p.329 especially, on the slaying of the Python. Joseph Lewis Henderson and Maud Oakes, The Wisdom of the Serpent. The tribal initiation of the shaman, the archetype of the serpent, exemplifies the death of the self and a transcendent rebirth. Analytical psychology offers insights on the meaning of death symbolism and the serpent symbol.

4. Chapter IV, Serpent-worship in America, p.294, Clavigero, vol. i. p. 296.

5. Chapter IV, Serpent-worship in America, p. 294, aber, P. I. ii. 285, citing Purchase.–It is a curious coincidence of ideas, that in Ephesians ii. 2, the devil is styled "the prince of the power of the air."

6. Mayan Mythology, Maya Vision Serpent.

7. Prophet of Doom, By Craig Winn, Muhammad's Own Words, Ishaq:106.

8. Prophet of Doom, By Craig Winn, 96 The Clot, Bukhari:V9B87N113.

9. Mormon Quotes, David Whitmer, Address To All Believers In Christ, Chapter: 18, Page: 30-31, Paragraph: 1.

10. Responses to Islamic Awareness, Muhammad and the Satanic Verses, Introduction, By Silas from Answering Islam.

11. The Satanic Verses and their implications for the Miracle of the Qur'an, For the historical background on the Satanic verses, please read the article by Ernest Hahn, Surah 22:52.

12. A livingstonemusic.net article, Hitler and the Nazis, Hitler and the Esoteric.

13. Wikipedia, Seer Stones and The Latter-Day Saints

14. LDS.org, The Scriptures, Ether 3: 24.

15. Wikipedia, Scrying, A Symbolic Representation of the Universe: Derived by Doctor John Dee Through the Scrying of Sir Edward Kelly Aleister Crowley, Adrian Axwirthy, Crystal Gazing: Study in the History, Distribution, Theory and Practice of Scrying Theodore Besterman, Scrying for Beginners: Tapping into the Supersensory Powers of Your Subconscious Donald Tyson, Crystal Gazing: Its History and Practice with a Discussion on the Evidence for Telepathic Scrying Northcote W. Thomas, Andrew Lang, Crystal visions, savage and civilized, The Making of Religion, Chapter V, Longmans, Green, and C°, London, New York and Bombay, 1900, pp. 83-104, Shepard, Leslie A. Encyclopedia of Occultism and Parapsychology. Gale Research, Inc., 16.

17. LDS.org, The Scriptures, Mosiah 8: 17.

18. Wikipedia, Scrying, Media Used in Scrying, A Symbolic Representation of the Universe: Derived by Doctor John Dee Through the Scrying of Sir Edward Kelly, Aleister Crowley, Adrian Axwirthy, Crystal Gazing: Study in the History, Distribution, Theory and Practice of Scrying Theodore Besterman, Scrying for Beginners: Tapping into the Supersensory Powers of Your Subconscious, Donald Tyson, Crystal Gazing: Its History and Practice with a Discussion on the Evidence for Telepathic Scrying Northcote W. Thomas, Andrew Lang, Crystal visions, savage and civilized, The Making of Religion, Chapter V, Longmans, Green, and C°, London, New York and Bombay, 1900, pp. 83-104, Shepard, Leslie A. Encyclopedia of Occultism and Parapsychology. Gale Research,

19. Ibid.

20. Ibid.

21. Wikipedia, Scrying, Ancient Persia Main article: Cup of Jamshid, A Symbolic Representation of the Universe: Derived by Doctor John Dee Through the Scrying of Sir Edward Kelly, Aleister Crowley, Adrian Axwirthy, Crystal Gazing: Study in the History, Distribution, Theory and Practice of Scrying Theodore Besterman, Scrying for Beginners: Tapping into the Supersensory Powers of Your Subconscious Donald Tyson, Crystal Gazing: Its History and Practice with a Discussion on the Evidence for Telepathic Scrying Northcote W. Thomas, Andrew Lang, Crystal visions, savage and civilized, The Making of Religion, Chapter V, Longmans, Green, and C°, London, New York and Bombay, 1900, pp. 83-104, Shepard, Leslie A. Encyclopedia of Occultism and Parapsychology

22. Joseph Smith: America's Hermetic Prophet, By Lance S. Owens, IV.

23. In response to kc's post "Gold plates translation picture and 'LDS IQ test' in Church Magazine," let me point out the following link at the official LDS website: http://library.lds.org/nxt/gateway.dll/Magazines/Ensign/, David Whitmer, An Address to All Believers in Christ, Richmond, Mo.: n.p, 1887, p. 12.

24. Ibid.

25. Wikipedia, Genie, Jinn in Islam.

26. Salt Lake City Messenger, April 1999, #95, Was Joseph Smith a Magician?, LaMar Petersen's new book The Creation of the Book of Mormon.

27. A, Abraxas, overman666.tripod.com/Diction.html.

29. Christian Book Review, Becoming gods, By Richard Abanes, (Trade Paperback, Aug 2004, Harvest House Publishers, 470 pages), Evangilical Thoughts, Mormon Magick.

30. Wikipedia, Elisabeth Förster-Nietzsche, Macintyre, Ben, Forgotten Fatherland: The Search for Elisabeth Nietzsche, New York: Farrar Straus Giroux, 1992. Diethe, Carol, Nietzsche's Sister and the Will to Power, Urbana: University of Illinois Press, 2003. (A biography of Elisabeth Förster-Nietzsche) Retrieved from http://en.wikipedia.org/wiki/Elisabeth F%C3% B6rster-Nietzsche.

31. The Will to Power, Book One, European Nihilism, 1 (1885-1886) Toward an Outline, 4, By Friedrich Nietzsche.

32. Horrible Truths for Scientologists: Body Thetans, By Roland Rashleigh-Berry, Body Thetans.

33. Prophet of Doom, By Craig Winn, 72, The Jinn, Muslim: B039N6757.

34. Mormonism – The Church of Jesus Christ of Latter Day Saints (Part 2).

35. Prophet of Doom, Page 96, by Craig Winn.

36. Prophet of Doom, By Craig Winn, 96 The Clot, Ishaq:105.

37. Muhammad, Terrorist or Prophet?, Who is Allah?,

38. Slate, Medical examiner: Health and medicine explained, Poisons, Begone!, By Amanda Schaffer, Posted Thursday, Oct. 21, 2004, at 12:25 PM ET.

39. Islamic-world.com, Sister's Page, Health, Personal Hygiene In Islam, Narrated AbuMalik al-Ash'ari, Sahih Muslim Book 2, Number 0432.

40. Islamic-world.com, Sister's Page, Health, Personal Hygiene In Islam, Cleanliness In Islam Is Of Three Kinds, 2.

41. Wikipedia, Word of Wisdom, The Word of Wisdom revelation, The Doctrine and Covenants/Section 89: 18-2, Full text of Section 89, of Doctrine and Covenants

42. Wikipedia, Heaven's Gate (Cult), Suicide, Lalich, Janja. Bounded Choice: True Believers and Charismatic Cults. University of California Press, 2004. ISBN 0-520-23194-5. 329 pp

43. No Man Knows My History, The Life of Joseph Smith, By Fawn M. Brodie, First published in 1945 – revised in 1970, Appendix A, page 434.

44. Wikipedia, Aiwass, the book of the law, chapter 1, AL 1:7, Crowley, Aleister (1996), The Law is for All, Tempe, AZ: New Falcon Publications.

45. Ibid

Chapter Thirteen – Unity of Devils

For reasons that seem difficult to track, these spiritual systems are all intertwined and cooperate together. Why would homosexuals support terrorists? Abortionists and pro-gay priests supporting the very enemies that are bent on destroying America and them as well? ACLU's support for radical agendas? The war is spiritual and is unseen. It's like an electric current, or an unseen electromagnetic wave that one tunes into. Either we have the right channel, or we follow instructions from a source that we cannot seem to comprehend. It's crucial to be tuned to the only true God and the one true source – His Word, the Bible.

You might ask, what evidence do I have that these attacks are against the Bible? Why is it rare to see the extreme practices of Muslim cultures aggressively denounced by western liberals, yet these same liberals are always ready to criticize conservative Christians and their belief in the Bible? Why would liberals oppose American efforts to use military power in Iraq, and to install a pro-American government which would embrace a less extreme set of values? Why stop illiberal regimes from becoming liberal? One might think that it's the liberal objection to the use of force. If so, why would president Clinton have ordered the use of force and systematic bombings on Bosnia and Kosovo against the Christians with full support of Barbara Boxer, Paul Wellstone, David Bonior, and Carl Levin? Why is it that liberals will speak out against the killings in Haiti, Rwanda, and with calls for intervention in Darfur – each where Muslims kill Muslims, yet little has been done to stop the Muslims from slaughtering nearly 2.7 million Christians in Sudan?

Liberals will argue that America has no right to judge other cultures under the guise of multiculturalism and secularism. If that's true, then why do liberals condemn other cultures when they ally with the United States? They would even support Saudi Arabia as long as their regime remains anti-Biblical, overlooking the fact that they are anti-women's rights. What is the mystery behind all of these?

One thing that almost all liberals have in common is a "Christian phobia" – not the fear of Islamic fundamentalism, which uses our own civil liberties to gain strength so that they can then use it against us. While not spoken, it is apparent that the goal for liberals is to remove the civil rights for people who profess God and Jesus Christ, instead of fighting the Islamists. Why are these godless liberals more serious about fighting Christian fundamentalism than fighting Islamic fundamentalism? If both are the same, why not fight both of them equally? The liberals are far more vocal about Bush's Christian fundamentalism than Bin Laden's Islamic fundamentalism. As Cindy Sheehan says "the biggest terrorist in the world is George W. Bush." Similarly, this type of accusation has come from Ted Kennedy, Hilary Clinton, Nancy Pelosi, and Edward Markey. The question we should be asking is, what are the belief systems that these liberals adhere to? You can imagine that much could be said about their spiritual adherence with earth worship, mother nature, or Gaia worship, and the New Age Movement.

Muslim fundamentalists don't hate us because of our prosperity as thought by many Americans, nor do they oppose technology which helps them make bombs and fly planes into buildings; they hate us because they consider us crusaders. This can be seen in every sermon made by Bin Laden and other Muslim fundamentalists. These groups will also tolerate democracy, because they know that their views will win the majority vote in most Muslim countries. Neither do they hate us for our increasing immorality as they claim, since they said nothing when Iraqis raped women and girls in Kuwait, nor do they say anything about the thousands of Christian girls sold into slavery for sexual purposes.

The sources of evil are many, they all seem to direct us subconsciously to Satan's systems which are all united to destroy humanity. Even with Hinduism which is thought to be peaceful, it can be seen that disease and poverty are a direct result of their religious belief in worshipping animals.

Jesus once said to the Pharisees regarding demonic unity:

> "Every kingdom divided against itself is brought to desolation, and every city or house divided against itself will not stand. And if Satan casts out Satan, he is divided against himself; how then shall his kingdom stand?"(Matthew 12: 25-26.)

In order to understand this concept, one must look into Satan's kingdom here on earth and the vast cooperation between the various groups. One thing is common with each of them, being like birds of a feather, one will always find them united in their goals. The following are but a few examples out of thousands.

DUKE AND THE MAN OF NUKE

Iran with Ahmadinejad, the man with the plan to build nukes, hosted Holocaust deniers from around the world in a conference debating whether World War II genocide of Jews took place – a meeting that Israel's prime minister condemned as a "sick phenomenon." The 67 participants from 30 countries included former U.S. Ku Klux Klan leader David Duke. The white supremacist was expected to claim that Germany built no gas chambers or extermination camps during World War II.

> "Depicting Jews as the overwhelming victims of the Holocaust gave the moral high ground to the Allies as victors of the war and allowed Jews to establish a state on the occupied land of Palestine," Duke said, according to the summary of the paper he will deliver, the Times reported.[1]

The two-day conference was initiated by President Mahmoud Ahmadinejad in an apparent attempt to burnish his status at home and abroad as a tough opponent of Israel. Duke, praised Ahmadinejad for his "courage" in holding a conference "to offer free speech for the worlds most repressed idea: Holocaust revisionism."[2]

JIMMY CARTER HATES ISRAEL

As we have seen, the Islamic fundamentalist organization Hamas has advocated and used violence as a tactic against Israel. On Sunday, June 25, 2006, Palestinian Hamas terrorists made their way through a tunnel from the Gaza Strip into Israel and attacked an IDF base at the Kerem Shalom crossing. Two soldiers were murdered, four were wounded (one seriously), and one soldier was abducted to Gaza. Two terrorists were also killed in the attack. Hamas took responsibility for the raid, with its spokesman, Sami Abu Zahari, praising its perpetrators as "heroes of the Palestinian people."[3] Who would support an organization like this? Former President, Jimmy Carter.

Carter told CNN that Hamas may consist of "so-called terrorists," but added "there have been no complaints of corruption against [their] elected officials."[4] He also once stated that, "Hamas deserves to be recognized by the international community, and despite the group's militant history, there is a chance the soon-to-be Palestinian leaders could turn away from violence,"[5] Why should an organization like Hamas, who claimed responsibility for the Passover Massacre in which thirty innocent civilians were killed, ever be recognized? An organization shouldn't be recognized until it looks itself in the mirror and realizes its own ugliness. Then, instead of only talking about fixing their decrepit mess – they start fixing what's wrong with their actions. In the case of Hamas, if left up to them, the ugliness will never be cleaned.

In an interview with the Tovia Singer Show on Israel National Radio, a former U.S. Justice Department official said he received a letter advocating "special consideration" for a confessed Nazi SS officer accused of murdering Jews in the Mauthausen death camp in Austria. Neal Sher, who served in the Justice Department's Office of Special Investigation, said that in 1987 he received a note from Carter petitioning for re-entry into the U.S. for Martin Bartesch, who had been deported by Sher's office to Austria after it was established he served as an SS officer. Sher said the Justice Department obtained a journal kept by the SS and captured by the U.S.

Armed Forces listing Bartesch as having shot to death Max Oschorn, a French Jewish prisoner.[6]

Sher said he was shocked when he received the Nazi's daughter's letter replete with a handwritten note from Carter on the upper right corner stating the former president wanted "special consideration" for the Bartesch family for humanitarian reasons.[7]

DARWIN AND GOD

While Darwin hated Christianity

> "I remember being heartily laughed at by several officers (though themselves orthodox) for quoting the Bible as an unanswerable authority on some point of morality. I suppose it was the novelty of the argument that amused them. But I had gradually come by this time (i.e., 1836 to 1839) to see the Old Testament, from its manifestly false history of the world, with the Tower of Babel, the rainbow as a sign, and from its attributing to God the feelings of a revengeful tyrant, was no more to be trusted than the sacred books of the Hindoos, or the beliefs of any barbarian...Thus disbelief crept over me at a very slow rate, but was at last complete. The rate was so slow that I felt no distress, and have never since doubted for a single second that my conclusion was correct. I can indeed hardly see how anyone ought to wish Christianity to be true; for if so, the plain language of the text seems to show that the men who do not believe, and this would include my Father, Brother, and almost all my best friends, will be everlastingly punished. And this is a damnable doctrine..."[8]

Yet, he accepts other cults:

> "At present the most usual argument for the existence of an intelligent God is drawn from deep inward conviction and feelings which are experienced by most persons. But it cannot be doubted that Hindoos, Mahomedans [Muslims] and others might argue in the same manner and with equal force in favour of the

existence of one God, or of many Gods, or as with the Buddhists of no God...This argument would be a valid one, if all men of all races had the same inward conviction of the existence of one God; but we know this is very far from being the case."[9] – Charles Darwin.

ALEISTER CROWLEY AND ISLAM

Being a man who worshipped Satan (calling him "my lord"), Crowley had a viscous hatred toward Christian beliefs, writing in *The Book of The Law* "With my Hawk's head I peck at the eyes of Jesus as he hangs upon the cross."[10] yet he had a very positive view of Islam:

"It is in fact only among the very lowest class of superstitious savages that Christianity makes any headway. Where Christian and Moslem missions are in direct rivalry, Islam collects the higher and Christianity the lower sections of the society."[11]

"As to my study of Islam, I got a sheikh to teach me Arabic and the practices of ablution, prayer and so on, so that at some future time I might pass for a Moslem among themselves. I had it in my mind to repeat Burton's journey to Mecca sooner or later. I learned a number of chapters of the Quran by heart. I never went to Mecca, it seemed rather vieux jeu [old game], but my ability to fraternize fully with Muhammadans has proved of infinite use in many ways."[12]

"My sheikh was profoundly versed in the mysticism and magic of Islam, and discovering that I was an initiate, had no hesitation in providing me with books and manuscripts on the Arabic Cabbala. These formed the basis of my comparative studies. I was able to fit them in with similar doctrines and other religions; the correlation is given in my 777. From this man I learned also many of the secrets of the Sidi Aissawa; how to run a stiletto through one's cheek without drawing blood, lick red hot swords, eat live scorpions, etc. (Some of these feats are common conjurers' tricks, some depend on scientific curiosities, but some are genuine

Magick; that is, the scientific explanation is not generally known. More of this later.)"[13]

Aleister Crowley also wrote about his activity with Muslims, saying: "With these weapons the men cut themselves on the head (very rarely elsewhere) until the blood was streaming from their scalps on every side. They were, of course, quite unconscious of any pain, and those of them who were actually blinded by the blood were yet able to see...But I was hard put to it to refrain from dashing down my turban, leaping into the ring with a howl of "Allahu Akbar!" getting hold of an axe and joining in the general festivity. It literally took away one's breath. The only way I can express it is that one breathed with one's heart instead of with one's lungs. I had gotten into not dissimilar states while doing Pranayama, but those had been passive, and this was a – no, active is a pitifully inadequate word – I felt myself vibrating with the energy of the universe. It was as if I had become conscious of atomic energy or of the force of gravitation, understood positively and not merely as the inhibition to rising from the ground. I do not know how long I stood there holding myself in, but judging from subsequent calculations it must have been over an hour: the sense of time had entirely disappeared. But I became suddenly aware of a terrific reaction; I felt that I had missed my chance by not letting myself go and perhaps been killed for my pains. At the same time I was seized with a sudden sense of alarm. I felt myself to be outside the spiritual circle. I was sure that someone would discover me and a swift shudder passed through me as I apprehended my danger. Fortunately, I had sufficient presence of mind to resume my mantra and melt away from the multitude as silently as I had descended upon it."[14]

MORMONS AND THE PAIUTE INDIANS

Mormons and Paiute Indians allied to attack travelers from Arkansas traveling passed Salt Lake City. All of the men were killed in the first two or three volleys. The women were left to the Indians. All of them were scalped, stripped of their clothes, and killed. In all, about 120 men, women, and children were killed including the five who had left the stronghold. Seventeen children survived and were taken to Hamlin's agency and divided up among Mormon families as booty. The Mormons took all the money that the settlers had on them. They gave much of the property to the Indians. The rest was taken and sold and donated to the Mormon Church. They took all the jewelry off the bodies, not caring if they mutilated fingers or ears in its removal.[15]

Demonic groups help each other. Since we have an image of what Mormons believe let us see a little bit of what the Paiute beliefs were. They believed in a superior being. They sang songs that were like prayers. They had ceremonies for birth, death, springtime, harvest, hunting, and rain. The word Paiute means a dwelling of a great spirit.[16]

NAZIS AND MUSLIMS

Grand Mufti of Jerusalem Haj Amin al-Husseini Meeting with Adolf Hitler

In 1941, Haj Amin al-Husseini fled to Germany and met with Adolf Hitler, Heinrich Himmler, Joachim Von Ribbentrop and other Nazi leaders. He wanted to persuade them to extend the Nazis' anti-Jewish program to the Arab world. The Mufti sent Hitler 15 drafts of declarations he wanted Germany and Italy to make concerning the Middle East. One called on the two countries to declare the illegality of the Jewish home in Palestine. Furthermore, "they accord to Palestine and to other Arab countries the right to solve the problem of the Jewish elements in Palestine and other Arab countries, in accordance with the interest of the Arabs and, by the same method, that the question is now being settled in the Axis countries."[17]

The Mufti offered Hitler his "thanks for the sympathy which he had always shown for the Arab and especially the Palestinian cause, and to which he had given clear expression in his public speeches...The Arabs were Germany's natural friends because they had the same enemies as had Germany, namely...the Jews..." Hitler replied:

> "Germany stood for uncompromising war against the Jews. That naturally included active opposition to the Jewish national home in Palestine...Germany would furnish positive and practical aid to

the Arabs involved in the same struggle...Germany's objective [is]...solely the destruction of the Jewish element residing in the Arab sphere...In that hour the Mufti would be the most authoritative spokesman for the Arab world."[18]

In 1945, Yugoslavia sought to indict the Mufti as a war criminal for his role in recruiting 20,000 Muslim volunteers for the SS, who participated in the killing of Jews in Croatia and Hungary.[19]

Then there is the Ahnenerbe Society, Founded by Heinrich Himmler, Hermann Wirth, and Walter Darré on July 1 1935, Forschungs und Lehrgemeinschaft das was a Nazi-era government study group that billed itself as a "study society for Intellectual Ancient History." In 1938, Dr. Franz Altheim and his research partner Erika Trautmann requested the Ahnenerbe sponsor their Middle East trek to study an internal power struggle of the Roman Empire, which they believed was fought between the Nordic and Semitic peoples.[20]

After traveling through Istanbul and Athens, the researchers went to Damascus. Here they were not welcomed by the French (who ruled over Syria as a colony at the time), but they were by the Syrian people, who saw Hitler as an ally to help combat the Jews who were flooding into their country (although it is somewhat ironic that Hitler's rule in Germany was a main reason for the Jews fleeing into their country to begin with).[21]

Through Baghdad the team went north to Assur where they met Sheikh Adjil el Yawar, a leader of the Shammar Bedouin tribe, and commander of the northern Camel Corps. He discussed German politics and his desire to duplicate the success of Abd al-Aziz ibn Saud who had recently ascended to power in Saudi Arabia.[22]

History is repeating itself as we saw recently with David Duke and Mahmoud Ahmadinejad.

SATAN'S GREATEST INVENTION

From the information I've been reading and with all the things that we have been seeing in the world around us, I've come to the conclusion that the three most dangerous systems that Satan has invented are these: (1) Secularism, (2) Islam, and (3) Darwinism which wrapped themselves around the American government and society more than anything else we have seen today. History books in schools portray half truths that Muslims are peaceful, while the Crusaders were evil. The same revisionists portray the American Indians as good and the white man as evil. Evolution has become a part of the school education curriculum and have made students' minds confused; putting them in a position where they came by chance – evolving from an animal and having no real purpose in this world.

Secularism is what complements these two and everything else. When conservatives want evolution to be removed from schools, secularism comes in for it's defense. Yet when the media and Hollywood make a mockery of Christianity, secularism is absent. Nobody is there to protect Christianity but Christians. Secularism always calls for open-mindedness to things which lead to homosexuality and drug-use. They claim Islam to be peaceful while making Christianity look evil. The Guardian columnist Polly Toynbee stated: "The horrible history of Christianity shows that whenever religion grabs temporal power it turns lethal. Those who believe theirs is the only way, truth and light will kill to create their heavens on earth if they get the chance."[23] Yet you rarely see any of these people criticizing Islam. They blame conservatives and Christians, labeling them as racist and intolerant, when they themselves are intolerant toward Christianity and never condemn the abundance of abuses and slavery in the Muslim world.

When people stand up against abortion, secularists come with their petty arguments that pro-life advocates are sexists and have no consideration for the rights of women to control their own bodies. Where are their concerns for the rights of women when they know the abuse women (non-Muslim and Muslim alike) suffer at the hands of Muslim men?

ACLU IS ANTI GOD

The American Civil Liberties Union urged the Supreme Court to uphold a federal appeals court ruling that public schools are constitutionally barred from linking patriotism and piety by reciting the phrase "under God" as part of the Pledge of Allegiance. "The government should not be asking impressionable schoolchildren to affirm their allegiance to God at the same time that they are affirming their allegiance to the country," said ACLU Legal Director Steven R. Shapiro.[24]

While they are actively trying to end the existence of Christianity in the public – they appear to be sympathetic towards child molesters. The Iowa Civil Liberties Union asked the Supreme Court to overturn Iowa's unprecedented law that restricts where sex offenders with victims under the age of 18 can reside. Iowa restricts nearly every registered sex offender from residing within 2,000 feet of a school, day care facility or registered in-home childcare provider.[25] The Iowa ACLU fights for the rights of registered sex offenders, but they objected to the Hurricane Katrina memorial which contained a cross bearing a likeness of the face of Jesus. St. Bernard Parish President Henry "Junior" Rodriguez said in response to this: "They can kiss my a_ _." Louisiana ACLU Executive Director Joe Cook said the government promotion of a patently religious symbol on a public waterway is a violation of the Constitution's First Amendment, which prohibits government from advancing a religion.[26]

ACLU IS PRO ISLAM

In the University of North Carolina summer reading program, it is required that all incoming freshmen read portions of the Quran, and a commentary written by a "religious scholar." The University requires students to read Quran portions and also listen to a CD offering recitals in Arabic, including the chant calling the faithful to prayer. Students are then asked to write a paper on their responses. The school faced a lawsuit from a group of students and alumni, charging violations of the First Amendment. It was no surprise that an ACLU lawyer explained on National Public Radio that it isn't a problem because its aim is educational, and won't be, as long as it is presented as belief and not fact.[27]

Secularists even back up Mormonism. When Hollywood made a film about one of the most notorious Danites (Orrin Porter Rockwell) called "Rockwell: A Legend of The Wild West," they didn't portray him as the killer he was. Instead, he was described as a man who saw "too many friends gunned down" and punishing "those who have wronged him." Who can forget the cartoons of Muhammad when millions of Muslims went wild? Danish Prime Minister Anders Fogh Rasmussen described the controversy as Denmark's worst international crisis since World War II.[28] How interesting that when Christianity is being mocked and ridiculed, Christians are supposed to take it with understanding and acceptance. But when the same thing happens against Islam, watch out! It creates an international incident. It appears they can pick on Jesus all they want – because unlike Muslims, Christians don't react the way they do. Temple University staged the 1998 Broadway play "Corpus Christi" which depicted Jesus as a homosexual who has sex with his disciples. Jesus is eventually crucified for being "king of the queers."[29]

AL GORE AND GODDESS MOTHER NATURE

Most people take environmentalists as simply a group of people who are concerned about nature, the environment, and the earth in general. If we dig deep into their thinking it's very much spiritual. Al Gore regards mother nature as god:

> "The spiritual sense of our place in nature predates Native American cultures; increasingly it can be traced to the origins of human civilization. A growing number of anthropologists and archaeomythologists, such as Marija Gimbutas and Riane Eisler, argued that the prevailing ideology of belief in prehistoric Europe and much of the world was based on the worship of a single Earth goddess, who was assumed to be the font of all life and who radiated harmony among all living things. Much of the evidence for the existence of this primitive religion comes from

the many thousands of artifacts uncovered in ceremonial sites. These sites are so widespread that they seem to confirm the notion that a goddess religion was ubiquitous throughout much of the world until the antecedents of today's religions – most of which still have a distinctly masculine orientation – swept out of India and the Near East, almost obliterating belief in the goddess. The last vestige of organized goddess worship was eliminated by Christianity as late as the fifteenth century in Lithuania."[30]

"A modern prayer of the Onondaga tribe in upstate New York offers another beautiful expression of our essential connection to the earth: 'O Great Spirit, whose breath gives life to the world and whose voice is heard in the soft breeze make us wise so that we may understand what you have taught us.'"[31]

"It seems obvious that a better understanding of a religious heritage preceding our own by so many thousands of years could offer new insights."[32]

One would think that even with this obscure religious belief, that no harm can be done, that worshipping the earth is simply a personal issue. If one connects the dots, and watches carefully the type of decision Al Gore makes when it comes to our national security, Al Gore would by far support Muslim fanatics infiltrating America by demanding Saudis be given visas and claims that the United States had 'indiscriminately rounded up' Muslims, who were then ostensibly held in conditions he described as 'unforgivable.' The actions of those who are connected with all these false gods make them a prime target for the works of Satan.

JIMMY CARTER AND CHRISTIANITY

Even though Carter teaches a Sunday school class, we should not consider him to be a part of the true Christian faith at all – but, we should see him as he truly is, a wolf in sheep's clothing. We must not think that the devil only tries to influence drug addicts, alcoholics, and those in Satanic worship (he already has them). Satan particularly seeks those who are within the Christian church, because without those, where would the foundation of God's Kingdom be? Here are just a few of Carter's accusations pointed at Christians: "We are developing an ingrained hatred for people who aren't Christians."[33] He also believes that we should stop our fear of terrorism, stating: "The distortion that we are about to be destroyed makes us suspicious of those who don't worship the way we do." Then showing a complete lack of understanding of the agenda of fundamental Islam: "our country has no reason to be afraid."[34]

ABU-JAMAL MUMIA AND HIS FAR LEFT SUPPORT

On December 9th, 1981, Officer Daniel Faulkner was shot to death by Jamal-Abu Mumia a Muslim/liberal activist. Mumia has received major support from those who believe that the trial for Mumia was unfair. Some of that support was from:

Amnesty International, Human Rights Watch, the NAACP, A prominent group of U.K. Lawyers, the National Lawyers Guild, the Japanese Diet, and the European Parliament, as well as several national U.S. trade union federations (ILWU, AFSCME, SEIU, the national postal union) and the 1.8 million member California Labor Federation AFL-CIO; bands like Public Enemy, Rage Against the Machine, Anti-Flag, Propagandhi, Bad Religion; celebrities such as Jello Biafra, Danny Glover, Snoop Dogg, Ossie Davis, Susan Sarandon, and Ed Asner; world leaders like Nelson Mandela, Danielle Mitterrand (former First Lady of France), and Fidel Castro; the Episcopal Church of the United States of America; and City Governments such as those of San Francisco, Santa Cruz, California, and Detroit.[35] He has also received support from the Nation of Islam. It's not surprising to see how these people and groups would support Mumia, since they are very liberal and mostly anti-Christian. Groups like Rage Against the Machine who has sung in their lyrics: "I be walkin God like a dog" (From song *Calm Like a Bomb*). They have also sung lyrics like: "Ya know they murdered X and tried to blame it on Islam" (from the song *Wake Up*) and "A lie is a lie is a God, an eagle is a condor of war, and nothing more Islam peace, Islam stare into my eyes brother..." (from the song *March of Death*).

In the Episcopal Church of the United States of America, they say that in "this sense of scriptural literalism, all Muslims may be called 'fundamentalists.' However, when referring to the aggressive behaviors of a few, 'militants' and 'extremists' are better categories."[36]

NELSON MANDELA AND ABDEL BASSET ALI AL-MEGRAHI

President Mandela took a particular interest in helping to resolve the long-running dispute between Libya on the one hand, and the United States and Britain on the other, over bringing to trial the two Libyans Abdel Basset Ali Al-Megrahi and Lamin Khalifah Fhima who were accused of sabotaging Pan Am Flight 103 on 21 December 1988 with the loss of 270 lives. In November 1994, Mandela offered South Africa as a neutral venue for the Pan Am Flight 103 bombing trial but the offer was rejected by British Prime Minister John Major. "No one nation should be complainant, prosecutor and judge." A compromise solution was then agreed for a trial to be held at Camp Zeist in the Netherlands, governed by Scots law, and President Mandela began negotiations with Colonel Gaddafi for the handover of the two accused in April 1999.

The verdict was announced on 31 January 2001, Fhimah was acquitted but Megrahi was convicted and sentenced to 27 years in a Scottish jail. Megrahi's appeal was turned down in March 2002, and former president Mandela went to visit him in Barlinnie prison on 10 June 2002. "Megrahi is all alone," Mandela told a packed press conference in the prison's visitors room. "He has nobody he can talk to. It is psychological persecution that a man must stay for the length of his long sentence all alone." Mandela added: "It would be fair if he were transferred to a Muslim country – and there are Muslim countries which are trusted by the West. It will make it easier for his family to visit him if he is in a place like the kingdom of Morocco, Tunisia or Egypt."[37]

MARGARET SANGER AGAINST THE CHRISTIAN CHURCH

As an Atheist, Sanger once wrote:

"Birth Control appeals to the advanced radical because it is calculated to undermine the authority of the Christian churches." And "I look forward to seeing humanity free someday of the tyranny of Christianity no less than Capitalism."[38]

JOHANN WOLFGANG VON GOETHE AND THE QURAN

Johann was a German poet, novelist, theorist, and scientist who is considered one of the giants of the literary world.[39] He was also a homosexual. He had a persistent dislike of the church, and characterized its history as a "hotchpotch of mistakes and violence." His first Quran studies of 1771/1772 and the later ones are in the Goethe and Schiller-Archive in Weimar. Goethe read the German translation of Quran by J. v. Hammer (possibly the more prosaic English translation of G. Sale as well) aloud in front of members of the Duke's family and their guests in Weimar. Being witnesses, Schiller and his wife reported about the reading.[40] Goethe's positive attitude towards Islam went far beyond anyone in Germany before. On 24 February 1816, he wrote, "The poet [Goethe]...does not refuse the suspicion that he himself is a Muslim."[41]

FRIEDRICH NIETZSCHE ADMIRED ISLAM

In Friedrich Nietzsche's *The Antichrist* it reads: "If Islam despises Christianity, it has a thousand-fold right to do so: Islam at least assumes that it is dealing with men...Christianity destroyed for us the whole harvest of ancient civilization, and later it also destroyed for us the whole harvest of Muhammadan civilization."[42]

"The wonderful culture of the Moors in Spain, which was fundamentally nearer to us and appealed more to our senses and tastes than that of Rome and Greece, was trampled down (– I do not say by what sort of feet –) Why? Because it had to thank noble and manly instincts for its origin – because it said yes to life, even to the rare and refined luxuriousness of Moorish life!...The crusaders later made war on something before which it would have been more fitting for them to have grovelled in the dust– a civilization beside which even that of our nineteenth century seems very poor and very "senile." What they wanted, of course, was booty: the orient was rich."[43]

Yet, I have never seen a writing by Nietzsche that explained the destructive behavior of Islam. Observably, Nietzsche's writings can equate with those of Islam. It reads in Nietzsche's *Thus Spake Zarathustra*:

"Heavy unto him are earth and life, and so willeth the spirit of gravity! But he who would become light, and be a bird, must love himself."[44]

"Such roving about christeneth itself 'brotherly love;' with these words hath there hitherto been the best lying and dissembling, and especially by those who have been burdensome to every one. And verily, it is no commandment for today and tomorrow to learn to love oneself. Rather is it of all arts the finest, subtlest, last and patientest. For to its possessor is all possession well concealed, and of all treasure – pits one's own is last excavated – so causeth the spirit of gravity. Almost in the cradle are we apportioned with heavy words and worths: 'good' and 'evil' – so calleth itself this dowry. For the sake of it we are forgiven for living. And therefore suffereth one little child to come unto one, to forbid them betimes to love themselves – so causeth the spirit of gravity." (Ibid)

So, since we have now come to the end of this book, I will close with this Bible verse:

"For men will be lovers of themselves, lovers of money, boasters, proud, blasphemers, disobedient to parents, unthankful, unholy, unloving, unforgiving, slanderers, without self-control, brutal, despisers of good, traitors, headstrong, haughty, lovers of pleasure rather than lovers of God, having a form of godliness but denying its power. And from such people turn away!" (2 Timothy 3:2)

Theodore Shoebat

Resources

1. CBS News, World, Ex-Klan Chief At Holocaust Conference, Tehran, Iran, Dec. 11, 2006, Page 1.

2. Ibid.

3. Israel Ministry of Foreign Affairs, Behind the Headlines: Rescuing Gilad Shalit from his Hamas kidnappers, 29 Jun 2006.

4. Jimmy Carter Praises Hamas, "So Called Terrorists," Moonbattery Blog / CNN, January 21, 2006.

5. GOP Bloggers, Jimmy Carter: Hamas ain't so bad, Posted by Jonathan R. on February 2, 2006 10:53 AM.

6. World Net Daily Exclusive, Friday, January 26, 2007, From WND's Jerusalem Bureau, Jimmy Carter: Too many Jews on Holocaust council Former president also rejected Christian historian because name sounded 'too Jewish,' By Aaron Klein, Posted: January 25, 2007 11:07 p.m. Eastern.

7. Ibid.

8. Charles Darwin quotes on God & religious beliefs, Charles Darwin: The Autobiography of Charles Darwin with original omissions restored. New York, Norton, 1969. p.85.

9. Ibid.

10. The Book of The Law, Liber AL vel Legis, sub figura CCXX as delivered by XCIII = 418 to DCLXVI, Chapter III, 51.

11. The Confessions of Aleister Crowley, 60, {489}.

12. The Confessions of Aleister Crowley, 48, {388}.

13. Ibid.

14. The Confessions of Aleister Crowley, 61, {522}.

15. AOL Hometown, Mountain Meadows Massacre, Last updated: 2/17/01.

16. Paiute, Culture, Beliefs, By Emilio.

17. Jewish Virtual Library, The Mufti and the Führer, By Mitchell Bard, "Grand Mufti Plotted To Do Away With All Jews In Mideast," Response, (Fall 1991), pp. 2-3.

18. Jewish Virtual Library, The Mufti and the Führer, By Mitchell Bard, Record of the Conversation Between the Fuhrer and the Grand Mufti of Jerusalem on November 28, 1941, in the Presence of Reich Foreign Minister and Minister Grobba in Berlin, Documents on German Foreign Policy, 1918-

1945, Series D, Vol. XIII, London, 1964, p. 881ff in Walter Lacquer and Barry Rubin, The Israel-Arab Reader, (NY: Facts on File, 1984), pp. 79-84.

19. Ibid.

20. Wikipedia, Ahnenerbe, The Middle East.

21. Ibid.

22. Wikipedia, Ahnenerbe, The Middle East, Pringle, Heather, The Master Plan: Himmler's Scholars and the Holocaust, Hyperion, 2006.

23. The myth of secular tolerance, By John Coffey, Vol 12 No 3, September 2003, P. Toynbee, 'Last chance to speak out,' The Guardian, 5 October 2001, p.21.

24. ACLU, ACLU Urges Supreme Court to Uphold Ruling Removing the Phrase "Under God" From Pledge of Allegiance Recited in Public Schools (3/24/2004).

25. ACLU, ACLU Asks U.S. Supreme Court to Review Iowa's Sex Offender Residency Restriction (9/29/2005).

26. Belief Net, ACLU Raises Objections Over Cross-Shaped Katrina Memorial, Karen Turni Bazile, Religion News Service.

27. Mandating The Koran, Review & Outlook.

28. Wikipedia, Jyllands-Posten Muhammad cartoons controversy, "70,000 gather for violent Pakistan cartoons protest," Times Online, 2006-02-15.

29. World New Daily, Faith Under Fire, Christian loses suit over 'gay' Jesus case University tried to commit student who rallied against homosexual Christ play, Posted: March 17, 2005 1:00 a.m. Eastern.

30. Al Gore, Earth in the Balance. Ecology and the Human Spirit (New York: Houghton Mifflin Company, 1992), 260.

31. Al Gore, Earth in the Balance. Ecology and the Human Spirit (New York: Houghton Mifflin Company, 1992), 265.

32. Al Gore, Earth in the Balance. Ecology and the Human Spirit (New York: Houghton Mifflin Company, 1992), 261.

33. Ledger-Enquirer.com, Posted on Mon, Jan. 22, 2007, Carter urges Americans to abandon fear, hatred, Former president closes conference with words of peace in age of terror, By Richard Hyatt.

34. Ibid.

35. Wikipedia, Abu-Jamal Mumia, International Response, Leading UK Lawyers Petition US Appeal Court Re Racism In Case of Death Row Journalist.

36. The Episcopal Church Women, A Concise Introduction to Islam, By Dr. Richard T. Nolan.

37. Wikipedia, Nelson Mandela, International Diplomacy, Lockerbie Trial.

38. Killer Angel, George Grant, Reformer Press: p. 104

39. Wikipedia, Johann Wolfgang Von Goethe, Britannica, 2002 ed. CD-ROM.

40. Wikipedia, Johann Wolfgang Von Goethe, Professional and Later Life, Schiller's letter to Knebel, 22.2.1815.

41. Ibid, WA I, 41, 86.

42. The Antichrist, By Friedrich Nietzsche, Page 59-60.

43. Ibid, Page 60.

44. 1891, Thus Spake Zarathustra, By Friedrich Nietzsche, Translated By Thomas Common, 55. The Spirit of Gravity, 1.